INDIAN

ZEN LEFORT

LAND

INDIAN LAND

Zen Lefort

For the First Nations
For Sophie

ECHOES
AND
RIPPLES

It is said that when Christopher Columbus first encountered the Indigenous population known as the Arawak, that the Arawak approached Columbus with gifts of their land. When the Europeans drew their swords, the Arawak grabbed the blades with their hands, not understanding that what was being offered in return for their gifts was violence.

If a camera had existed to capture this moment of the collision of the Old World with the new one, it would have captured the Arawak slicing their hands on the blades of the swords they had so innocently grabbed onto. Flash and click, a photograph of Indigenous blood dripping into the earth.

Blood has an echo. It is red and shiny and lasts for the generations that follow.

After Columbus arrived in the New World, and during the formation of the United States of America, Indigenous language, culture, and history were slaughtered and, in many cases, completely buried.

The government took every effort to make Native Americans invisible; and over decades of practices, which still exist today, Indigenous sacred sites are often overrun or permanently destroyed by new infrastructure or the exploitation of natural resources on their land. Theirs have been hands that have held the stones of hardship. They awaken each new day to the continued theft of their land under constant threat, whether that be drilling for a new pipeline, or the wreckage to an ecosystem that is already fragile.

The echoes of this environmental destruction are plenty. The howl of the wind. The cry of the grasses. The creaking of the sky under the weight of plastic stars. In the chaos of climate change, it is the Indigenous populations that will be most affected. Those whose land had been dismantled, reshaped, destroyed, and now left like bones on the ground.

At the time of this publication, one in three Native Americans are living in poverty. Housing is that of crumbling walls, empty cabinets, and in some cases the very absence of electricity and running water. There is a general lack of access to health care and education. In the echoes of empty land, empty government promises, and even emptier solutions, living on reservations comes with some of the highest rates of unemployment in the country. For Native youth, suicide is the second leading cause of death. One cannot help but make the connection between the loss of culture and the loss of one's own identity to the emotional pain that follows.

It isn't just the hardship of poverty that Indigenous lives face; it is also a continued violence. As a society, we're left with the shocking realization that Native American women and girls are murdered ten times more than any other group in the United States. Added to those startling figures, Native Americans are killed by police at the highest rate seen in this country.

There are ripples that come from these moments of destruction. Ripples that cast across the waters of time. These ripples smell as ancient as the earth. They carry the sound of the shifting mud. They speak with the ominous warnings from the elders and their traditions.

I was raised with the Cherokee spirit by my mother Betty. As I listened to the stories passed down through generations of my family, I was inspired. Stories where the leaf met the forest, bringing centuries of culture alive. As a child, I would stand on the hills of southern Ohio, reaching to the sky, my ear laid to the past, listening for the voices of those who have come before me. This is why one of my favorite photographs in this powerful collection is of the woman standing by the red car with the three young girls on top of it. There are two horses nearby, the ropes in the hands of the girls.

In the culture of my Cherokee ancestors, women were the leaders and thinkers. More than that, it is said the land was born from them. I see that ancient story in this very contemporary photograph. The car is but a prop, while the woman and the three young girls are the heart of a people that has not stopped beating. And what the girls hold in their hands is not a rope, but the connection to the earth around them, the horses standing witness to the relationship that, in the modern world, has been tested, but not yet broken.

This photo is just one of many in this commanding collection that make this point, as protestors and activists within each tribe fight for Indigenous land and their human and environmental rights. You see the strength of the individuals in these photos. The resilience of them saying, "You have not erased me." This book is testimony that Native lives matter. They fill these pages with their presence.

Zen Lefort is a remarkably gifted photographer who uses the lens of his camera to help give a voice to the generations who have been systemically silenced. In a world of stolen land, culture, history, and lives, these photographs magnify the hearts and minds of those who refuse to be removed. Lefort has captured not only the souls of his human subjects, but the soul of the landscape around them. His artistic eye is sharp, capable of catching the astounding truth.

This volume of work solidifies Lefort as an artist searching the world around him to find the causes and issues that deserve amplification. In doing so, he's inviting the world to take a look through his camera at the varied and complex realities of Native lives today. In his skilled hand, each photo possesses a unique voice but collectively are saying,

"We are still here."

I think now of a spider web I once saw in the fork of a branch across the river my ancestors long ago dipped their own toes in. The web was ravaged by wind, or perhaps by a bird flying through. Instead of moving on, the spider stayed to patch the holes. The newly spun threads glistened in the sun, until what had been destroyed was once more repaired. I see in each of these photographs another strand added to the web. Another way to repair what has been destroyed, and find the way back home. Like the spider web, there is the chance to rebuild, so that what glitters in the sun is the power of a people who have survived.

May you carry these photographs with you as ripples of the enduring strength of the Indigenous spirit.

Tiffany McDaniel

"I see a time of seven generations when all
the colors of mankind will gather under the sacred
tree of life and the whole earth will become
one circle again."

Crazy Horse's prophecy,
1877

TWO
WORLDS

This story begins in 1492, when the Genoa navigator Christopher Columbus set foot in the New World and decided to call "Indians" the people living there. Half a millennium later, the tribes which didn't disappear following this colonization were deported to reservations all across the United States. They are living the American Way of Life, submitted to assimilation policies aiming to destroy their ancestral cultures. On the damaged roads of the reservations, churches and fast food restaurants have sprung up like mushrooms. The tepees of the large plains and the "hogans," as we call traditional Navajo dwellings, have been replaced by mobile homes. On the road leading to Window Rock, the capital of the Navajo Nation, we can witness a man wandering on the side of the road, like a lost soul, in between the noises of large SUVs. He wears a cap "Native Veteran," as well as an eagle feather. He holds a sign. Written on the rotten cardboard, one can read: "We are still here!"

"Nowadays, I'm split between two worlds.
There is of course my Indian culture, our songs,
our dances, and our food. And then there is money,
who's gonna drive the biggest car, who will have
the best TV, who'll own the coolest pair of Jordans.
What do we do when all this materialistic stuff
takes center stage over the rest of our lives?"

Chanse Zavalla,
Chumash tribe

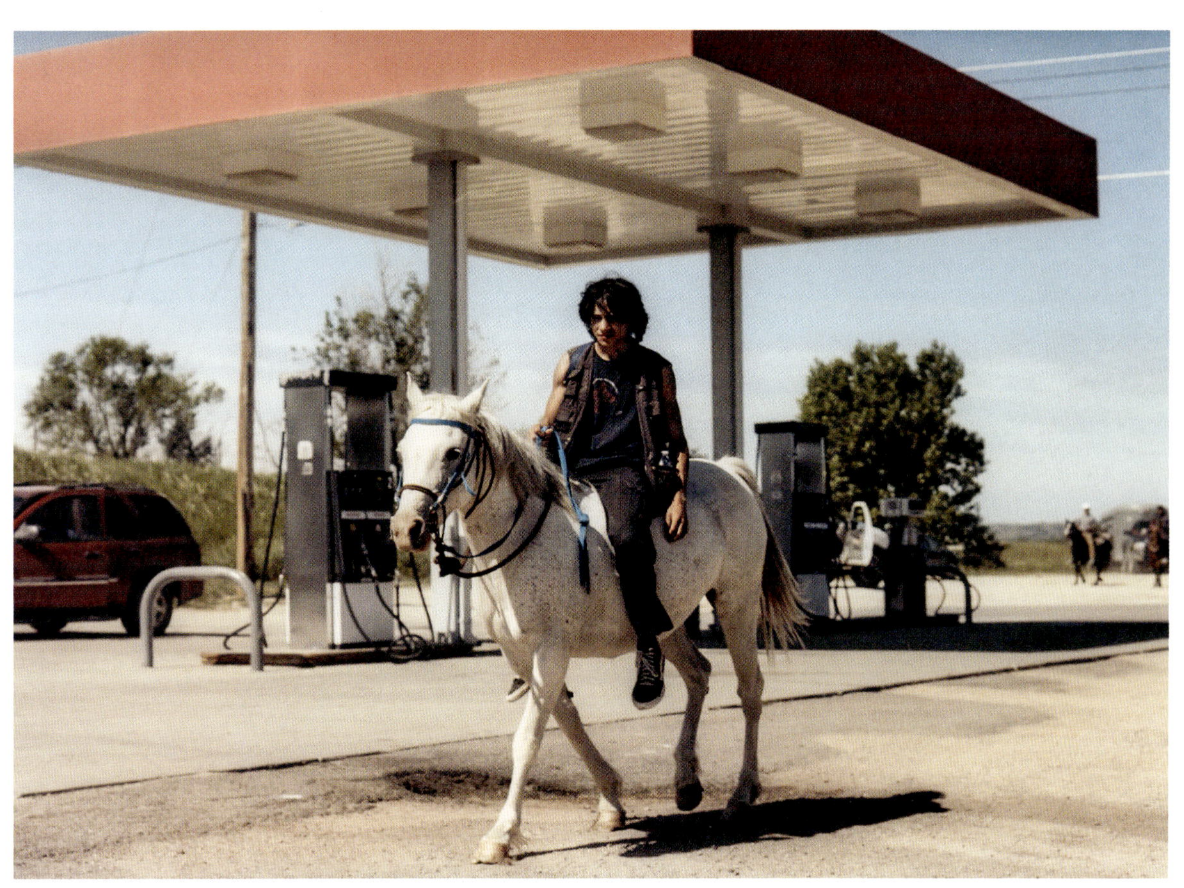

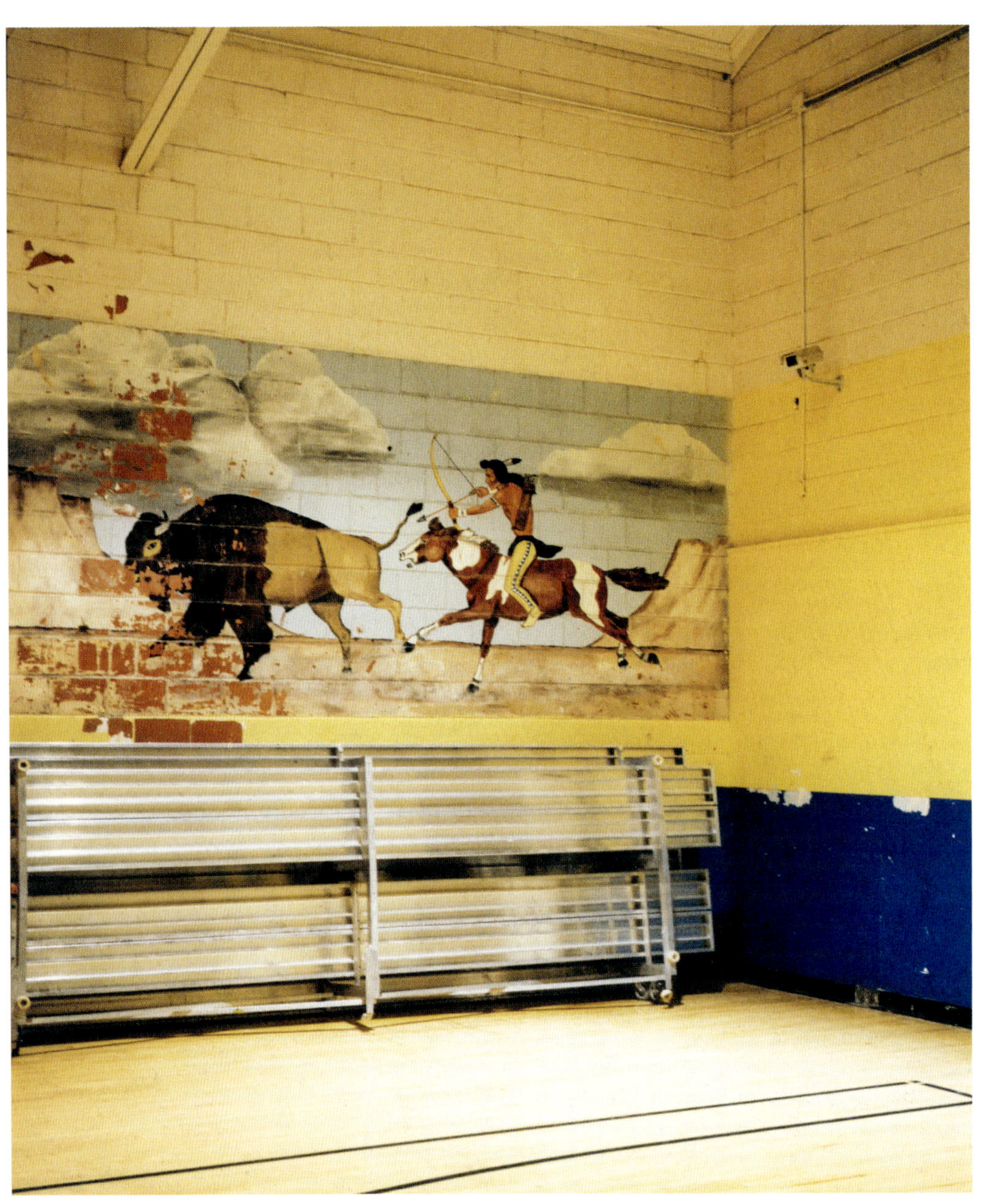

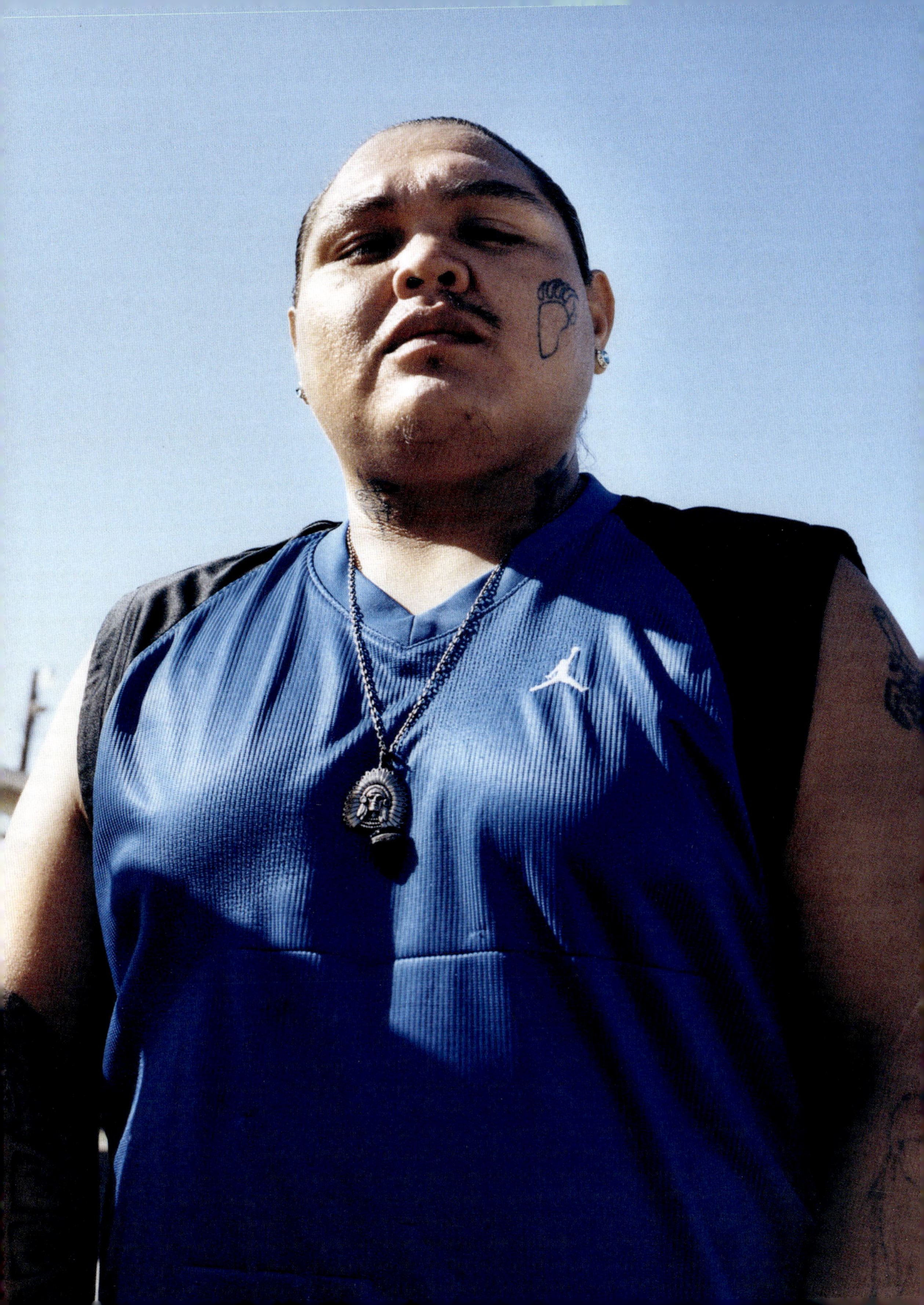

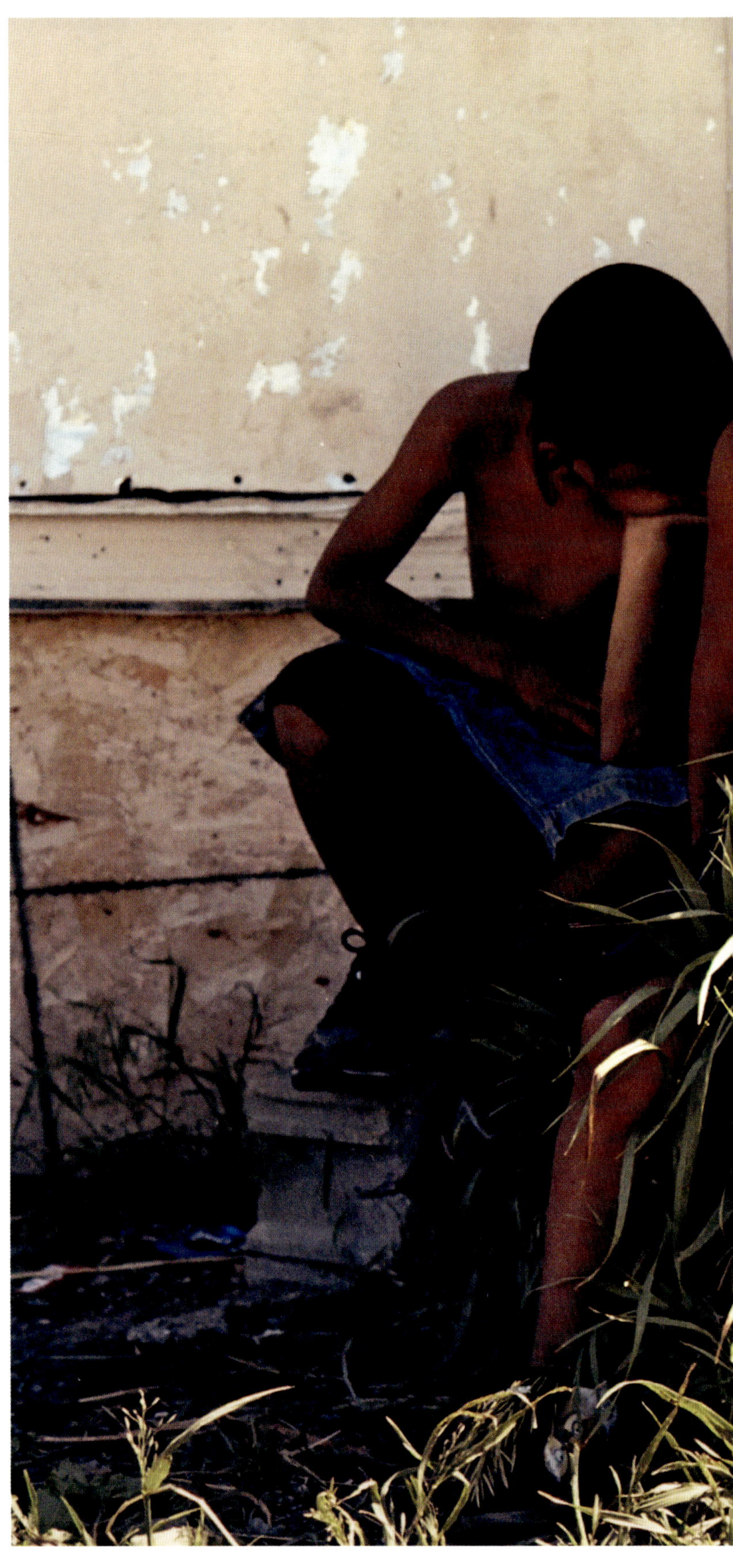

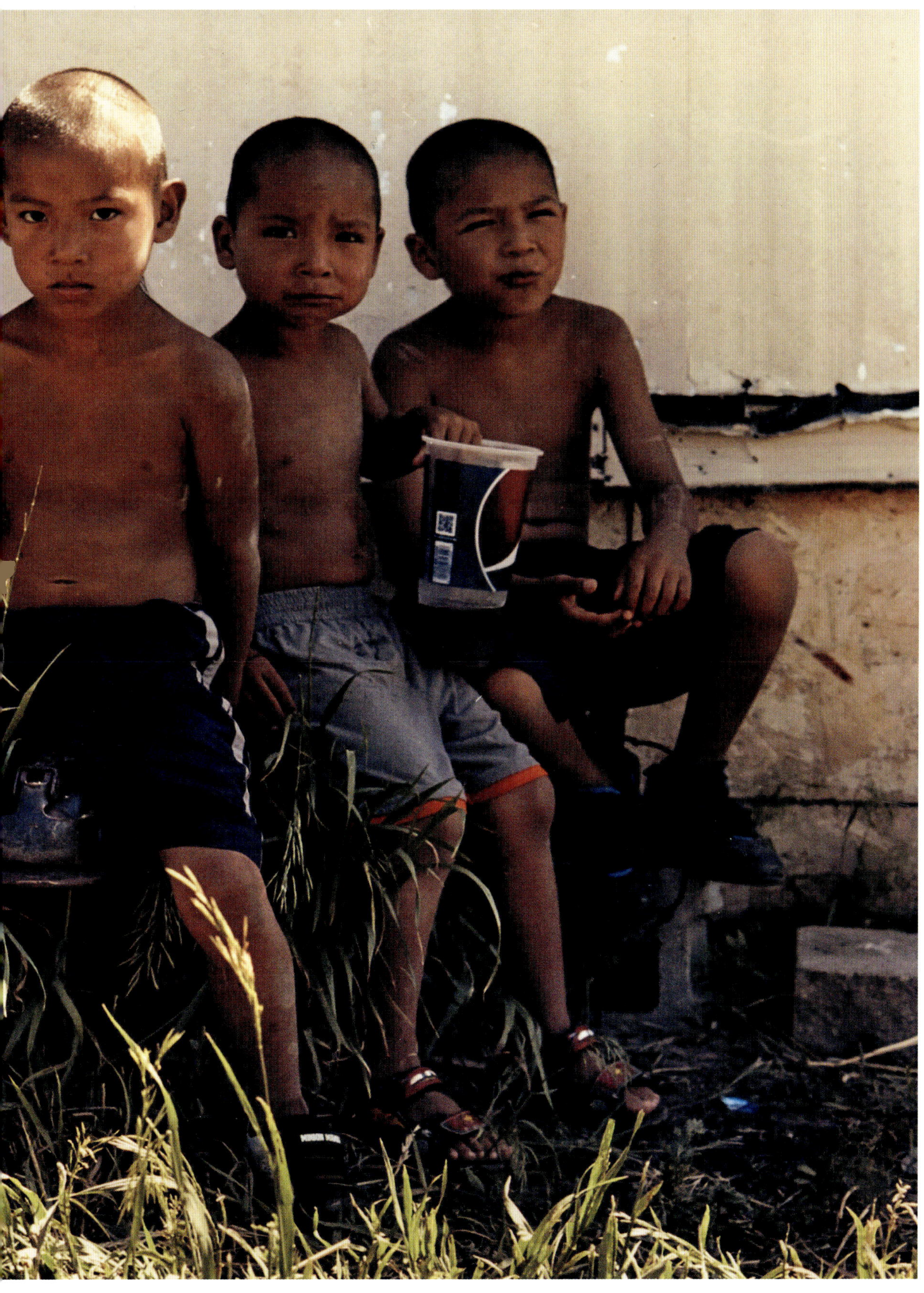

"Our language will never die; it is part of our daily life. We've simply, in recent years, had to invent new words like 'bathroom' or 'smartphone,' which we call 'omás'aphela.' We have created these new words to adapt and to not lose our language."

Alex White Plume,
Lakota tribe

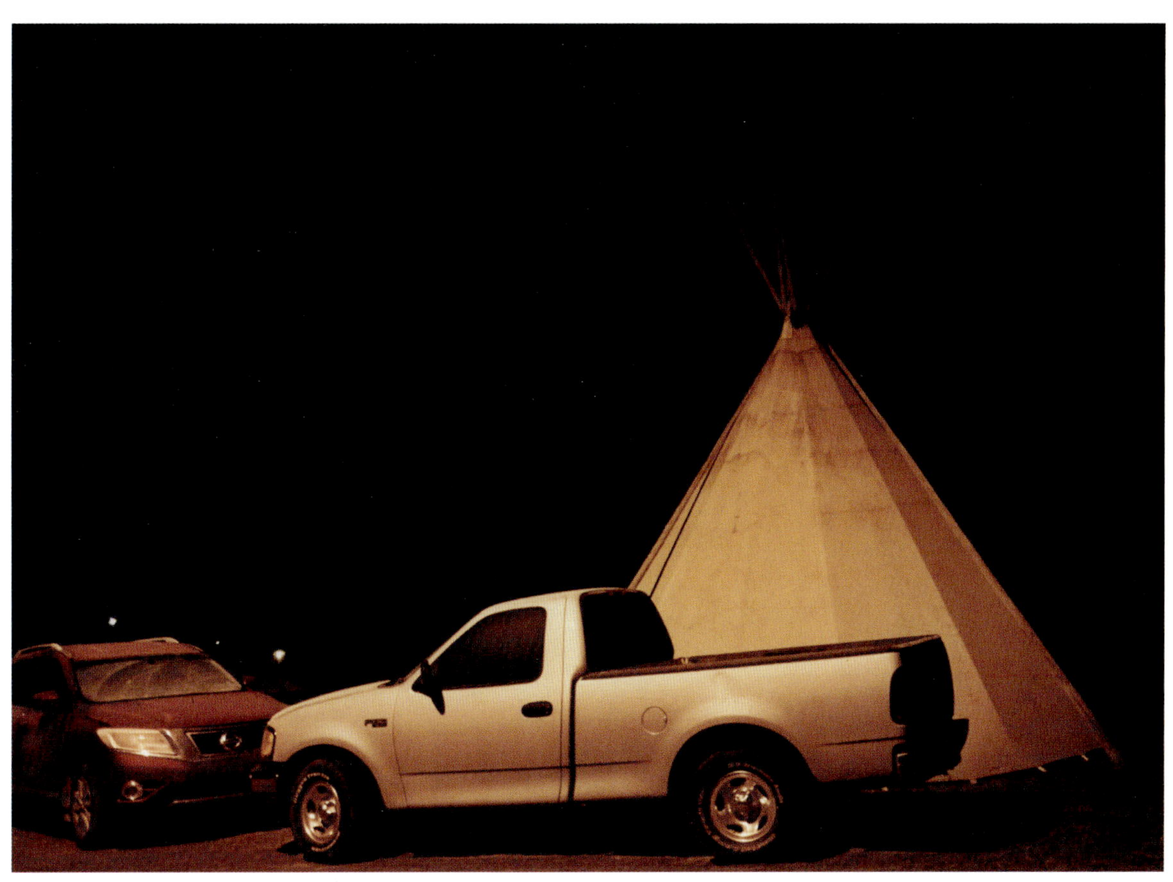

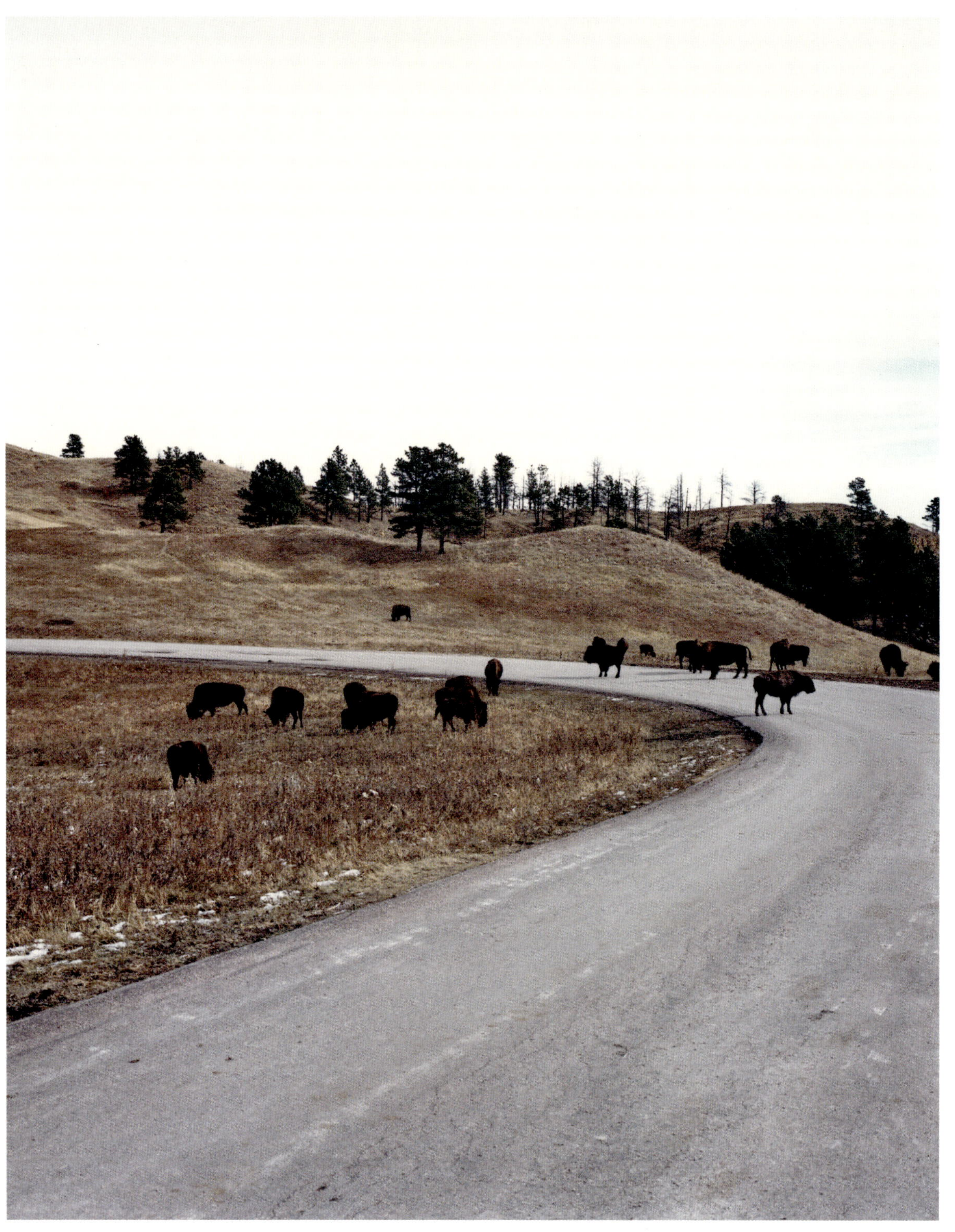

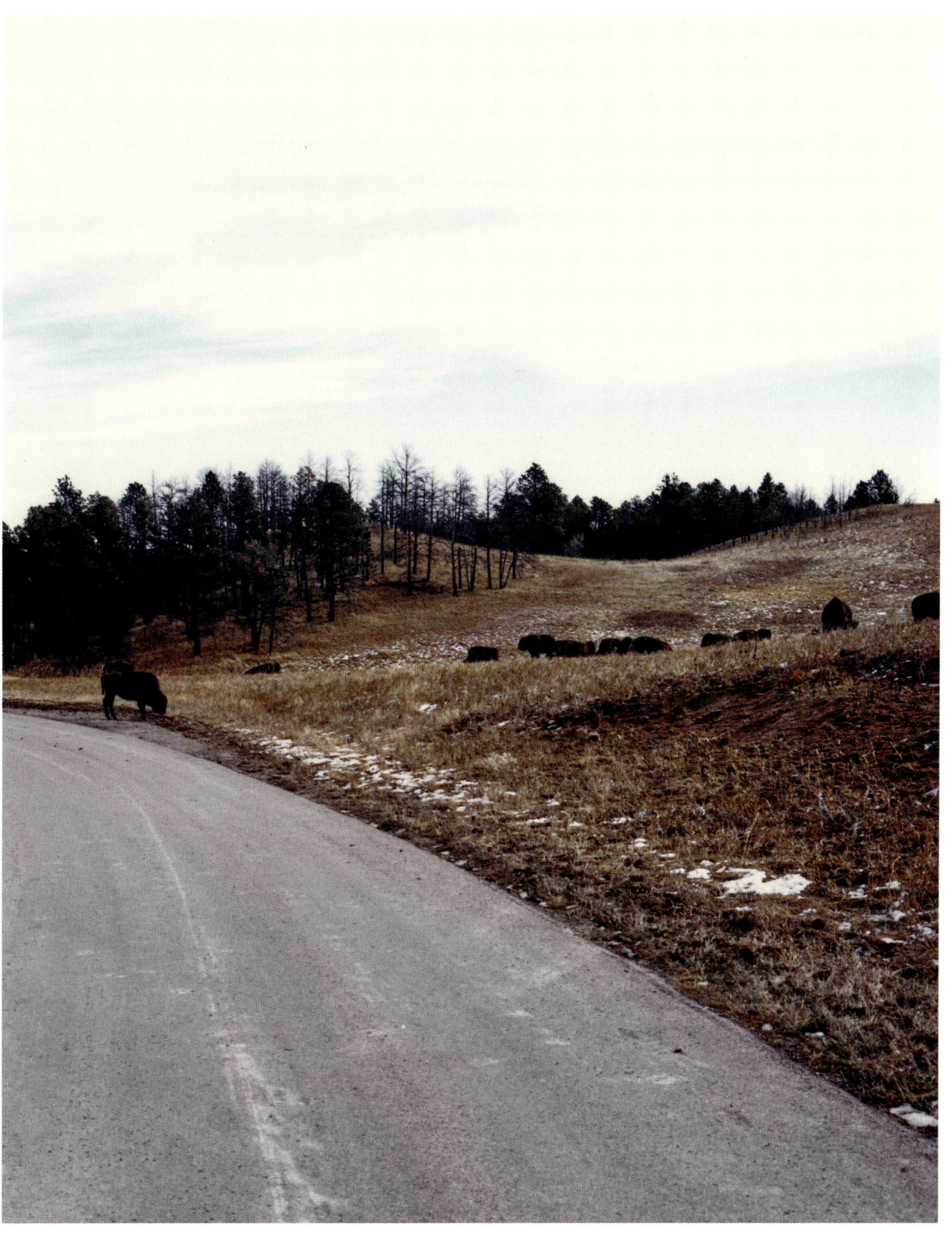

"Living on reservations made by the white government is like living in a wide open land of prison. But, still, it is our Homelands."

Gibby Jones,
Navajo Nation

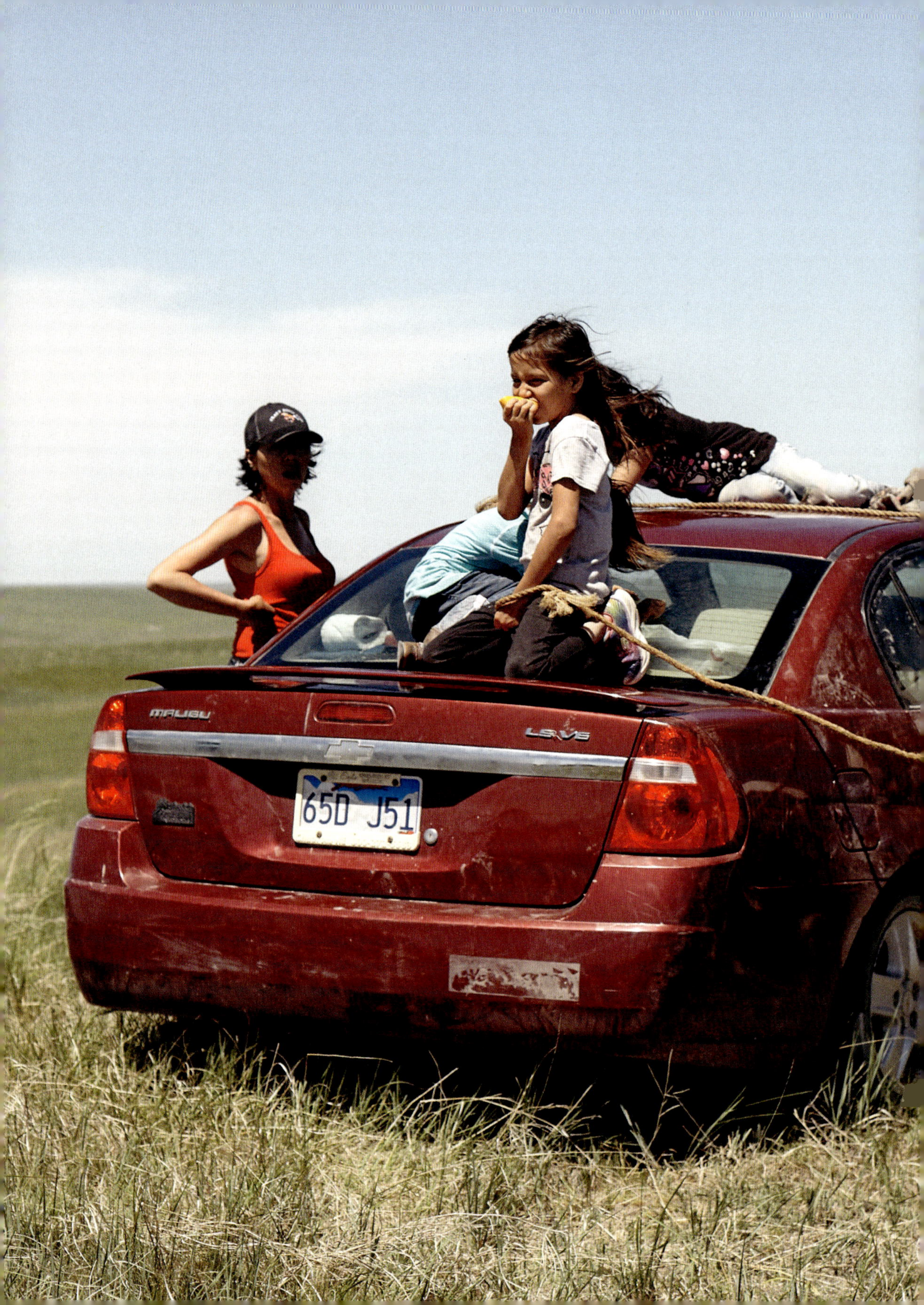

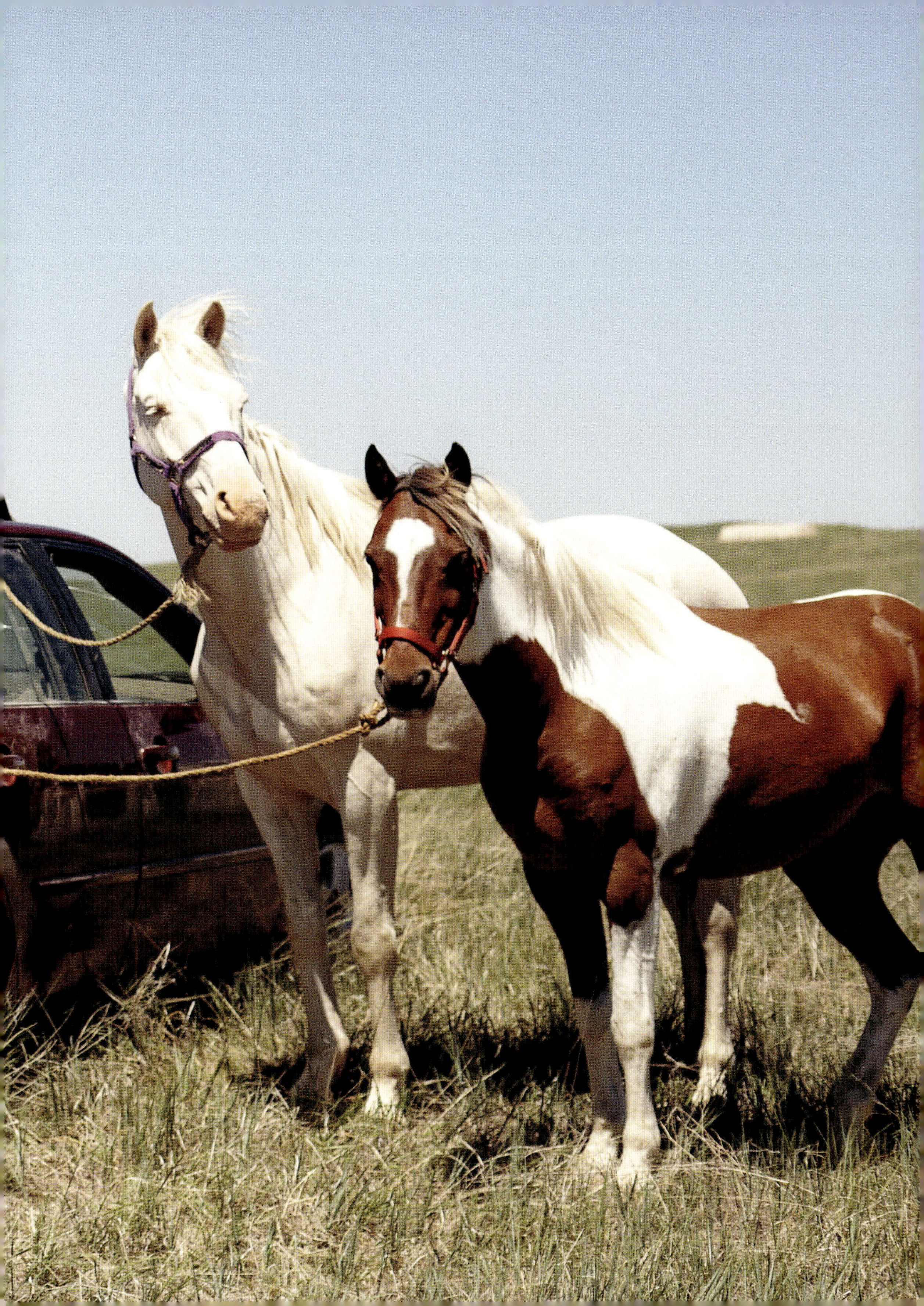

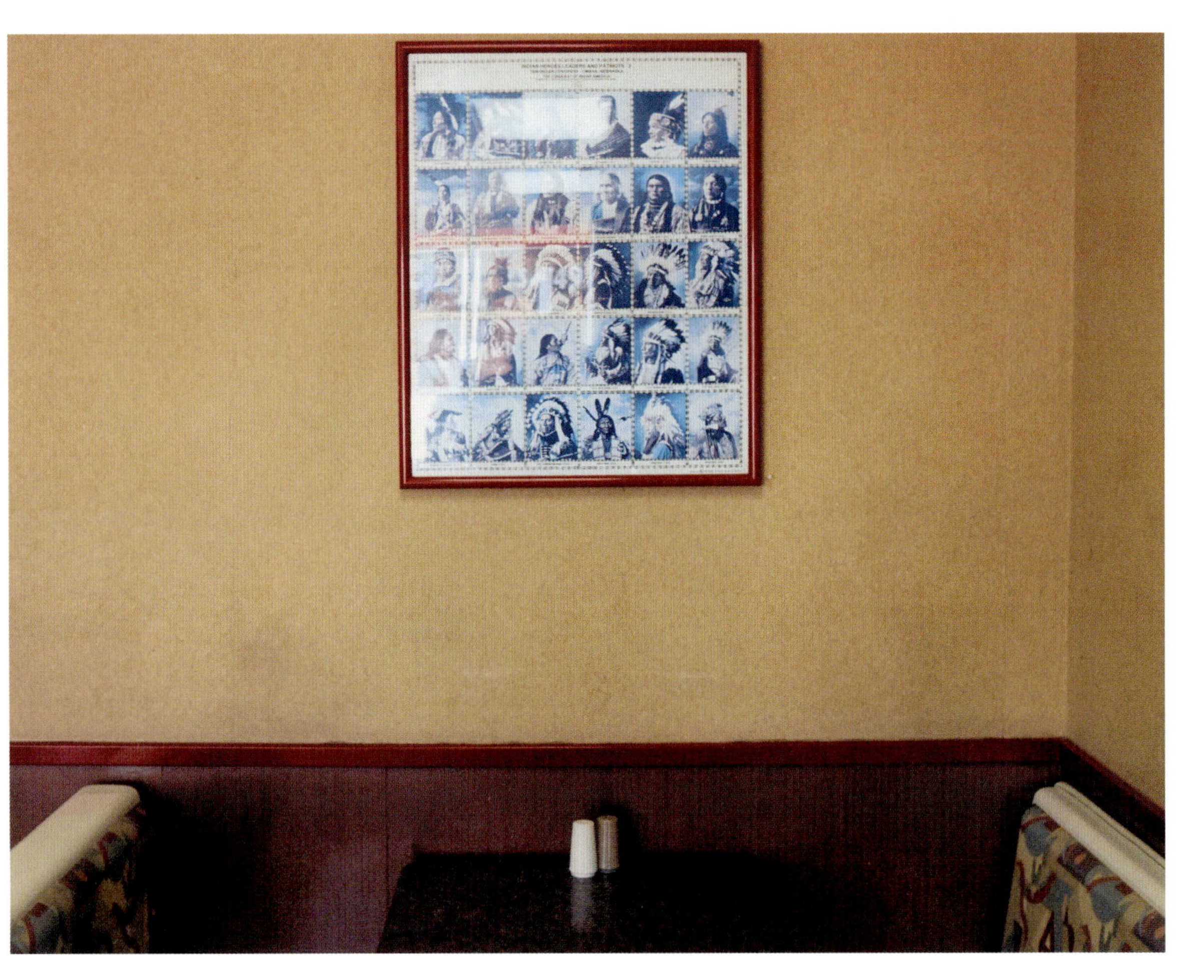

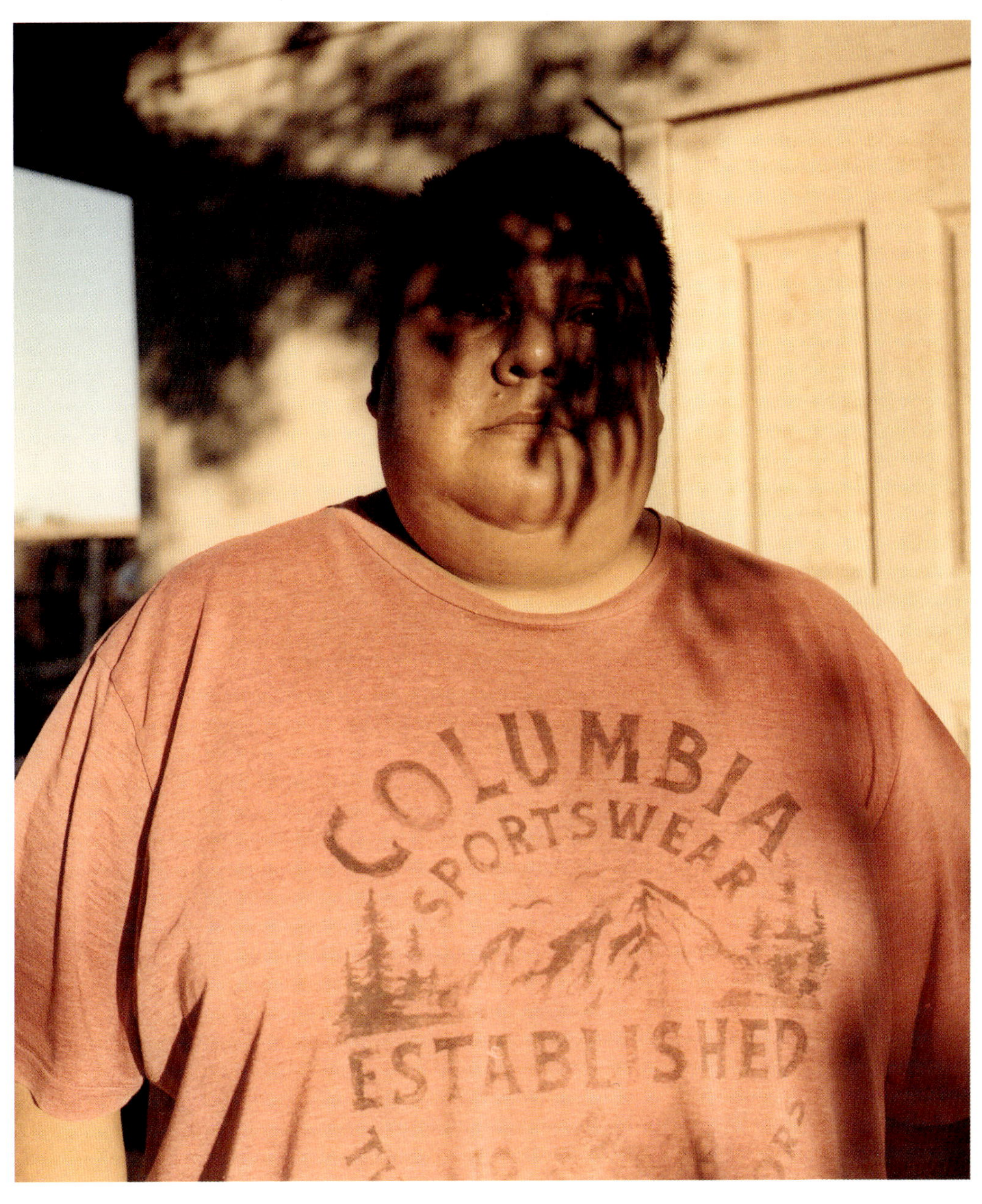
COLUMBIA
SPORTSWEAR
ESTABLISHED

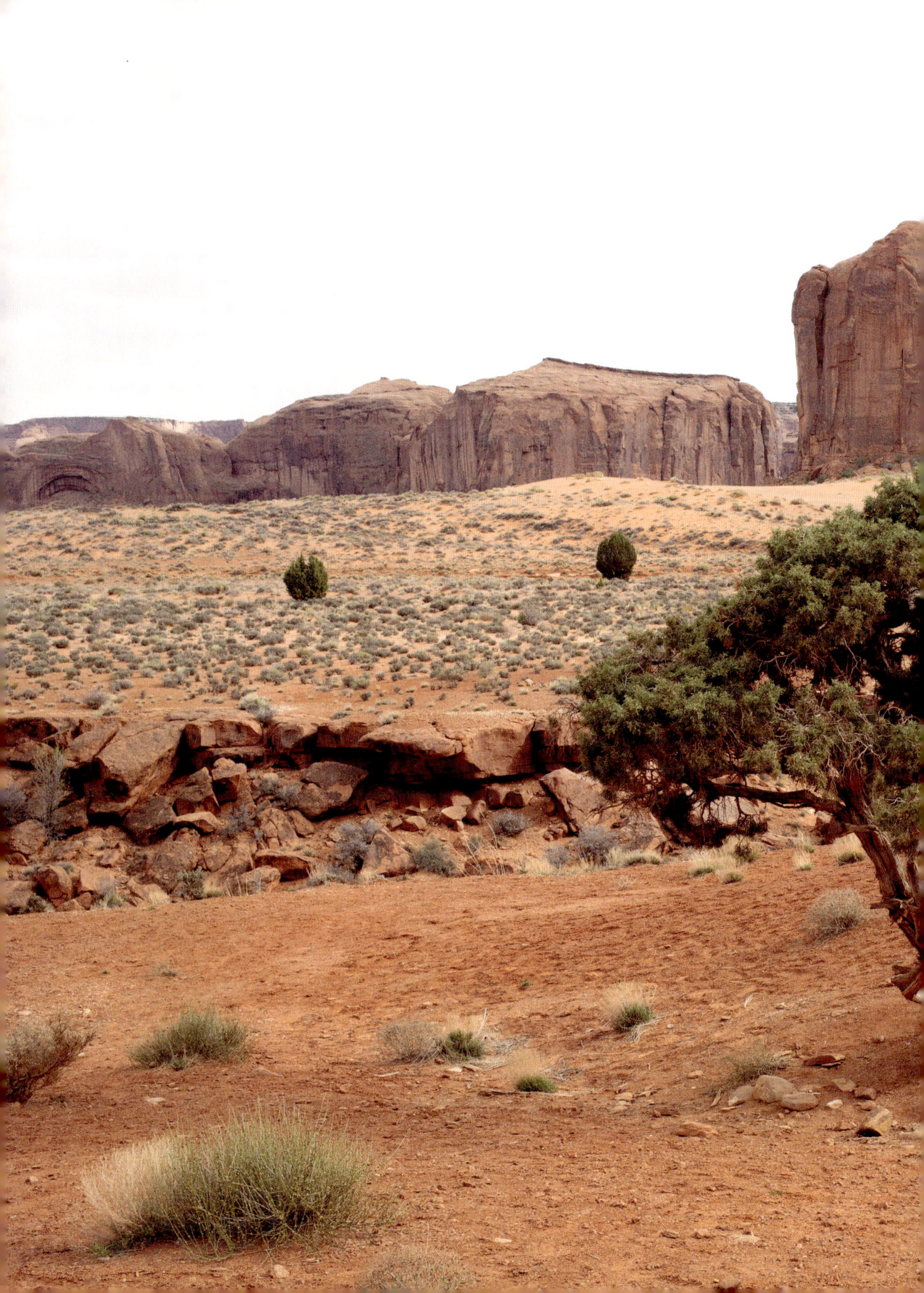

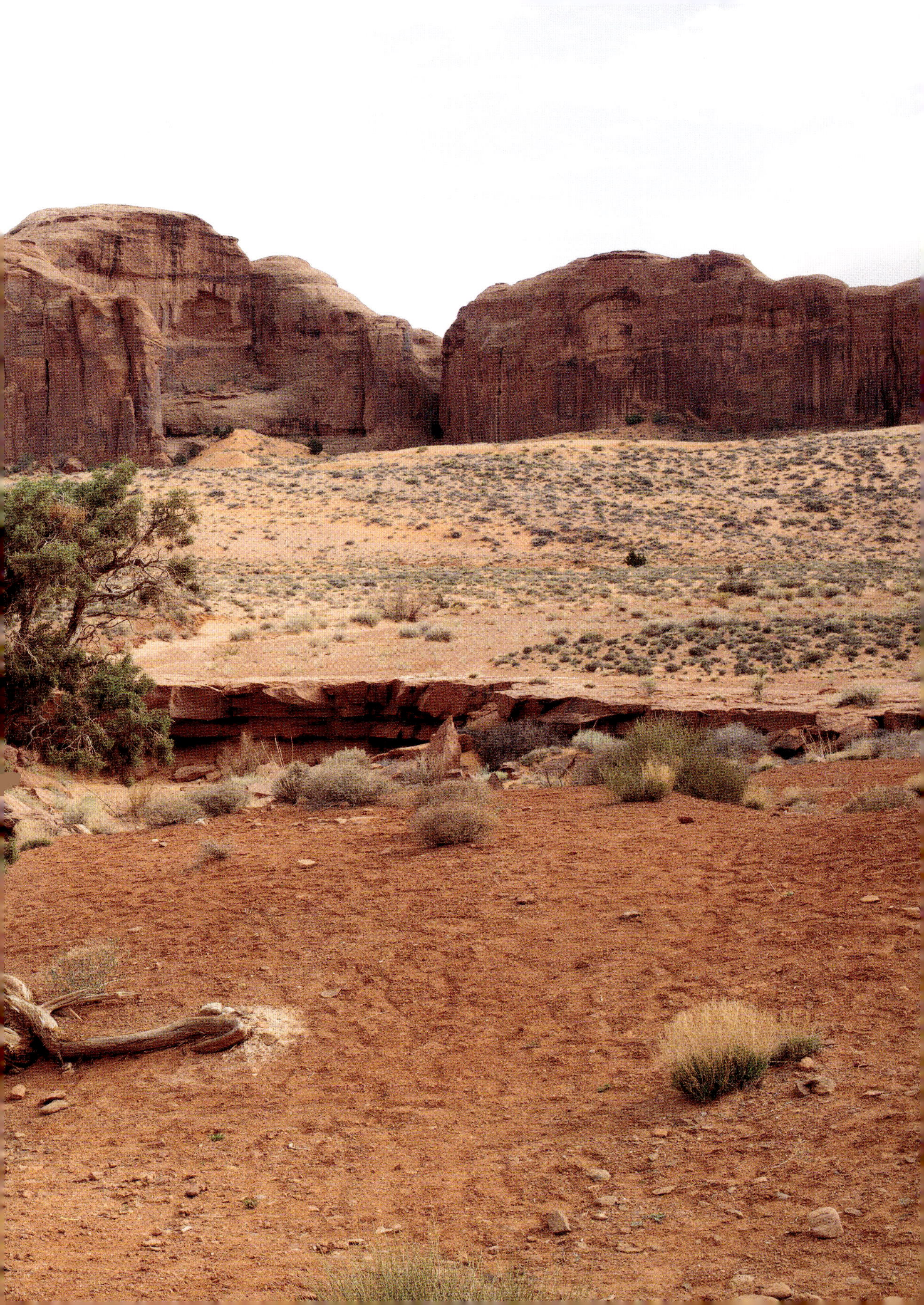

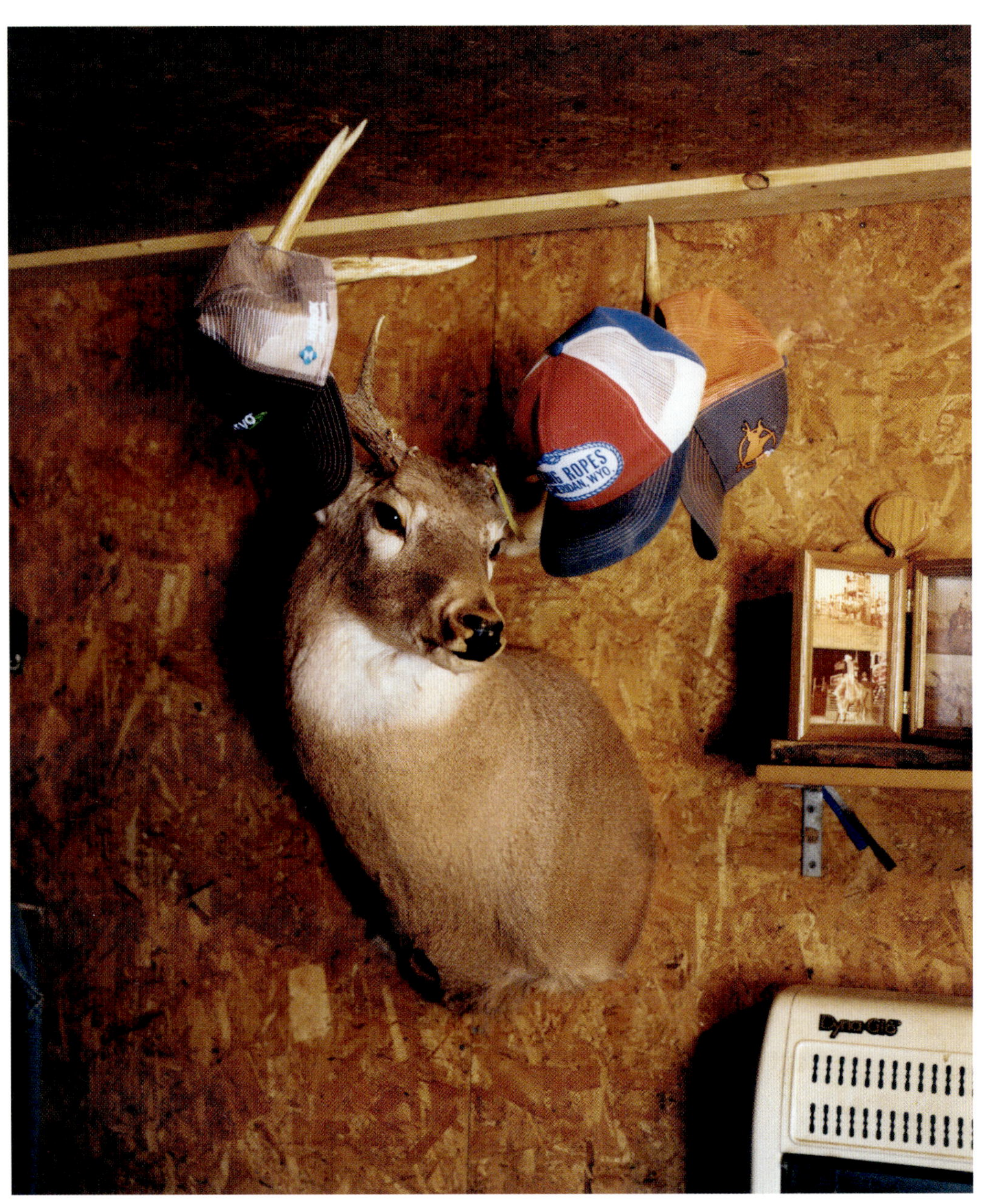

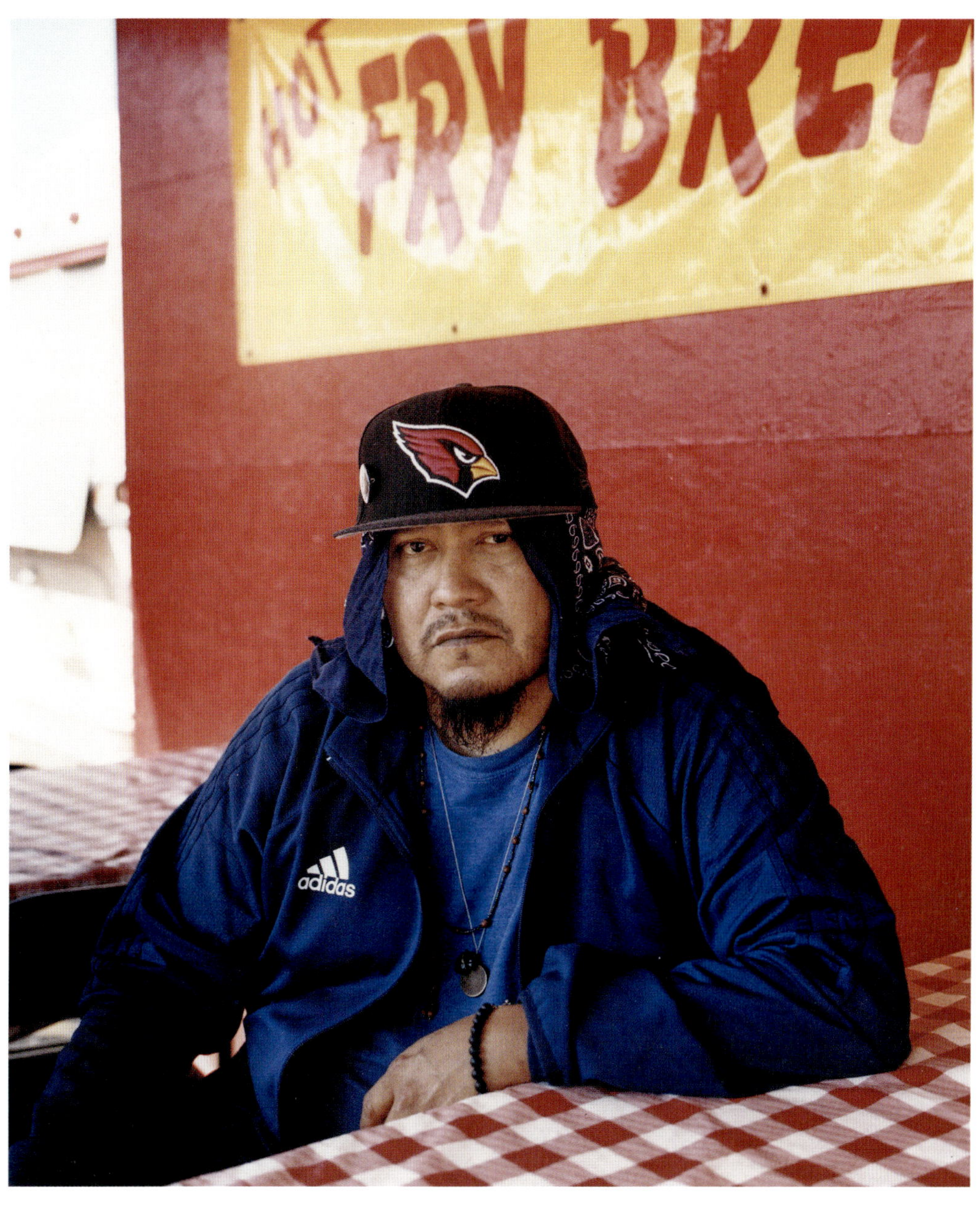

HOT FRY BREAD

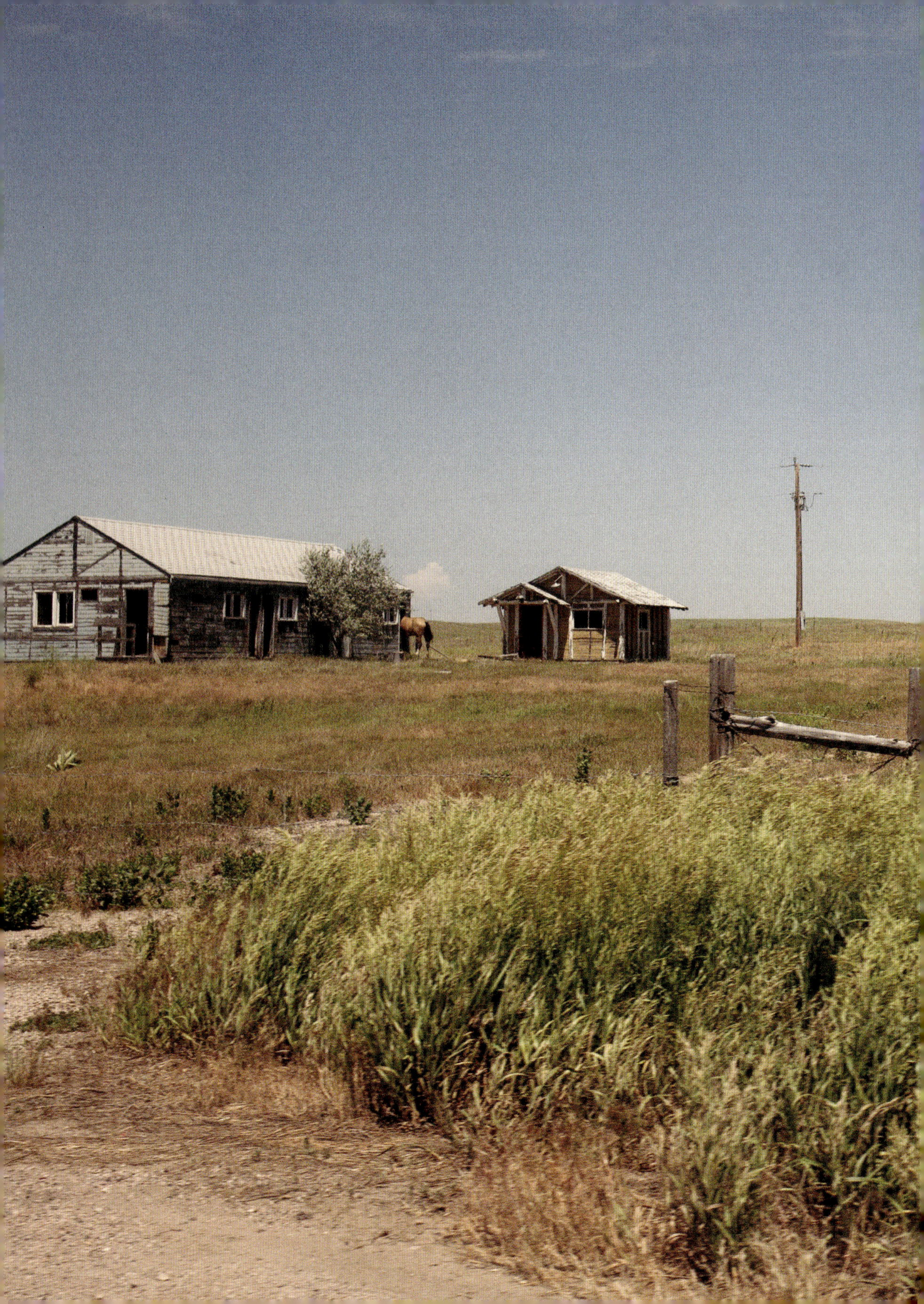

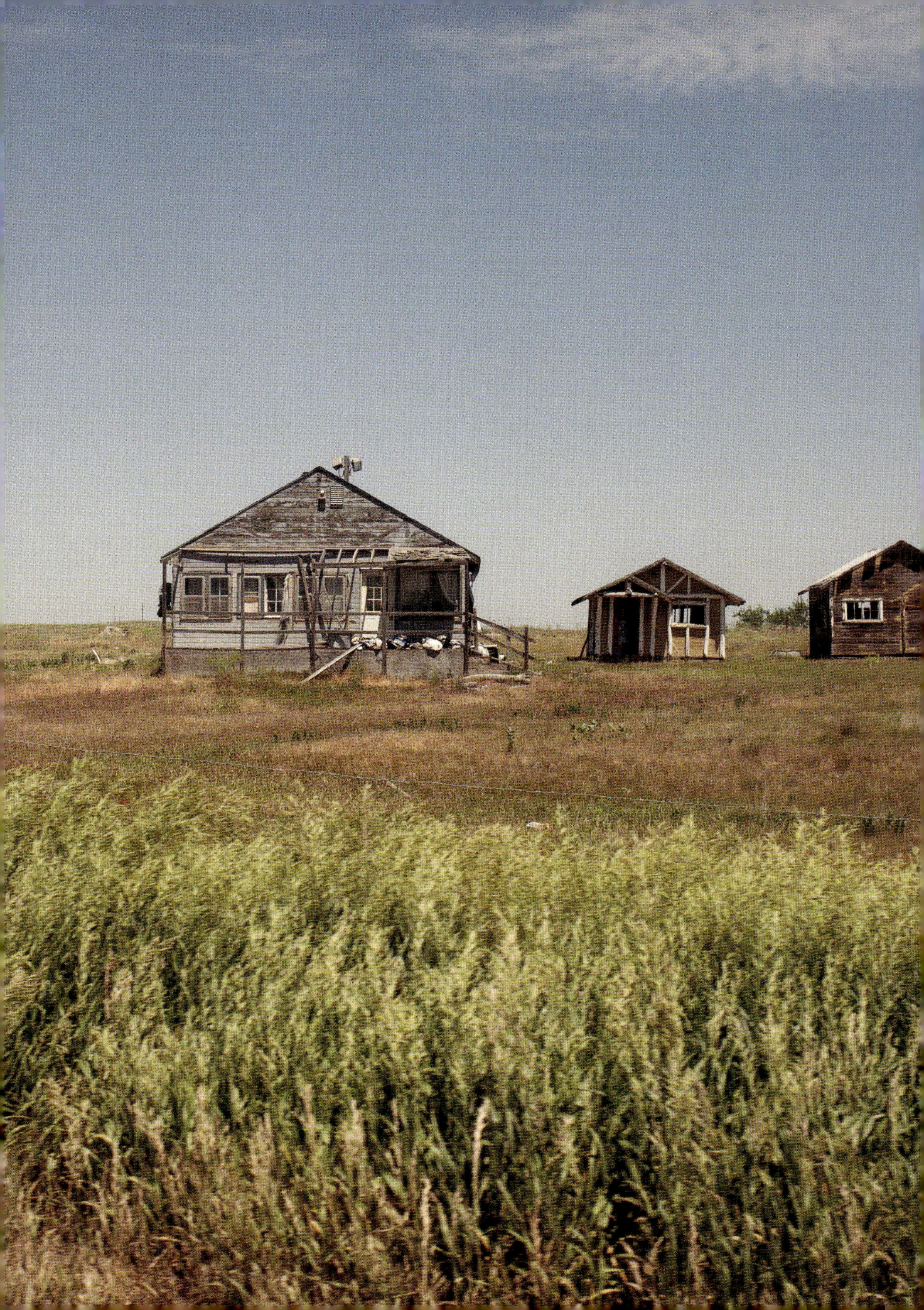

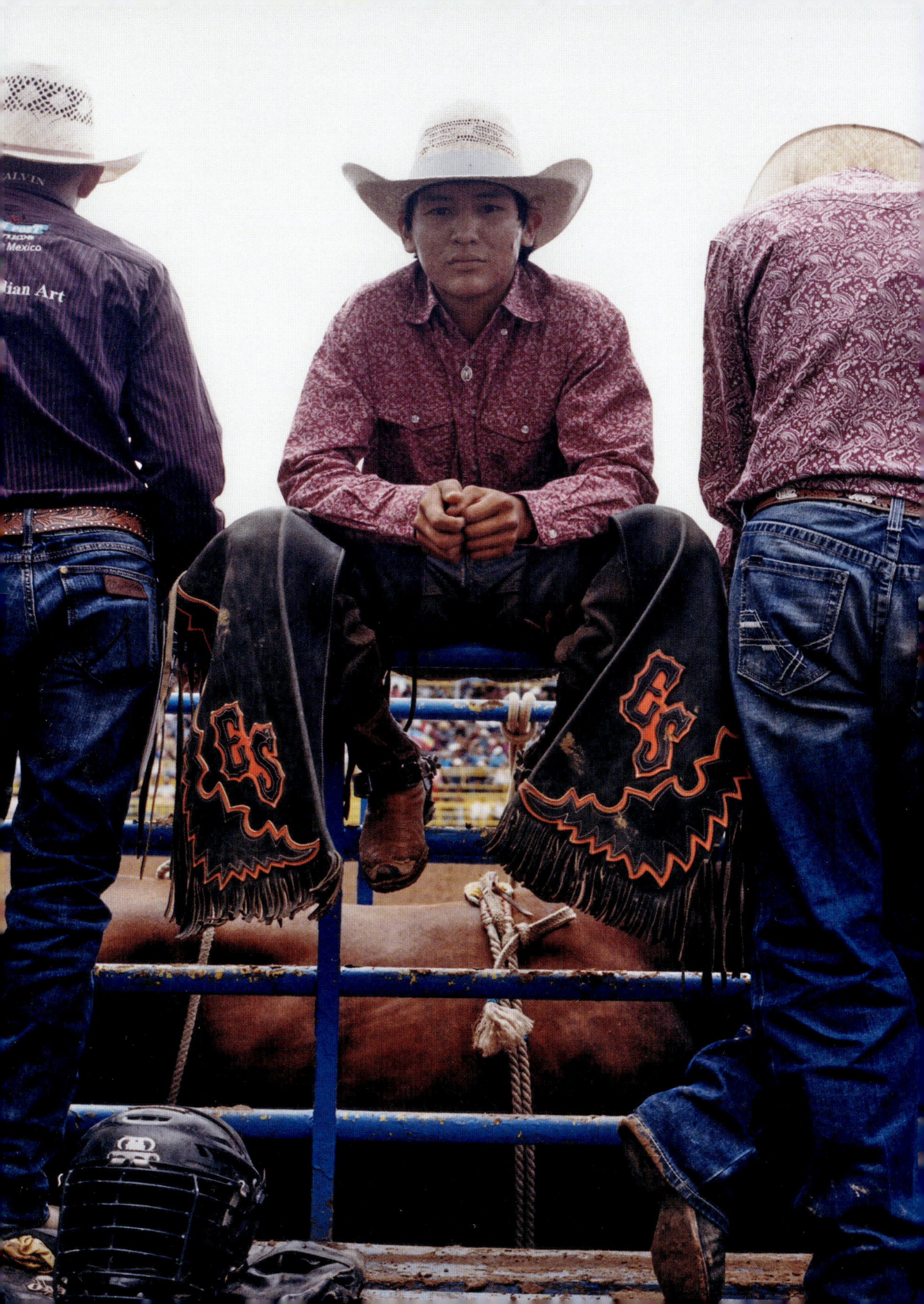

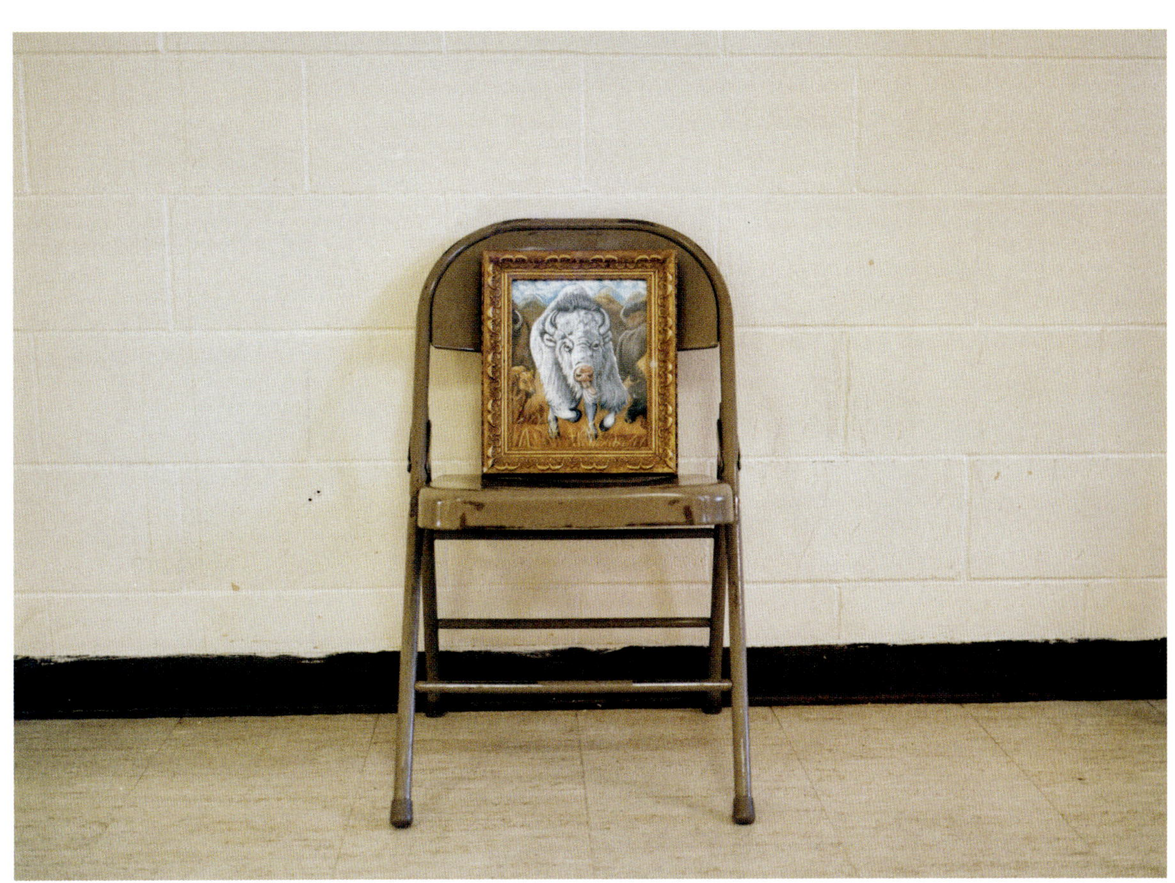

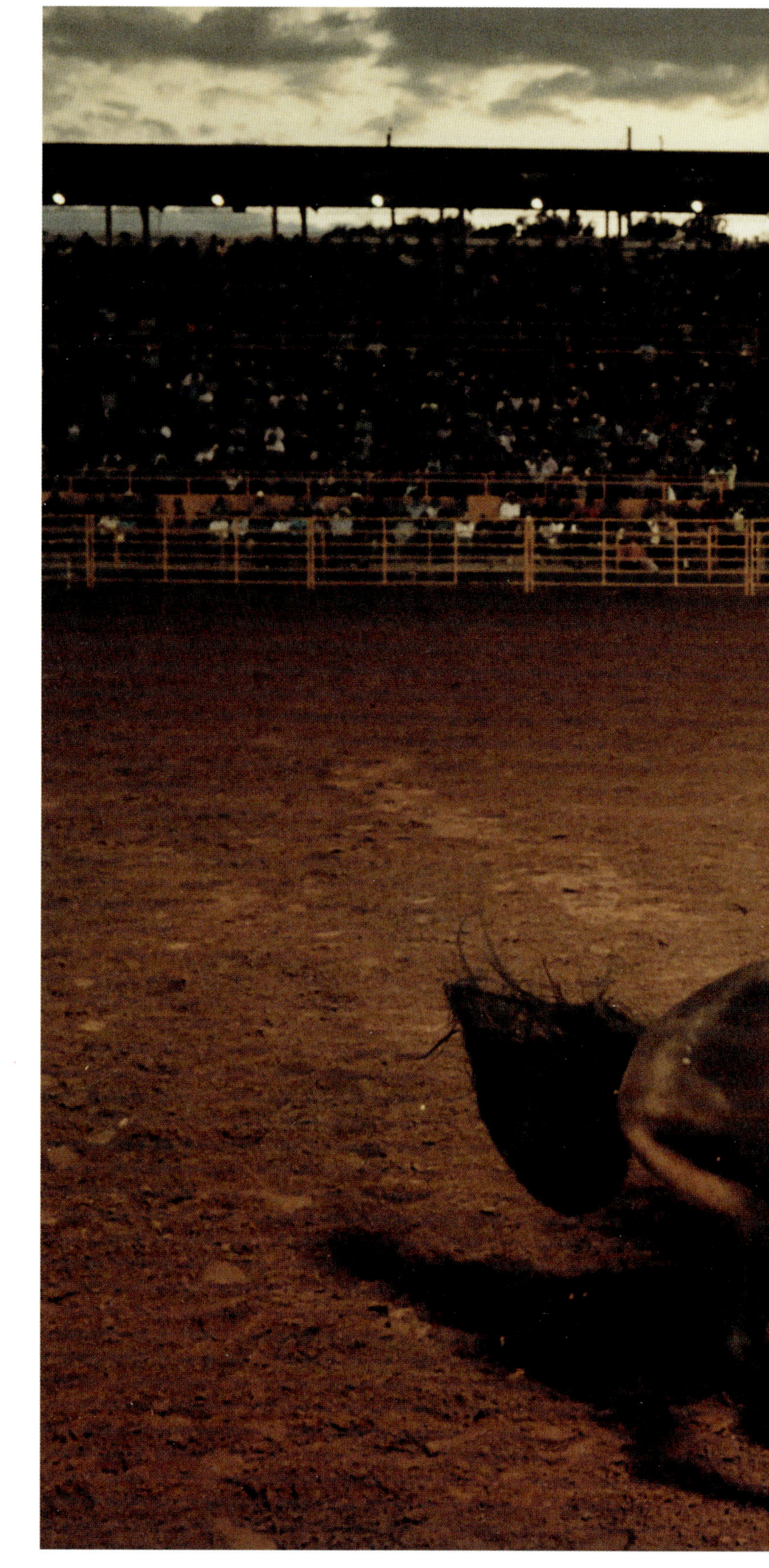

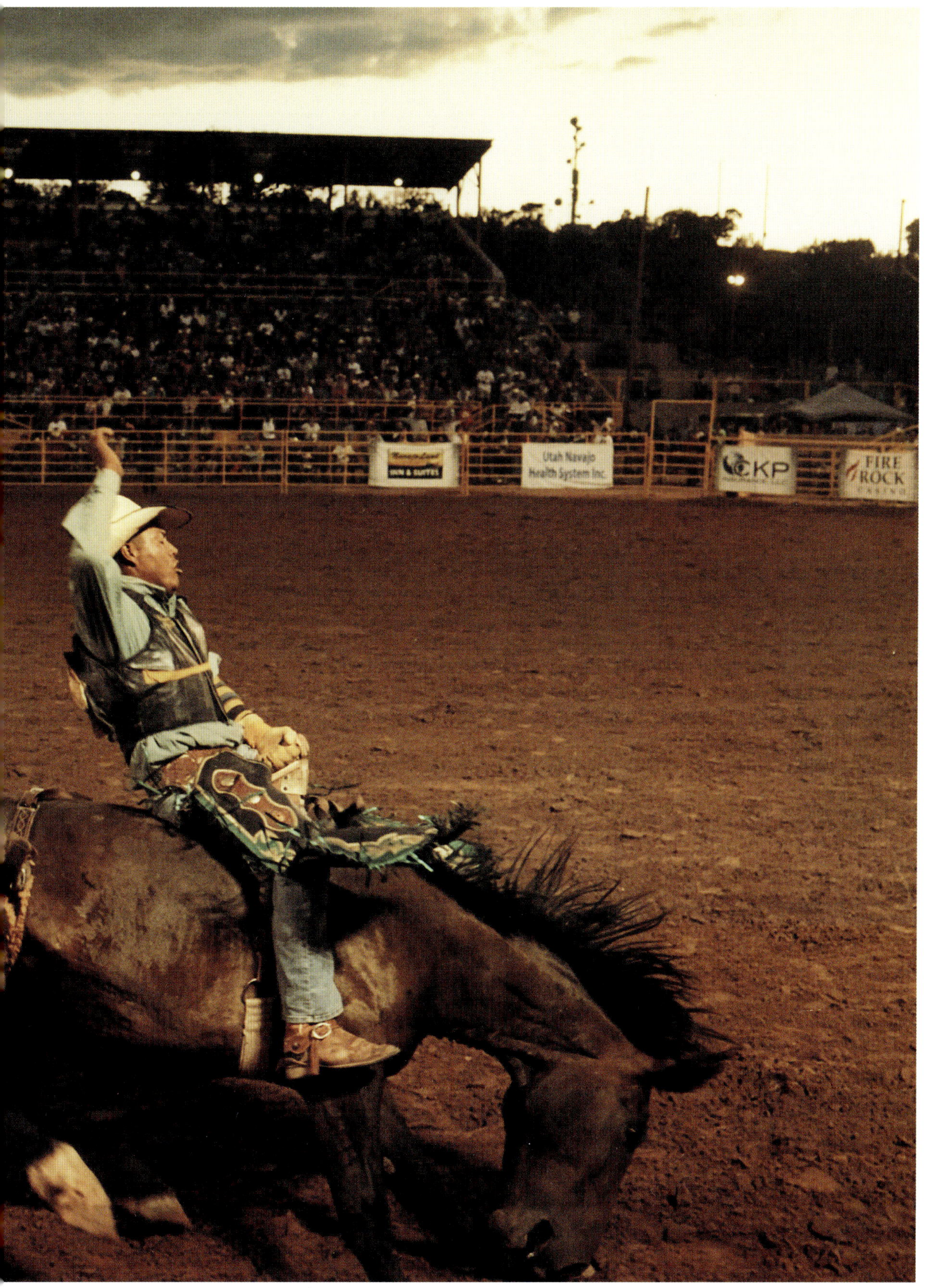

Utah Navajo
Health System Inc.
CKP
FIRE ROCK

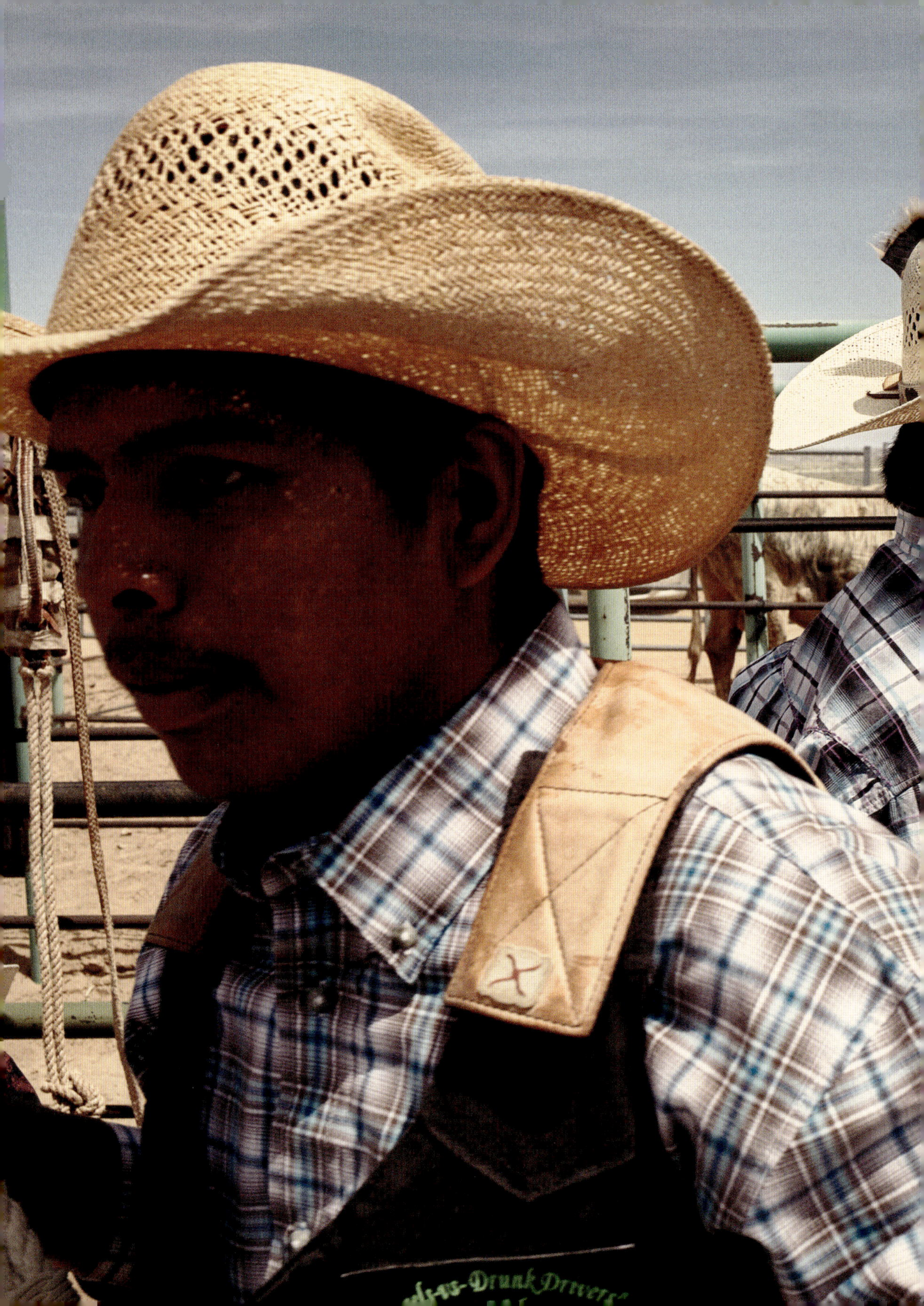

-Drunk Drivers

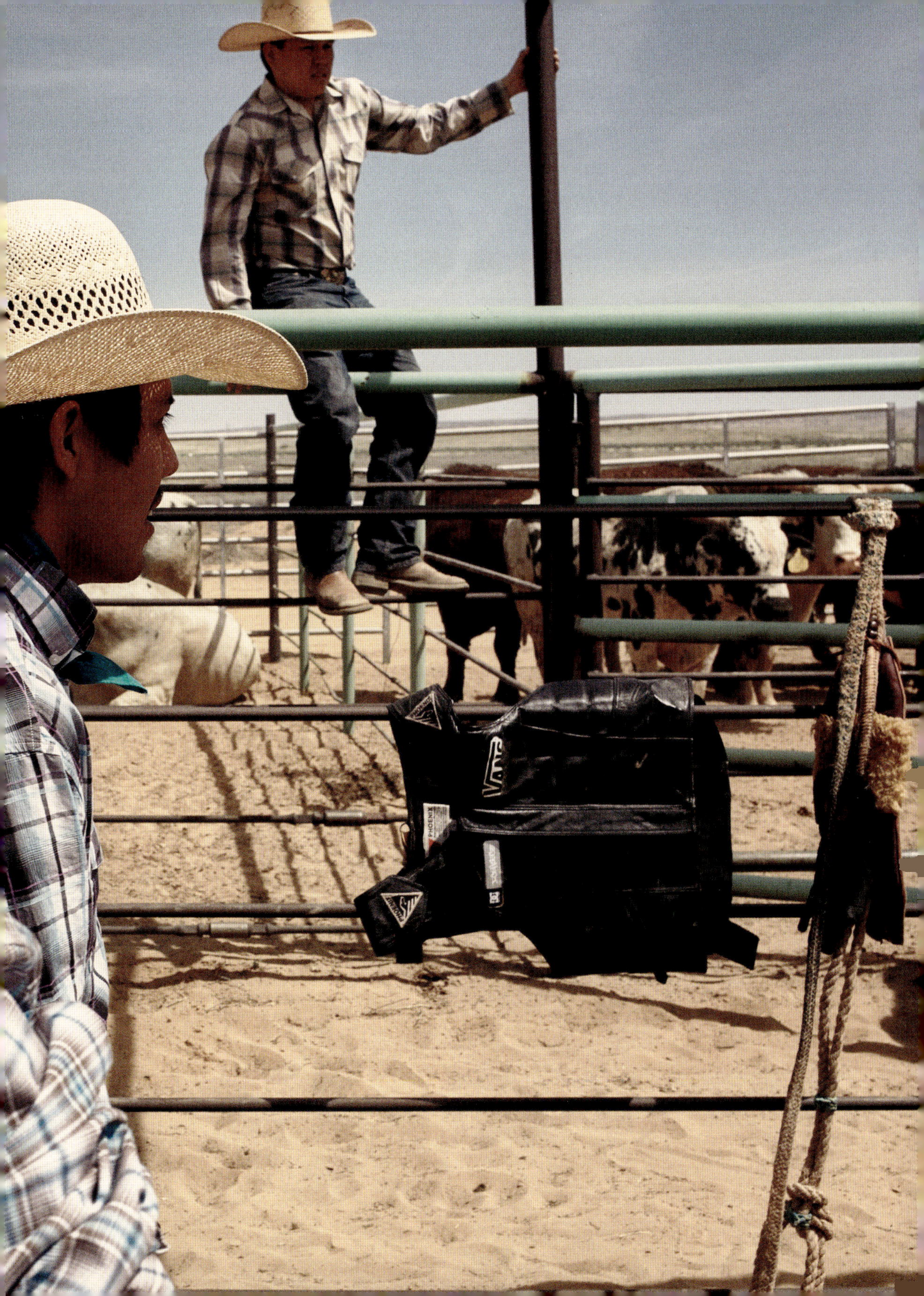

"The unemployment rate on the reservation
is above 60 percent. Most end up leaving
the reservation for work. Like myself, many go out
to not only improve one's life but to return one day
and help change the lives of the reservation.
I will go back home and face our problems head on."

Greyhorse,
Navajo Nation

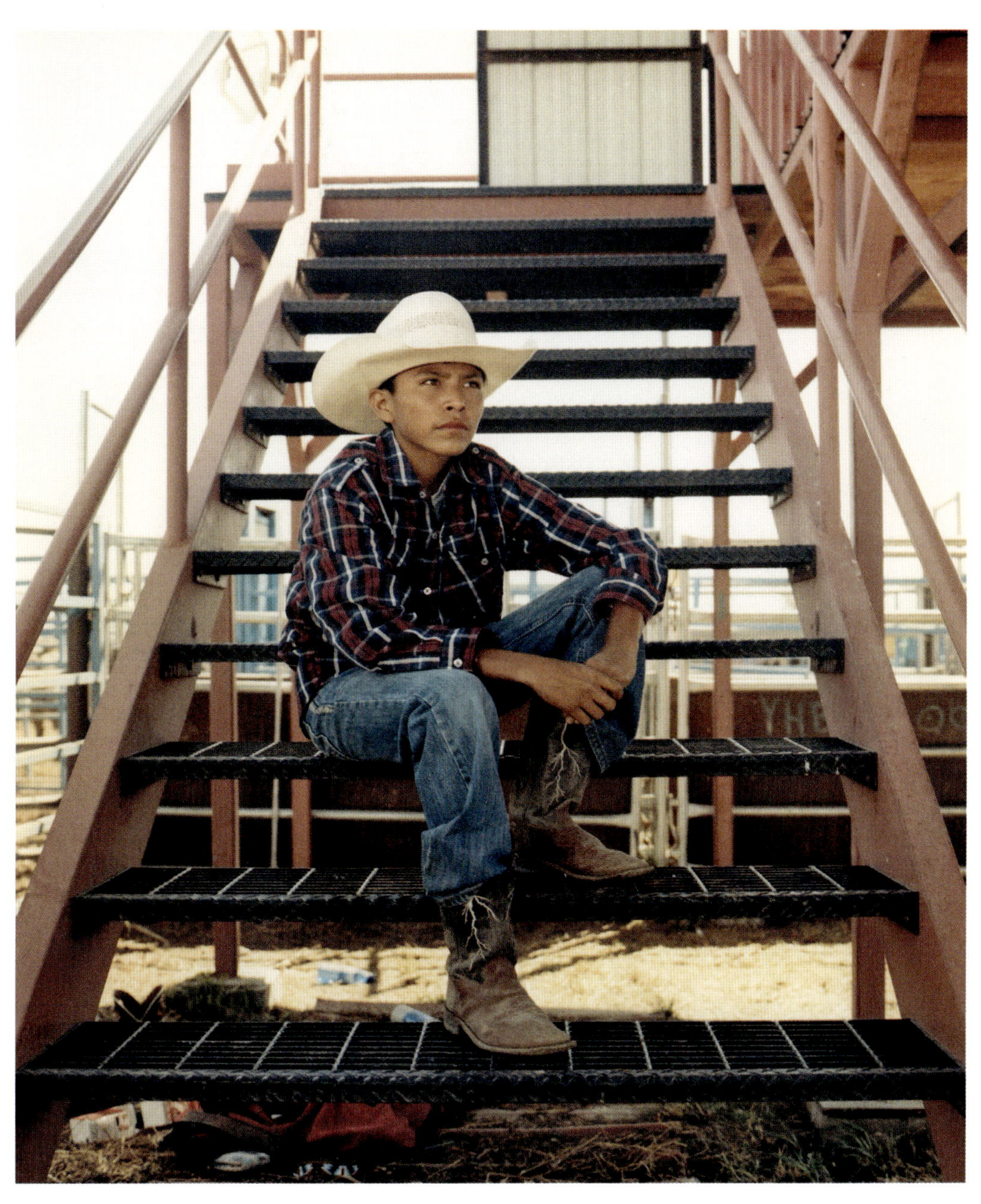

"In 1966, I became a chief. They put a headdress
on me and people started calling me 'elder' yet
I was only twelve years old. From that moment,
I had the responsibility of the sacred pipe,
I had to start learning the sacred language,
to avoid foul language, and to give up holding
a gun in my hands."

Chief Arvol Looking Horse,
Lakota tribe

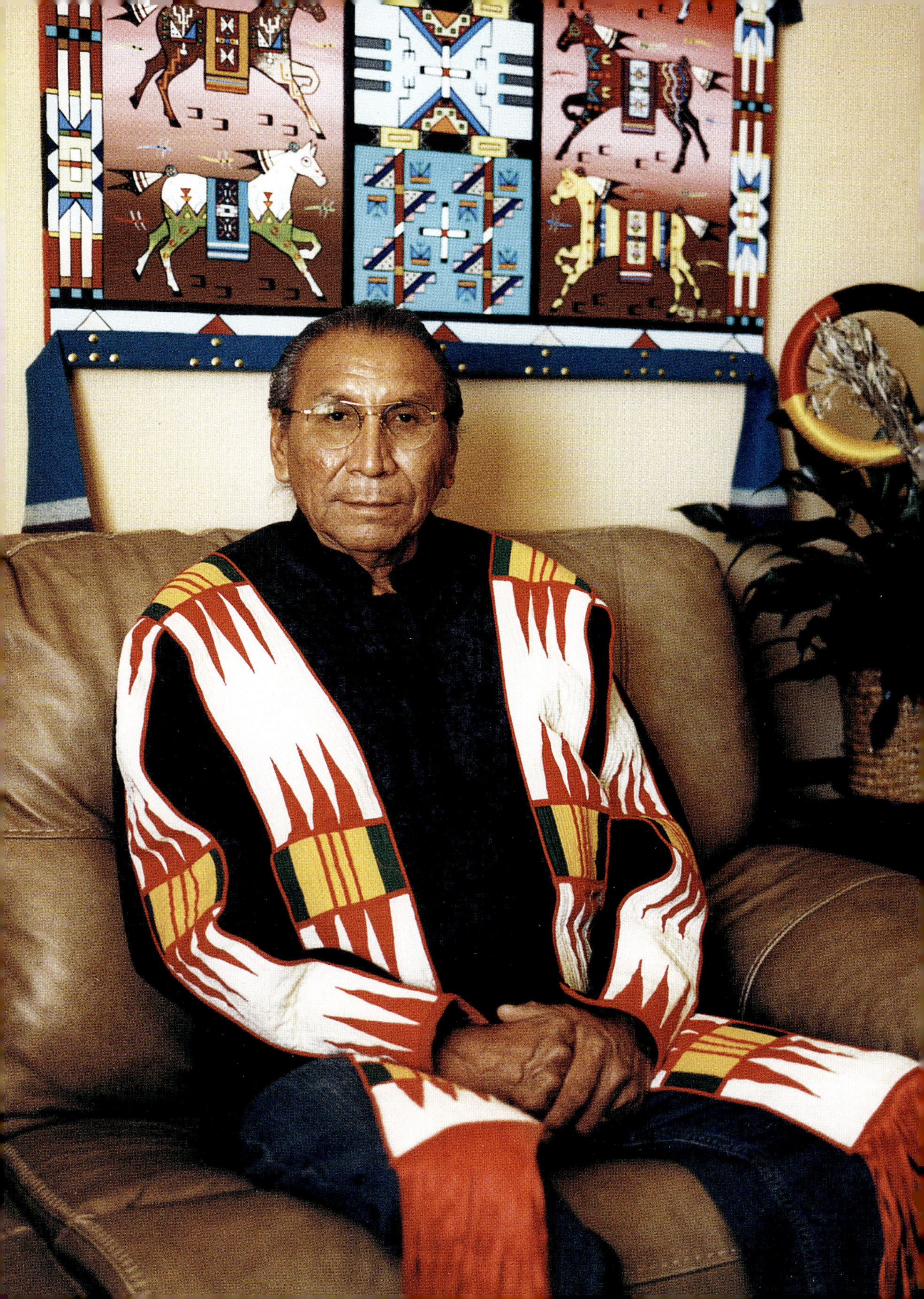

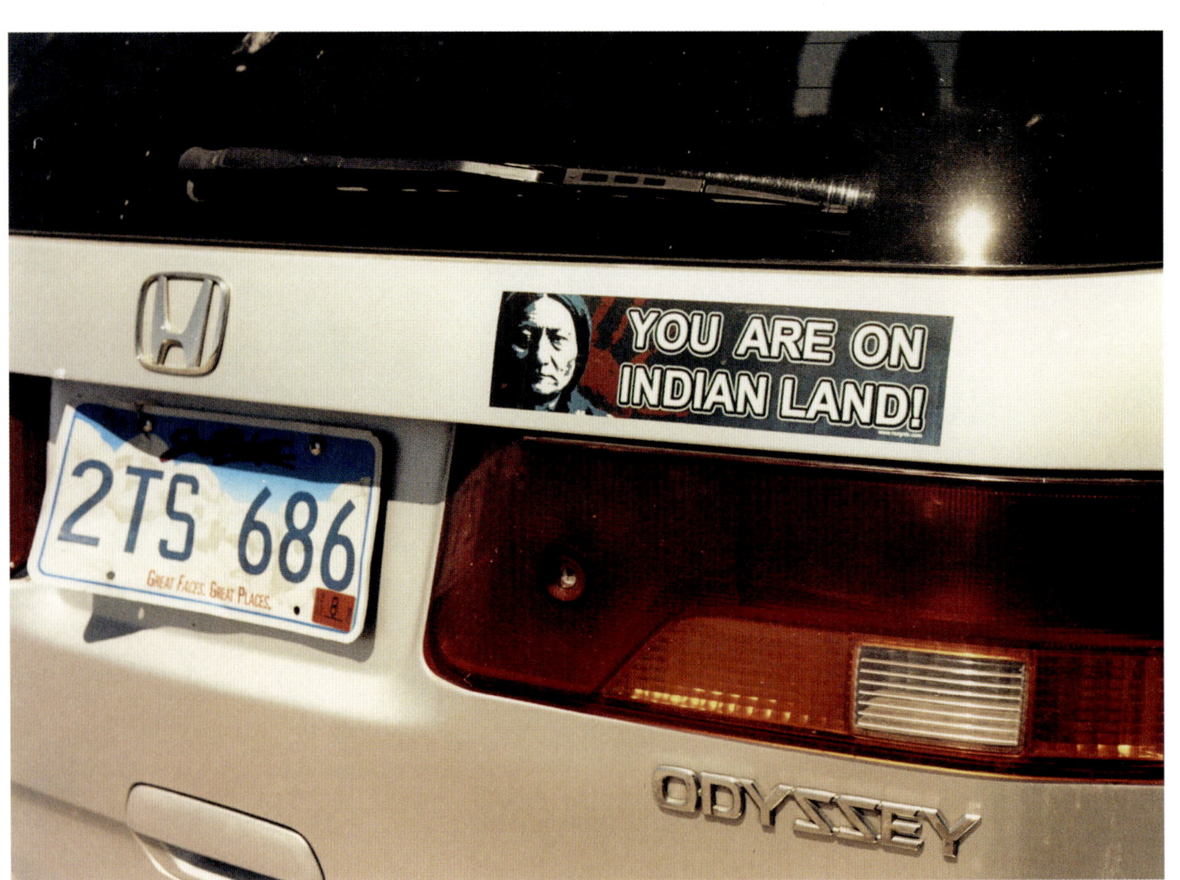

YOU ARE ON INDIAN LAND!
2TS 686
GREAT FACES. GREAT PLACES.
ODYSSEY

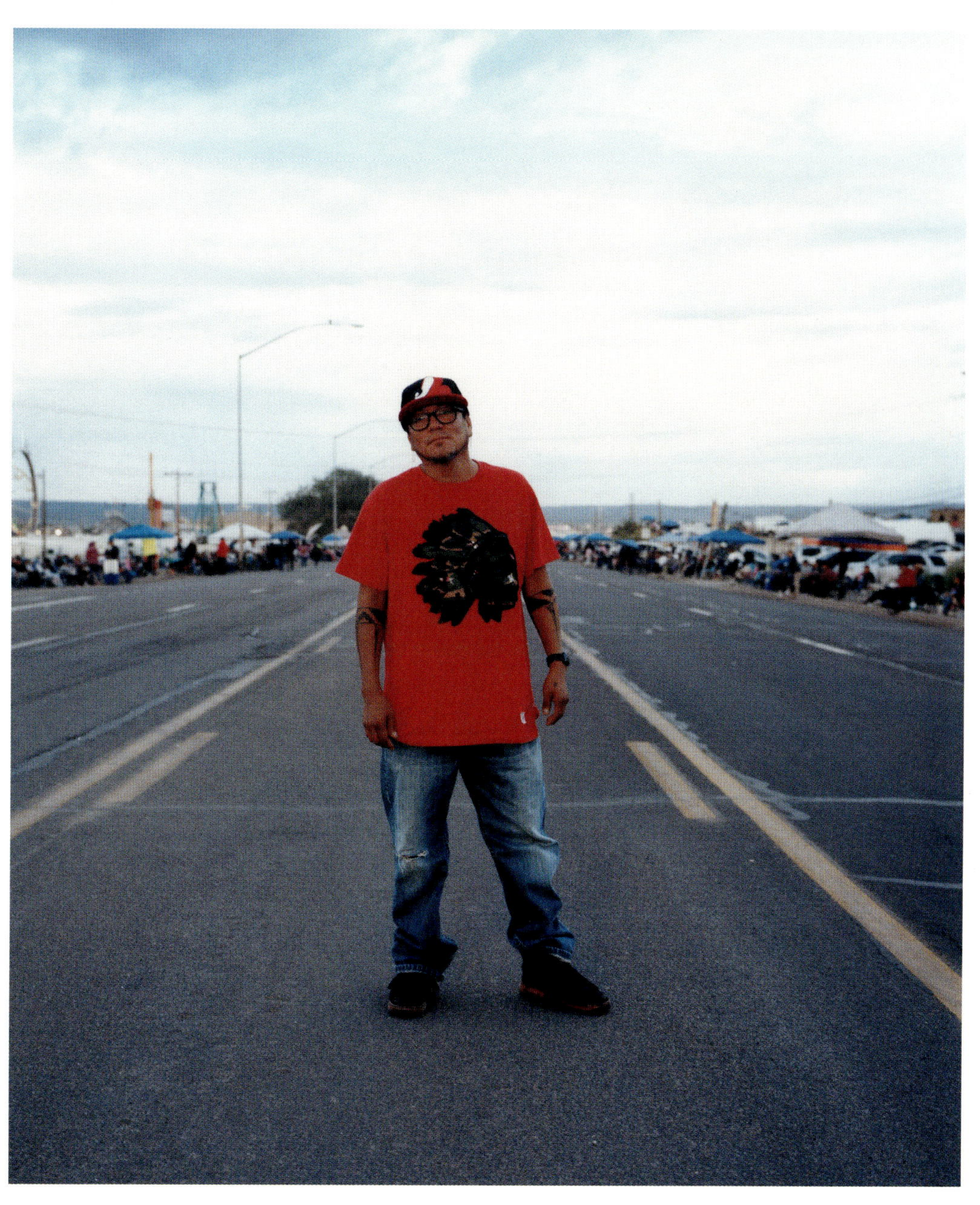

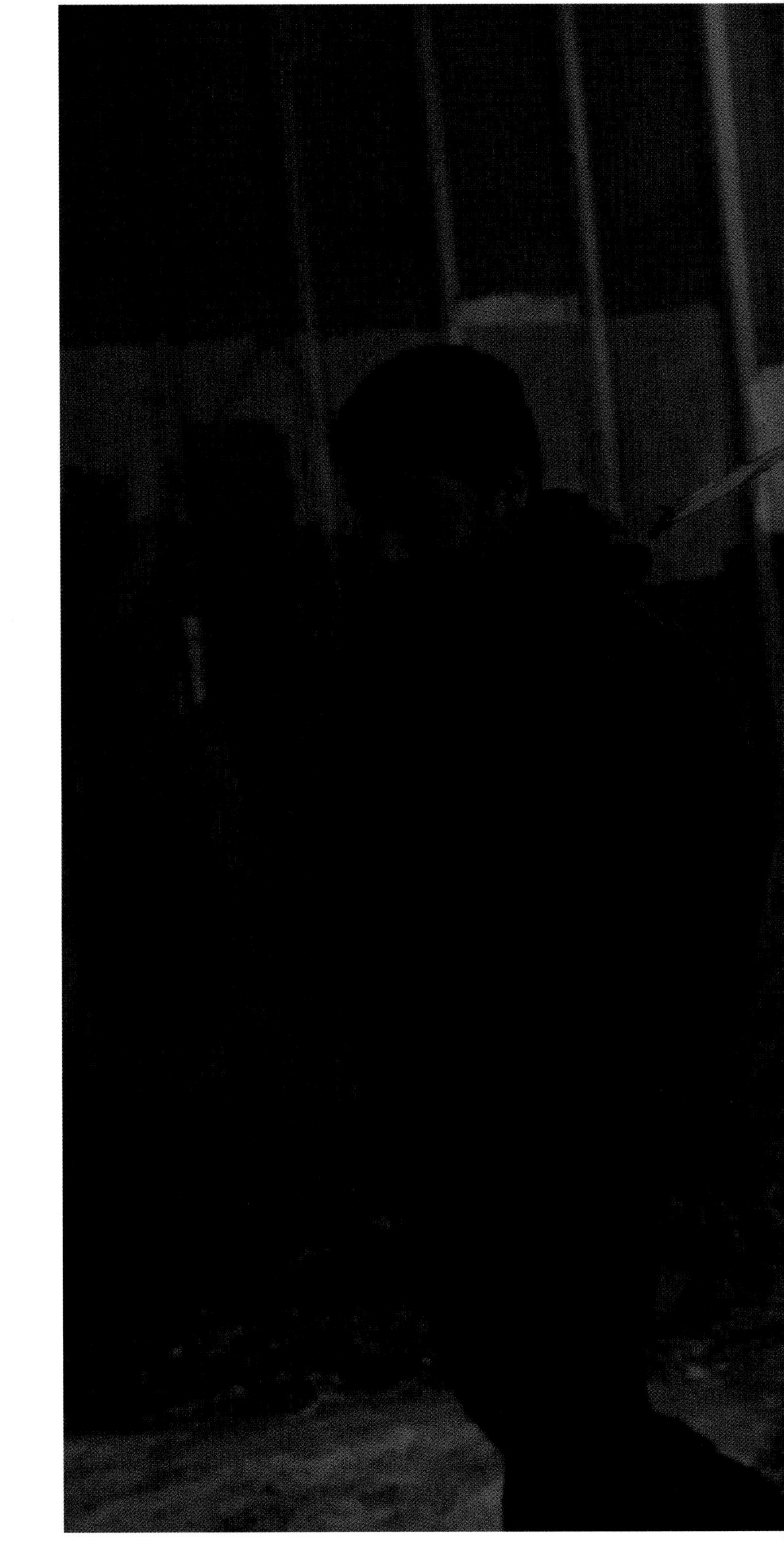

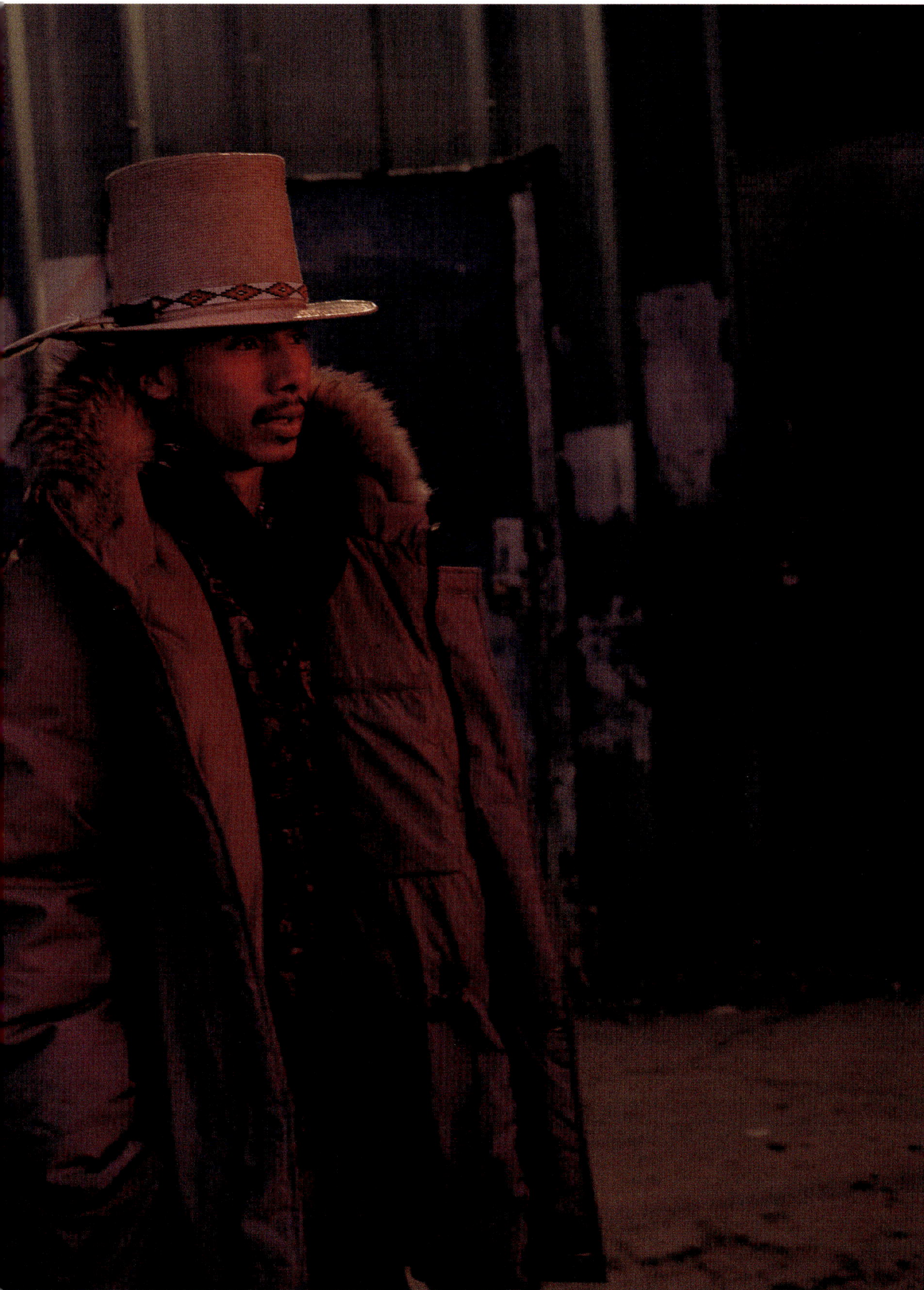

"Our generation of youth is coming into power. We're starting to step up and take leadership roles across the country. You're seeing young Native people rise up and run for public office, for state governments, for the federal government, for their city governments. I myself, I've worked for a local official in Chicago. And I'm able to help push and fight for Native issues because I am a Native person. I'm able to be in that office and constantly remind them that everything we do is going to affect Indigenous people here in the city."

Anthony Pochel,
Lakota tribe and Saulteaux tribe

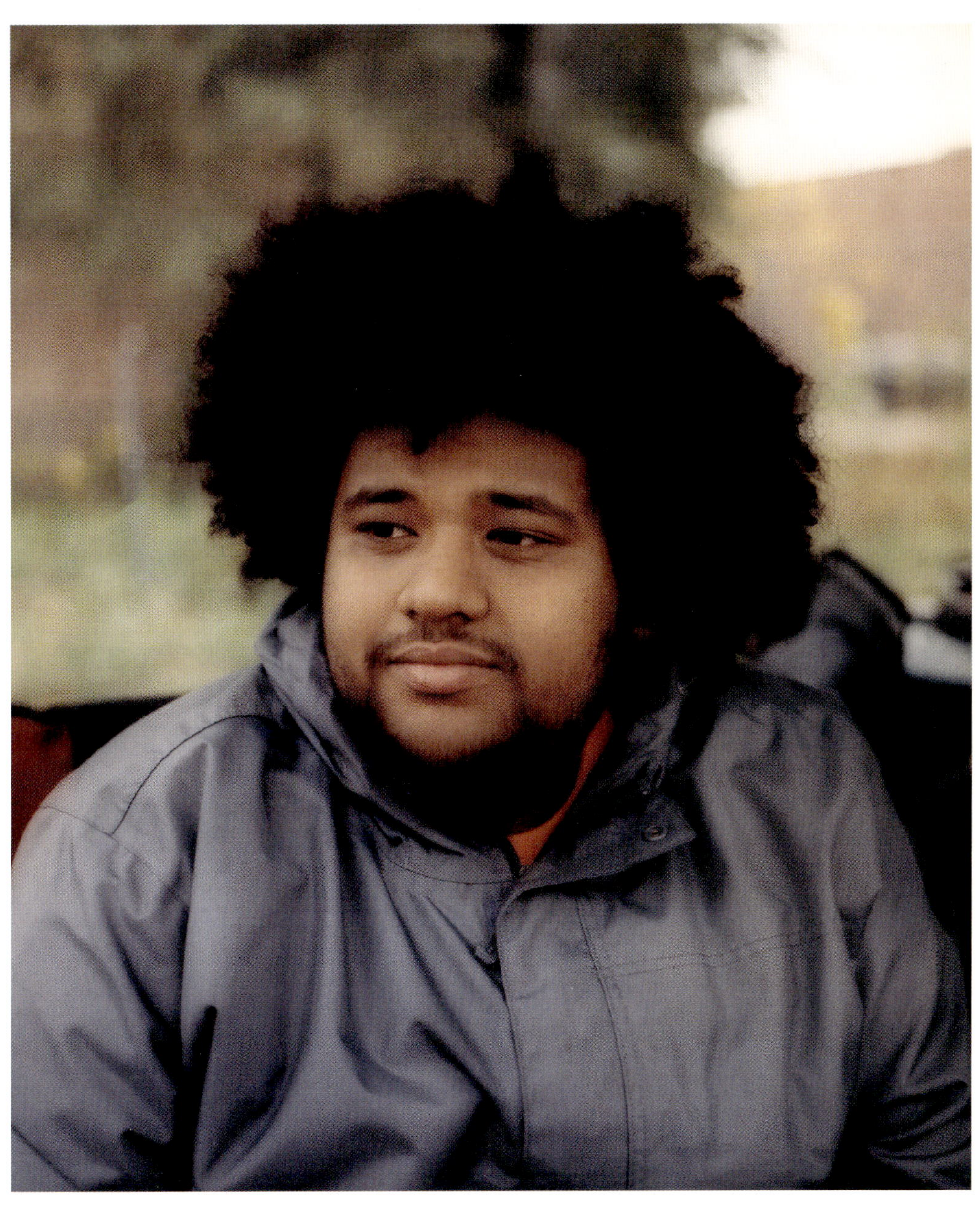

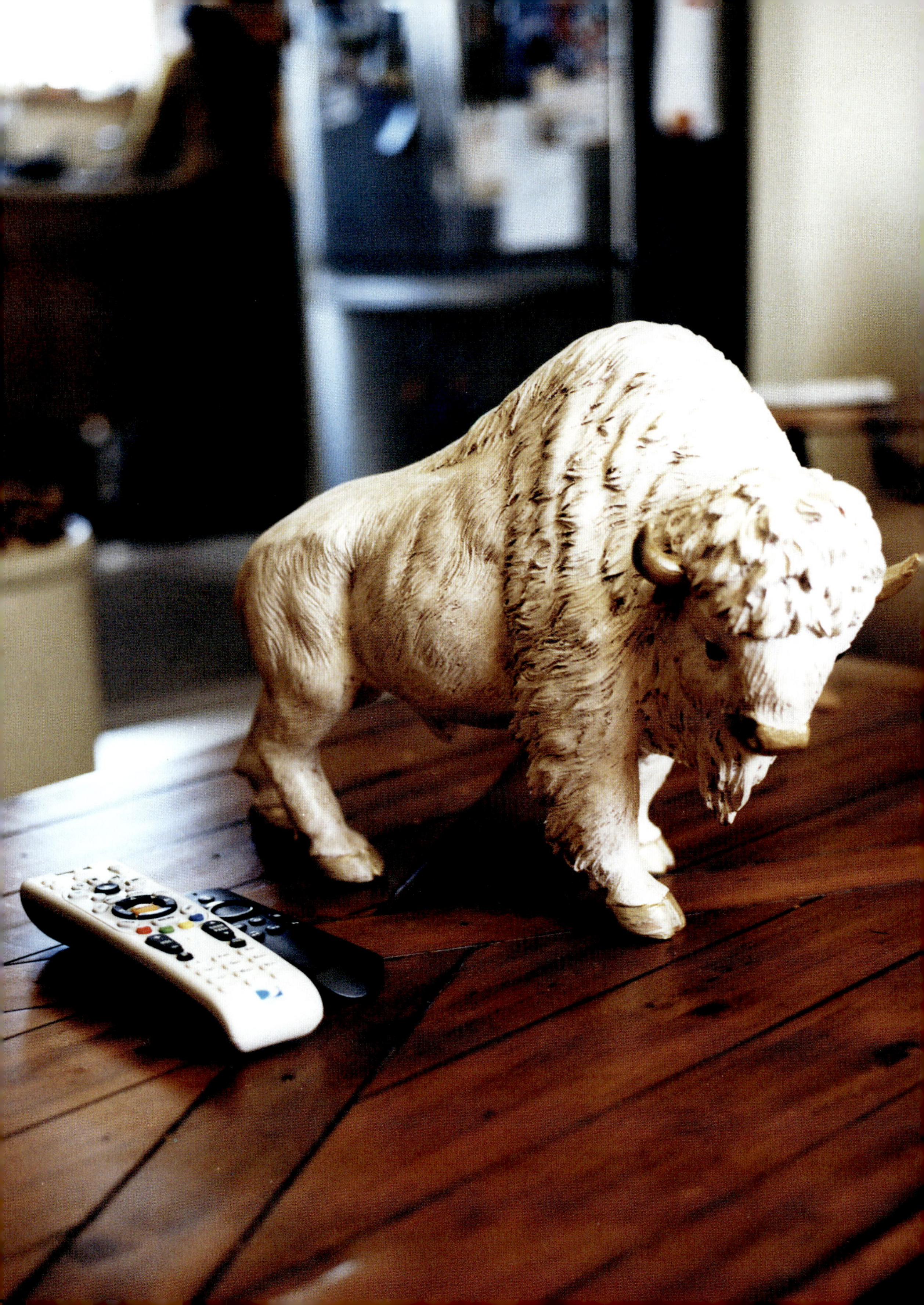

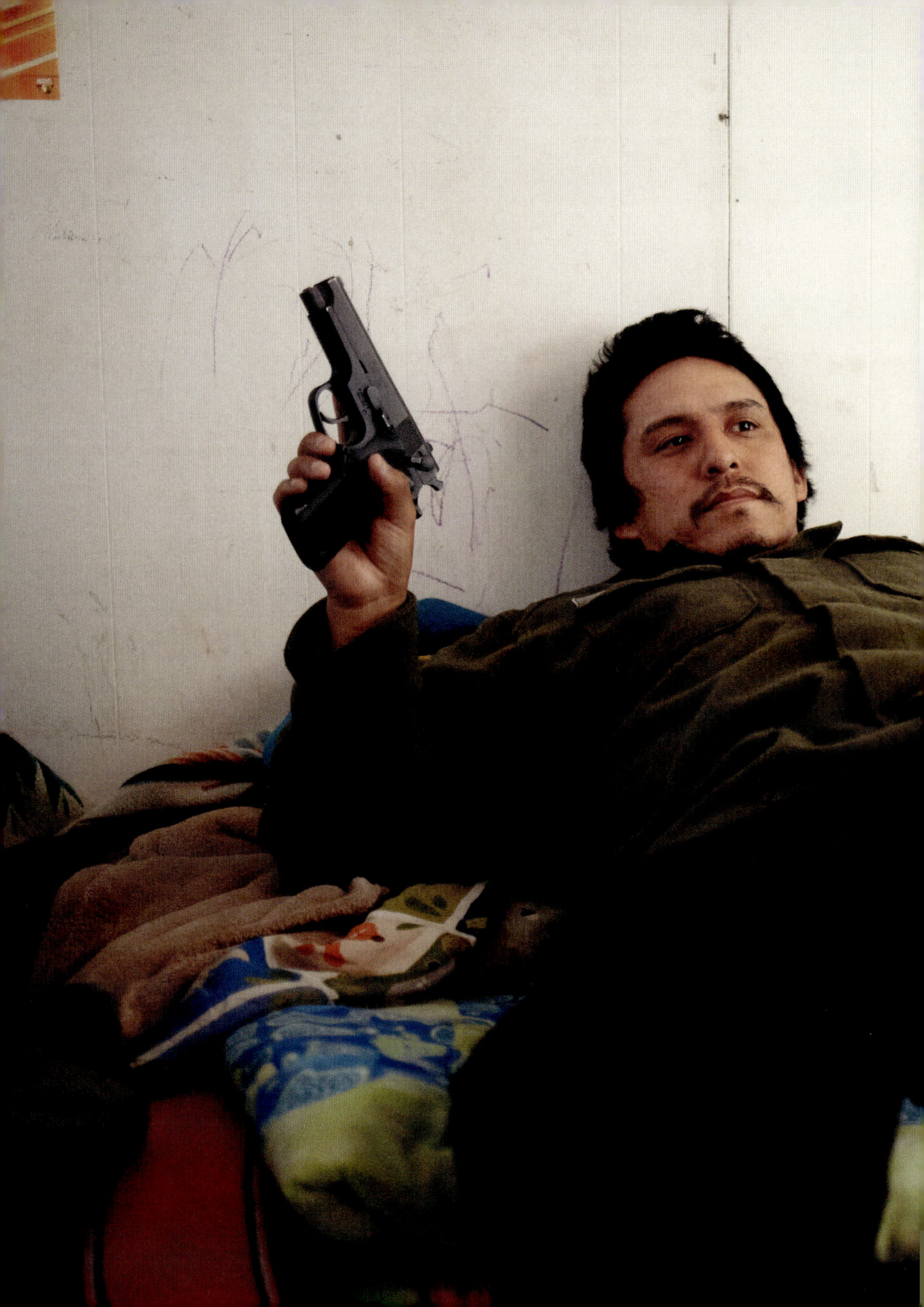

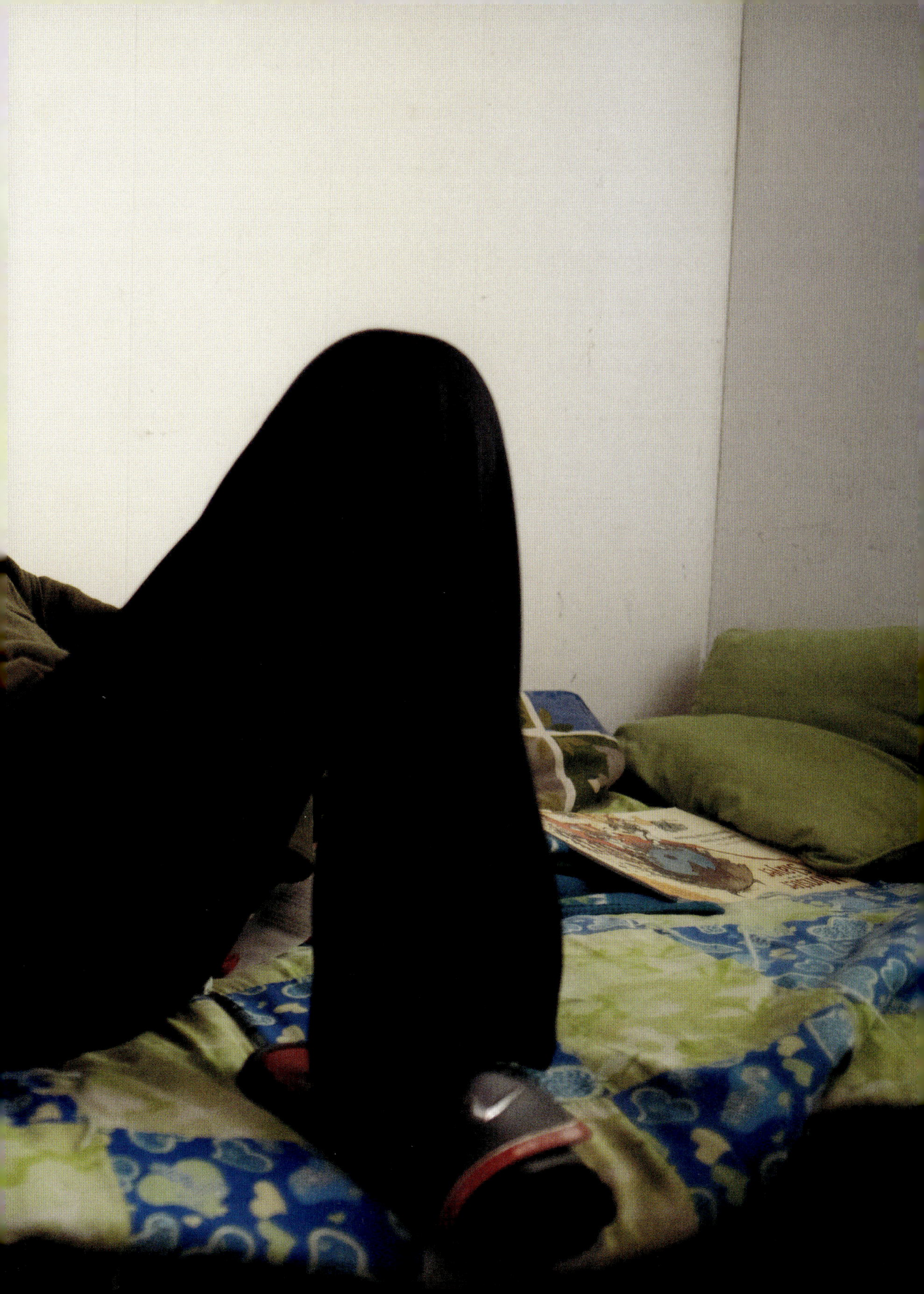

INDIAN SUMMER

On the central ring of the powwow, the grass yellowed by the August sun will soon be trampled by hundreds of dancers coming to dance to the rhythms of the drums. In the parking lot, between two pickup trucks, people trade their jeans and T-shirts for traditional costumes decorated with pearls and eagle feathers; they leave their old sneakers in the car to put on leather mocassins. At nightfall, lampposts light up to finally reveal the shadows dancing in a trance on the ground. Under the gaze of the elders sipping lemonade while sitting on camping chairs, the bells of the costumes tinkle following the beat of the drummers. This is how the soft summer evenings on the reservation go by. Tomorrow, they will have to put on their clothes to go to work. The powwow costume will be put away in the closet; it will not see the light again until next summer.

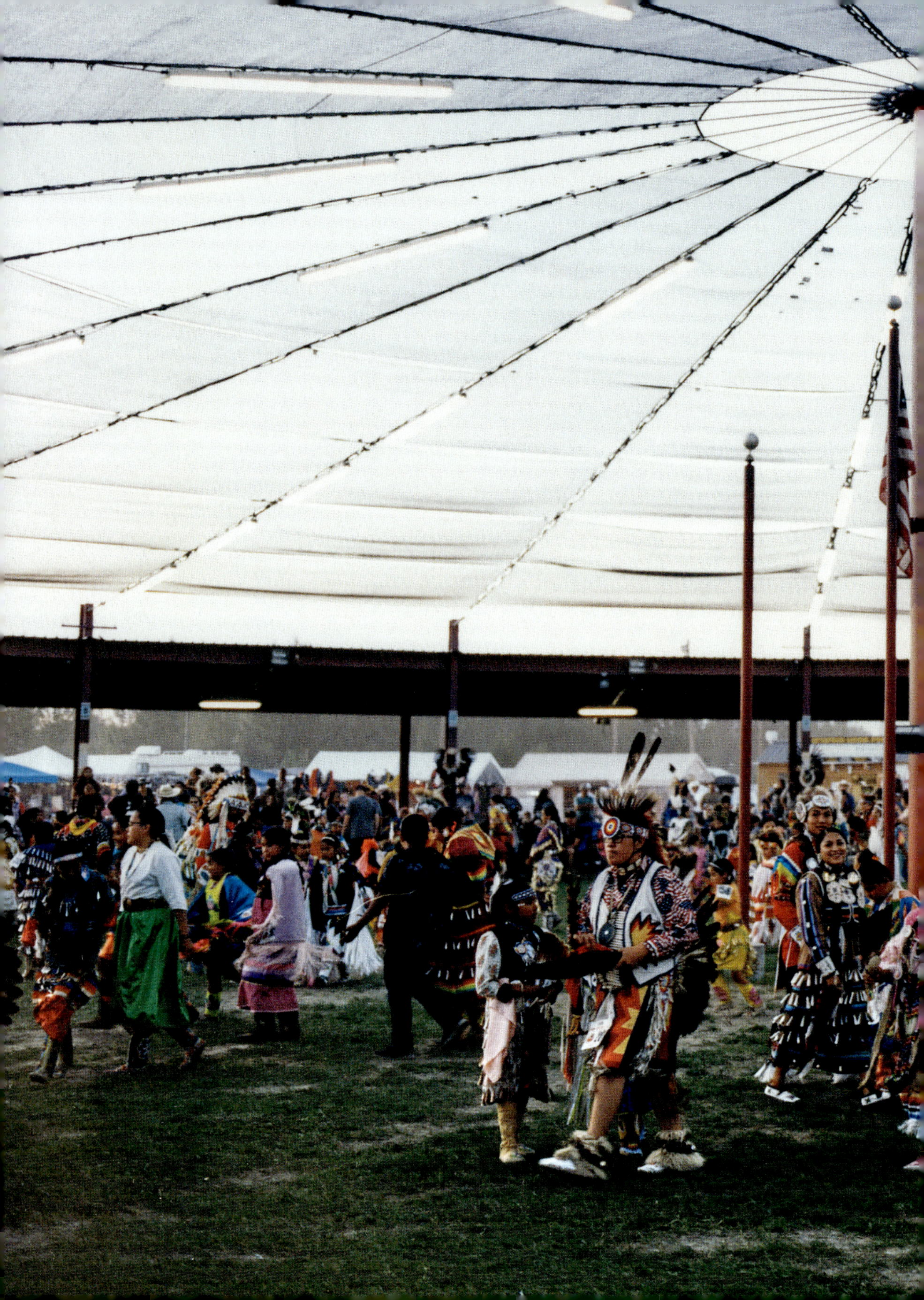

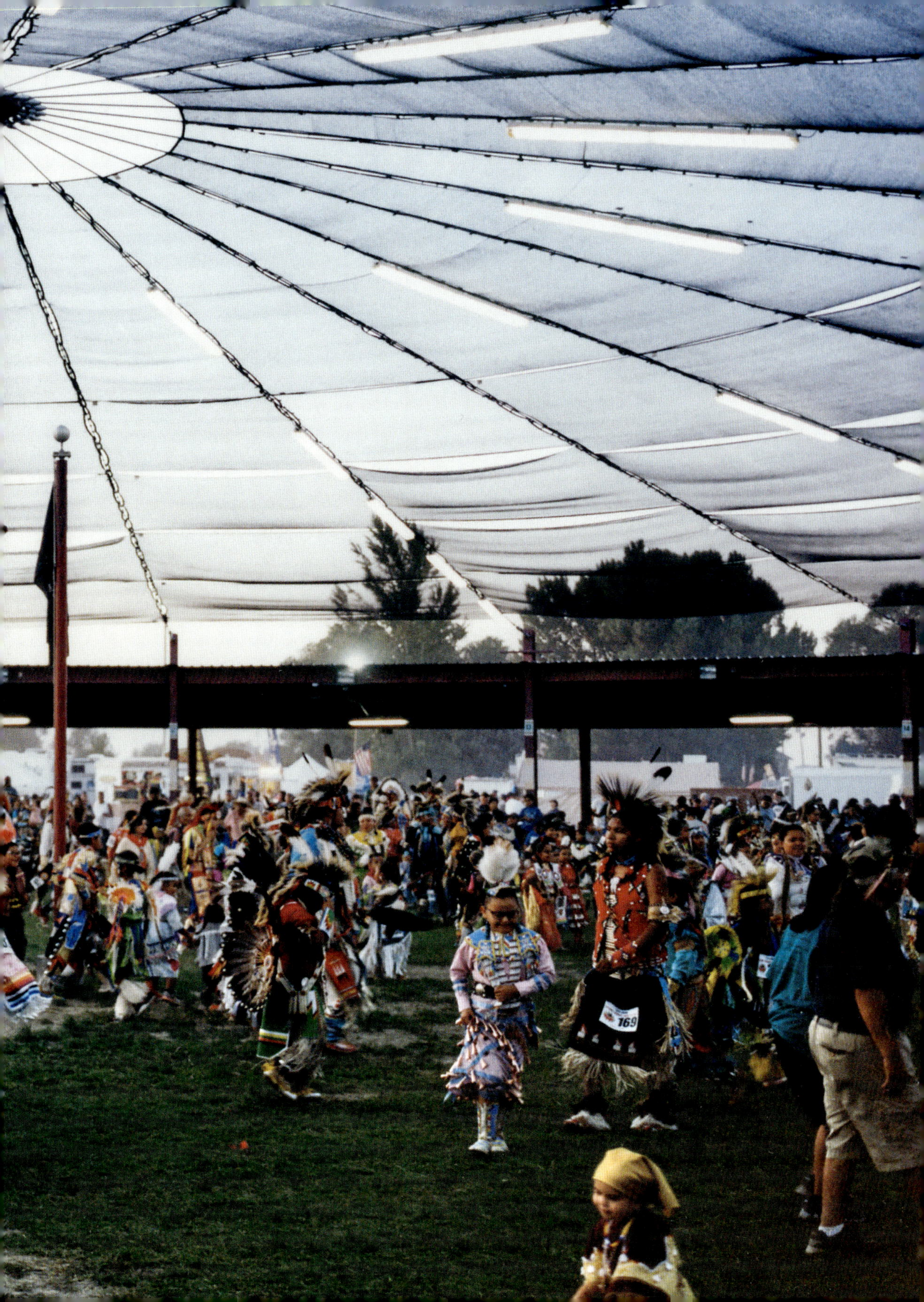

"Going to these ceremonies, it makes you feel good, powerful, happy, chills . . . It's kind of hard to explain . . . That spark feeling on the inside. I see our ceremonies as important because they speak of our culture, language, stories. A healing technique to connect back to our ancestors, gods, family, and Mother Earth. Without our ceremonies we wouldn't be here today."

Gibby Jones,
Navajo Nation

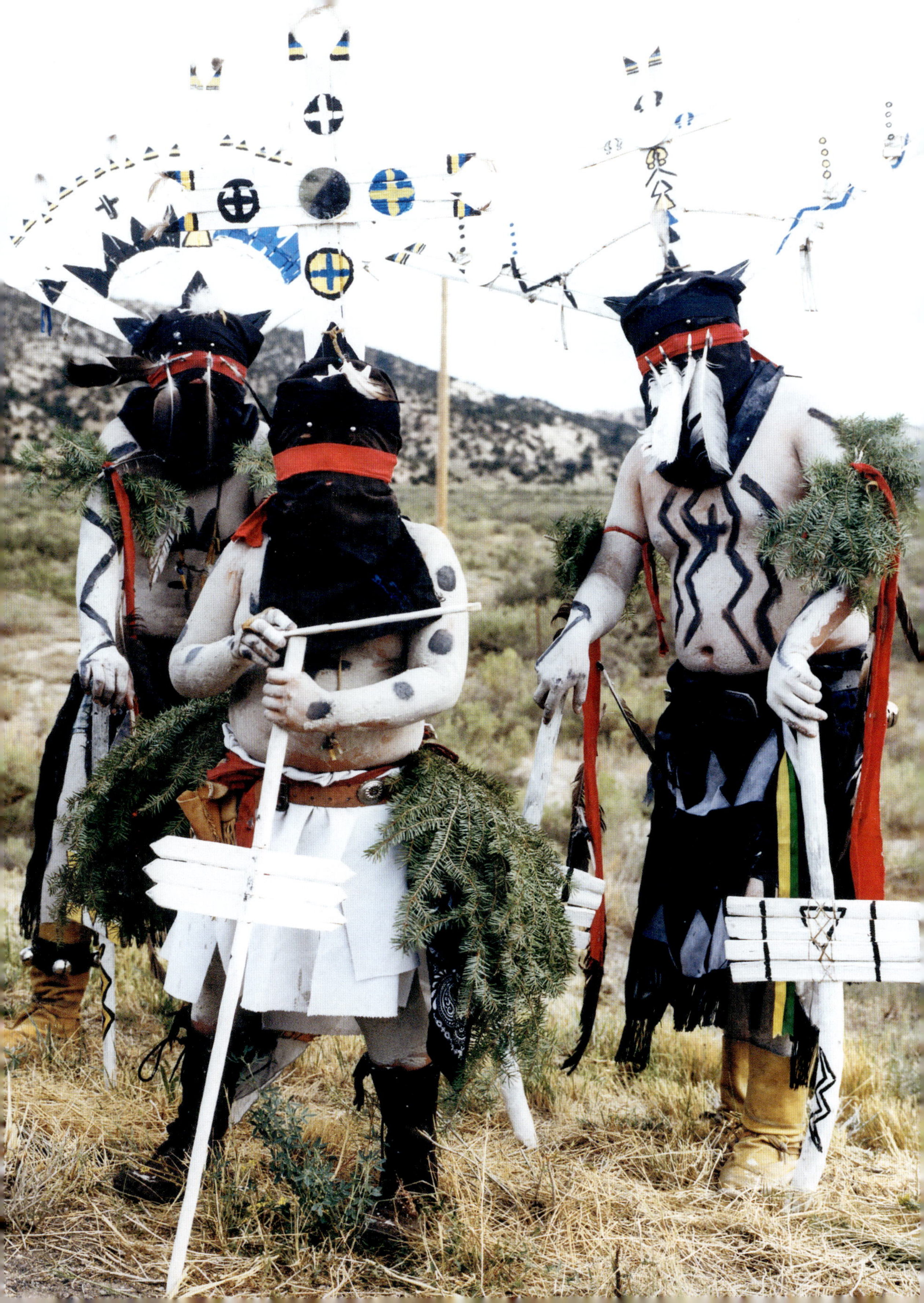

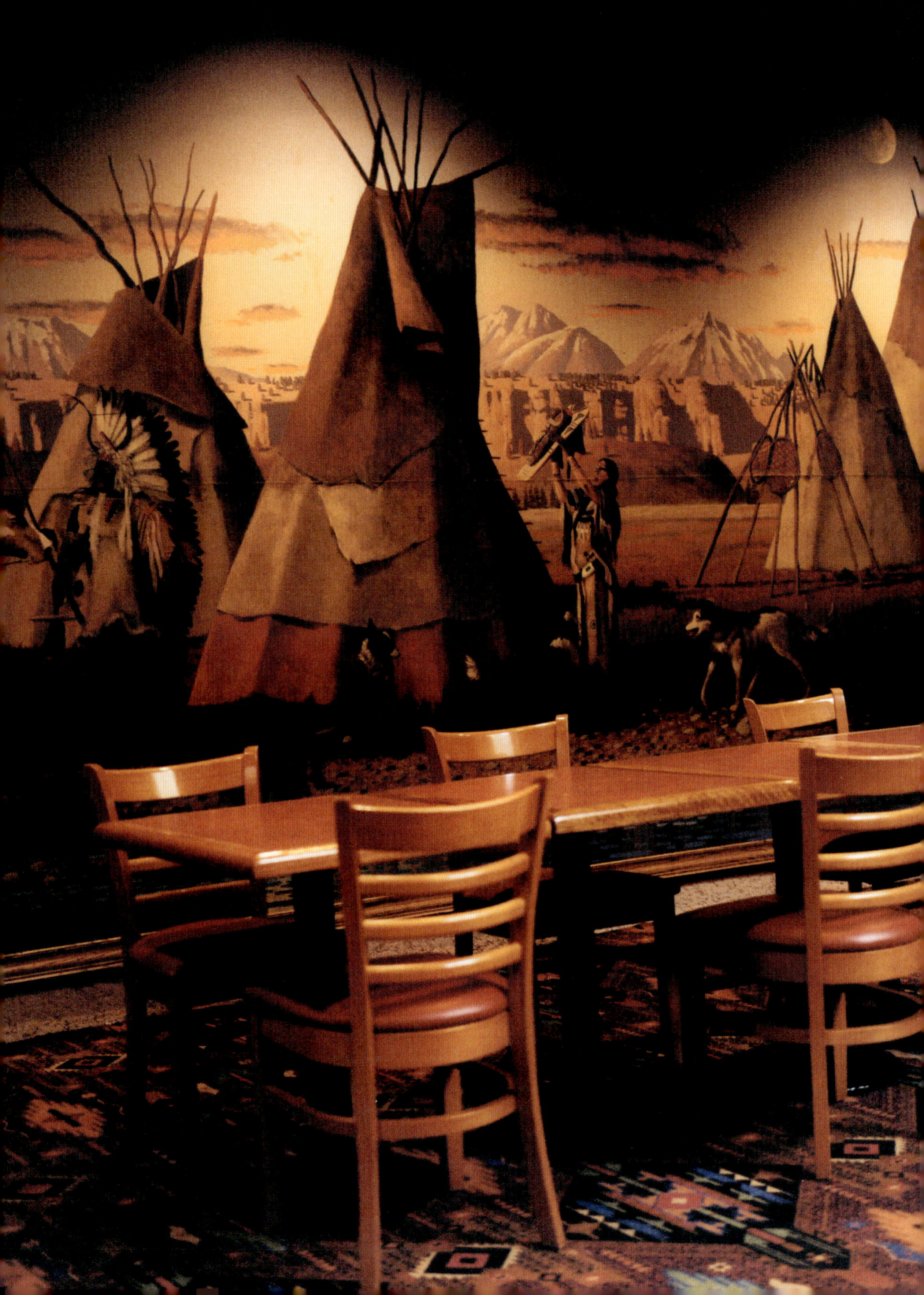

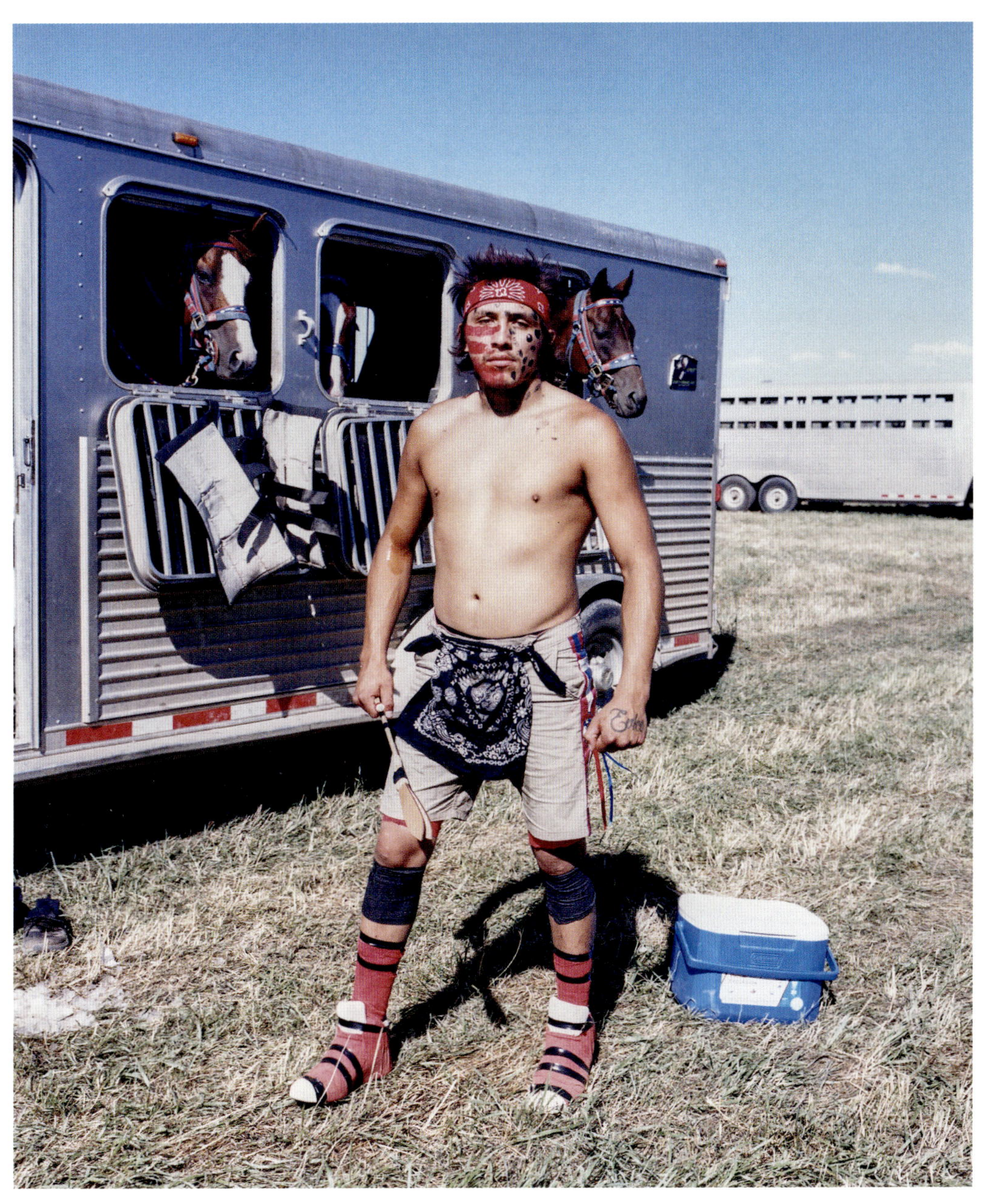

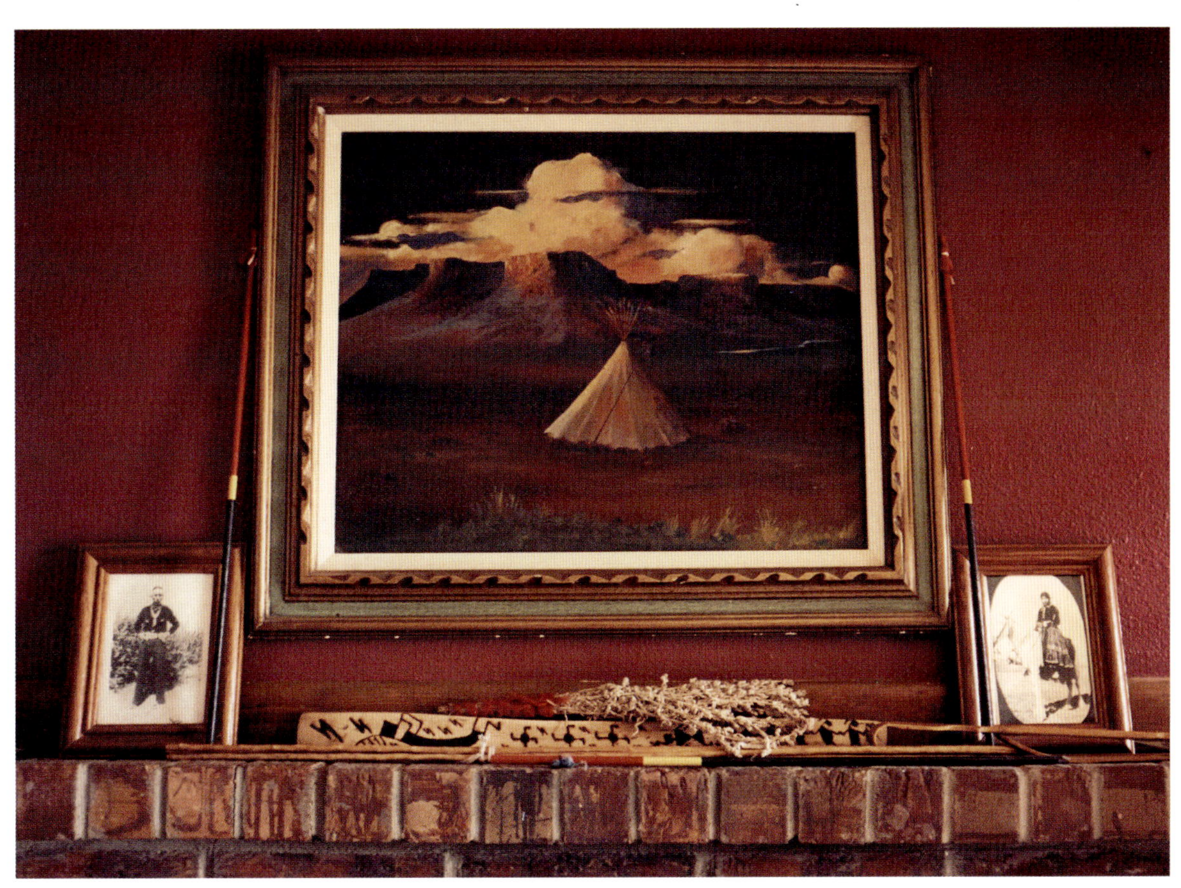

"Throughout my years in college, I really saw
a disconnect between our youth and our elders.
So my platform as Miss Navajo Nation
is to encourage our youth and our elders to find
a common ground where we can come together and
learn from one another, because I think that we are,
the youth of today, in an era of iPads and iPhones
and instant social media, YouTube, and their
entertainment is so instant. Whereas our elders
and our older adult population, they are unfamiliar
with this."

Shaandiin Parrish,
Miss Navajo Nation 2019,
Navajo Nation

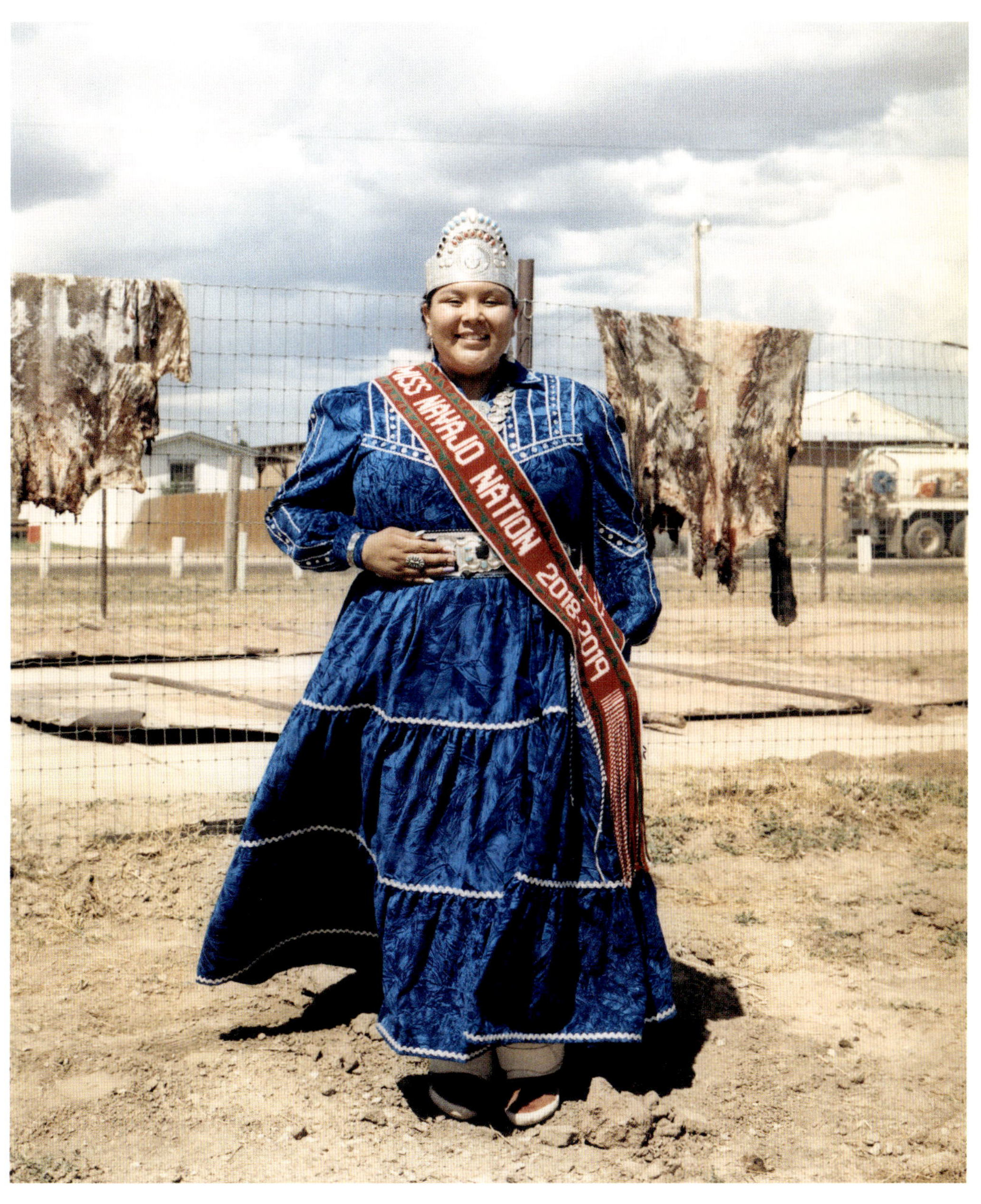

MISS NAVAJO NATION 2018-2019

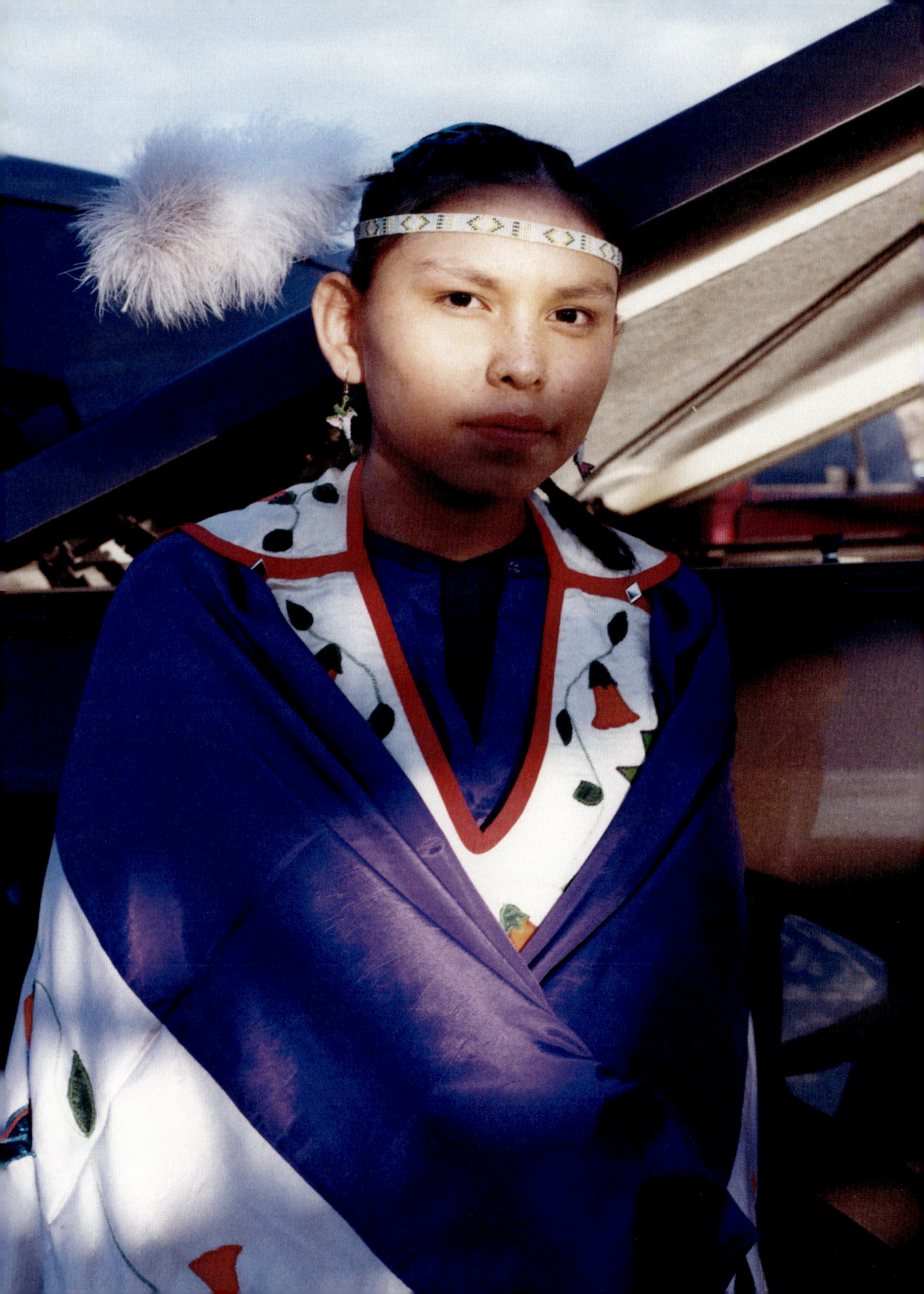

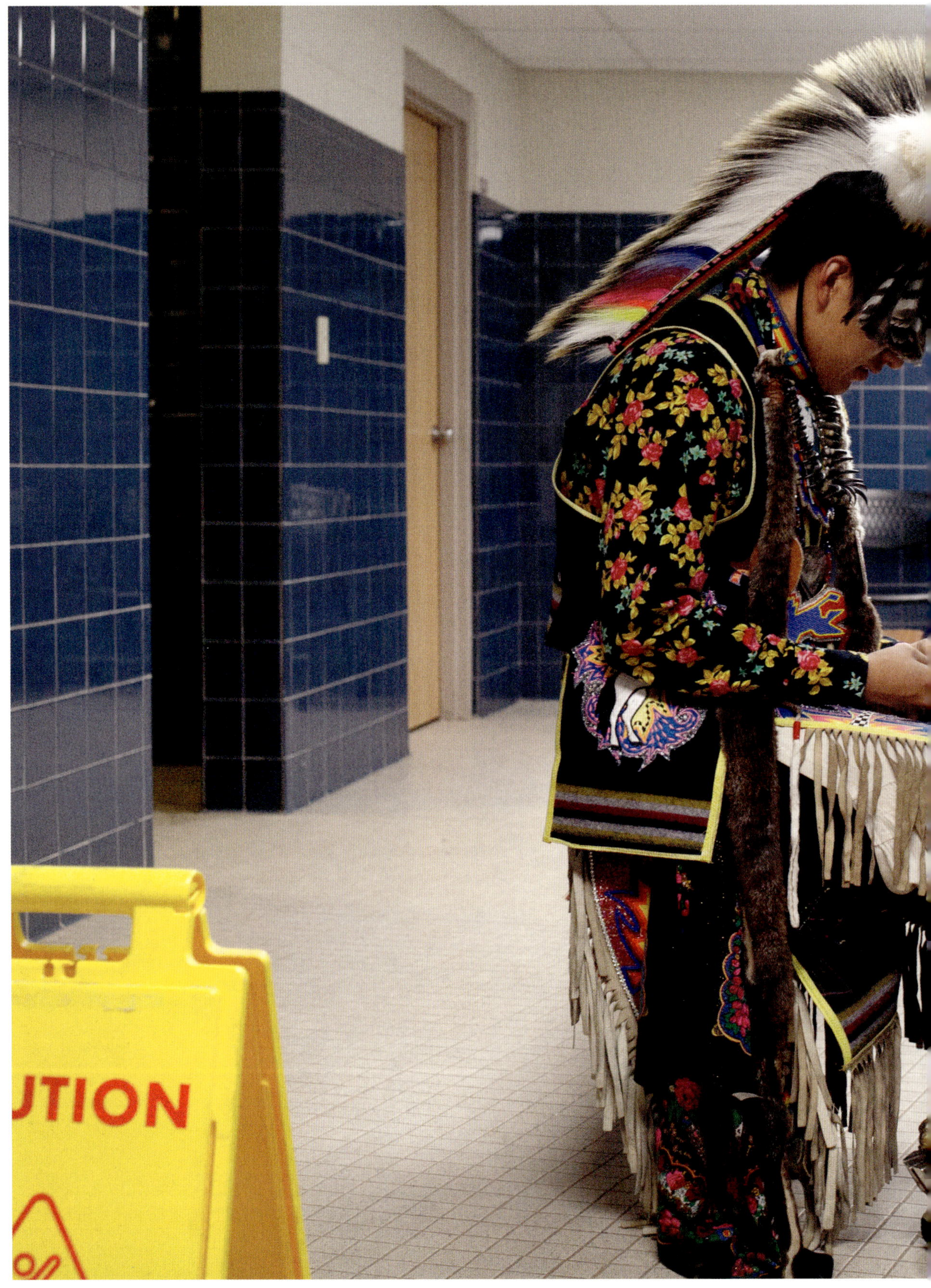
UTION

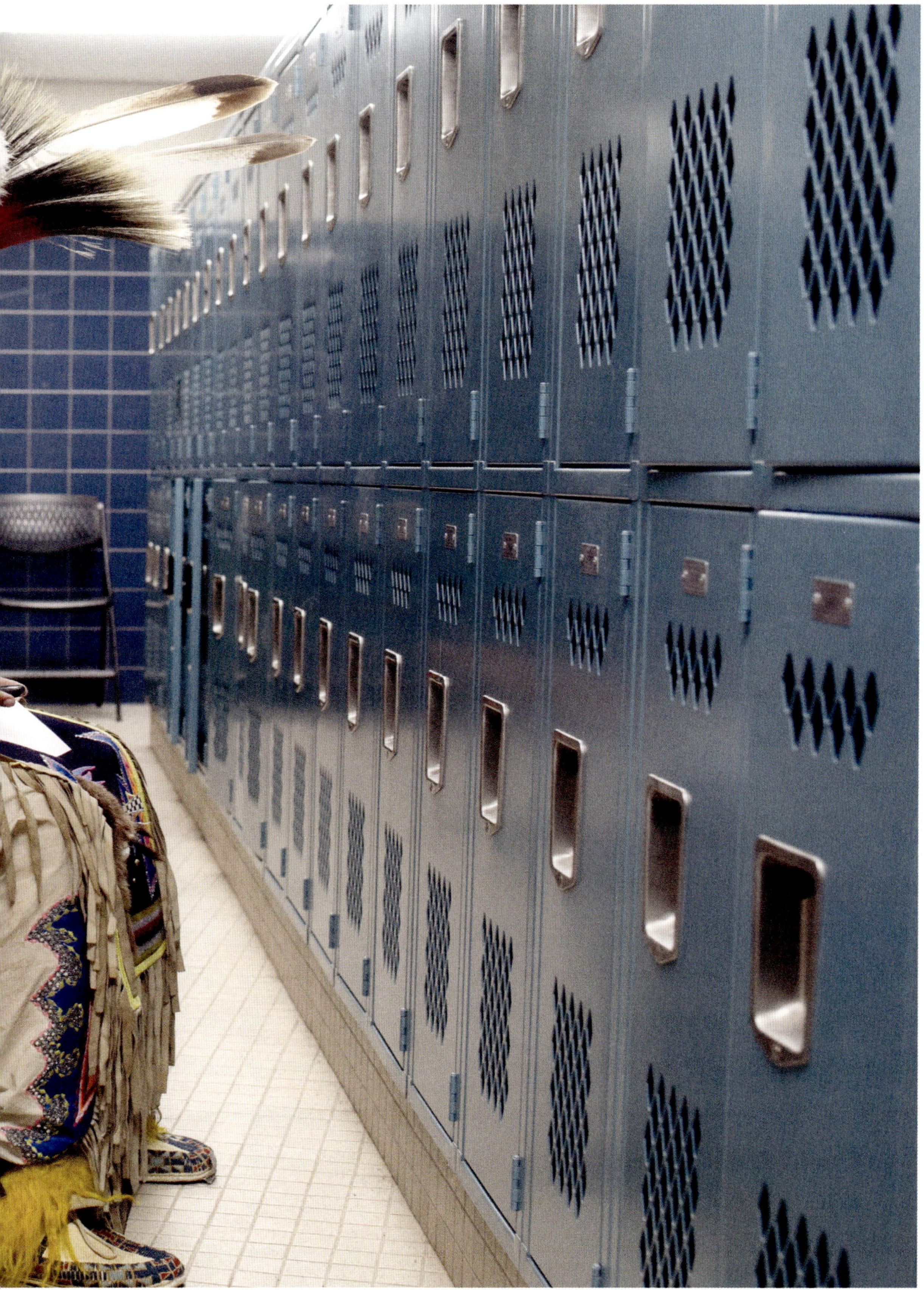

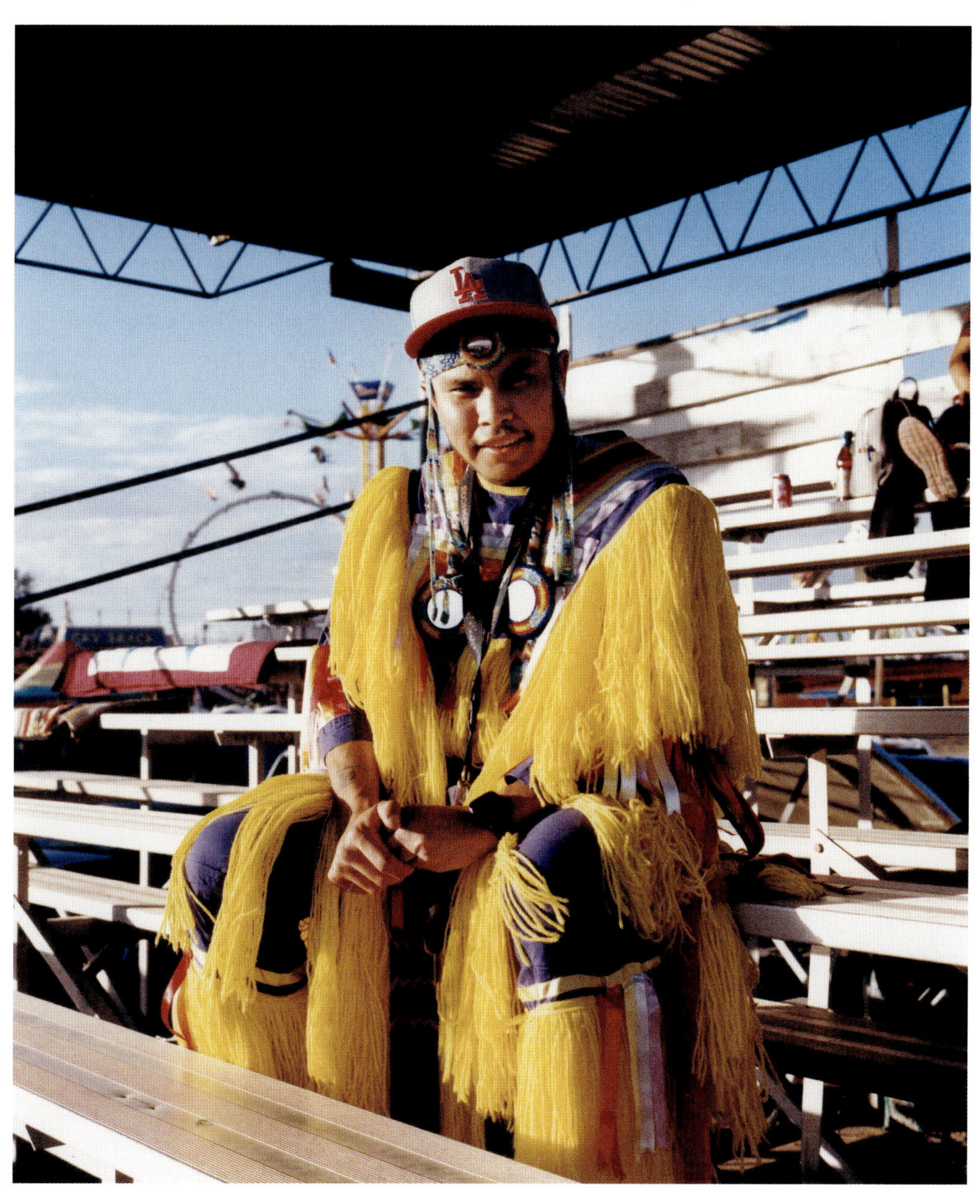

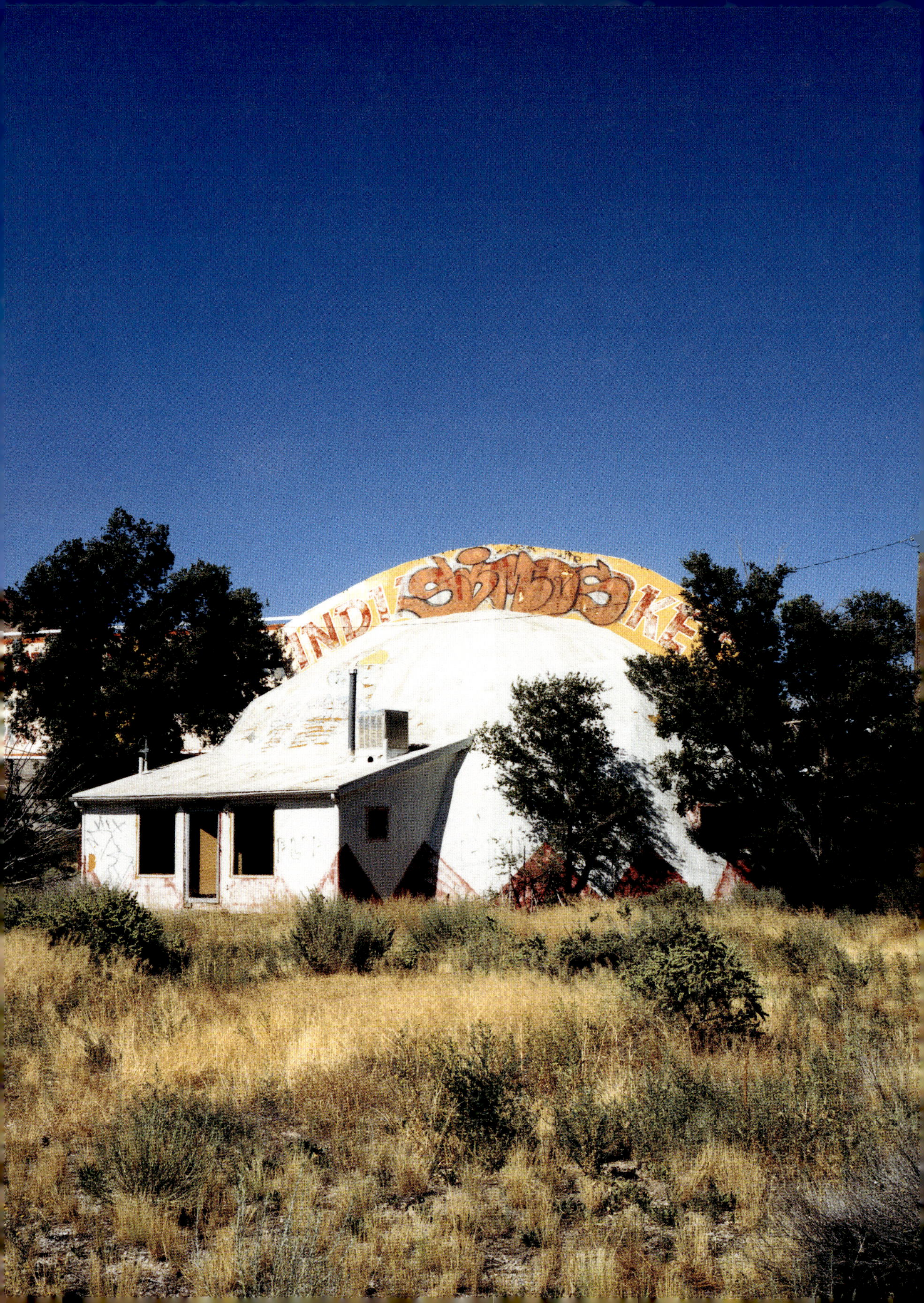

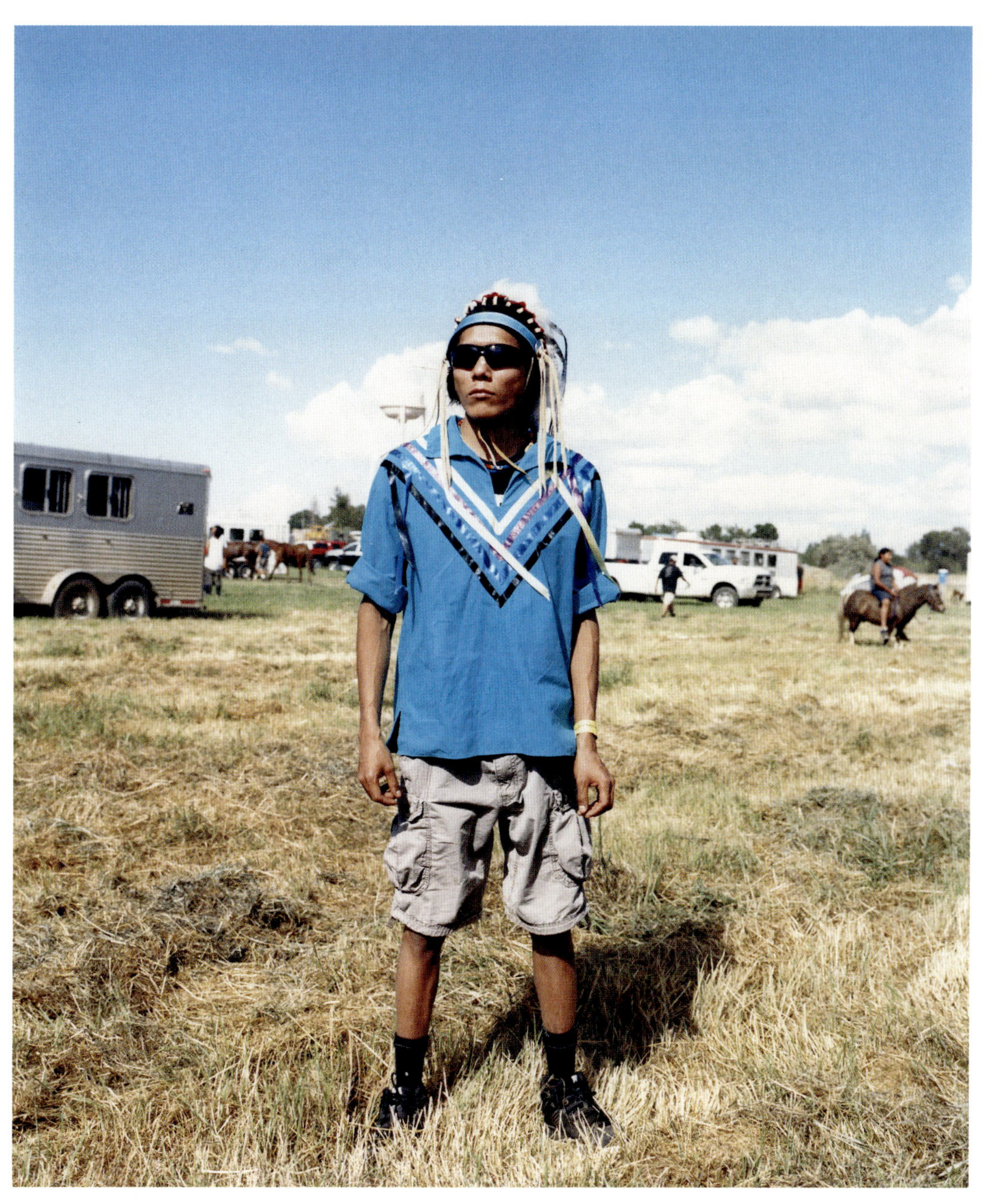

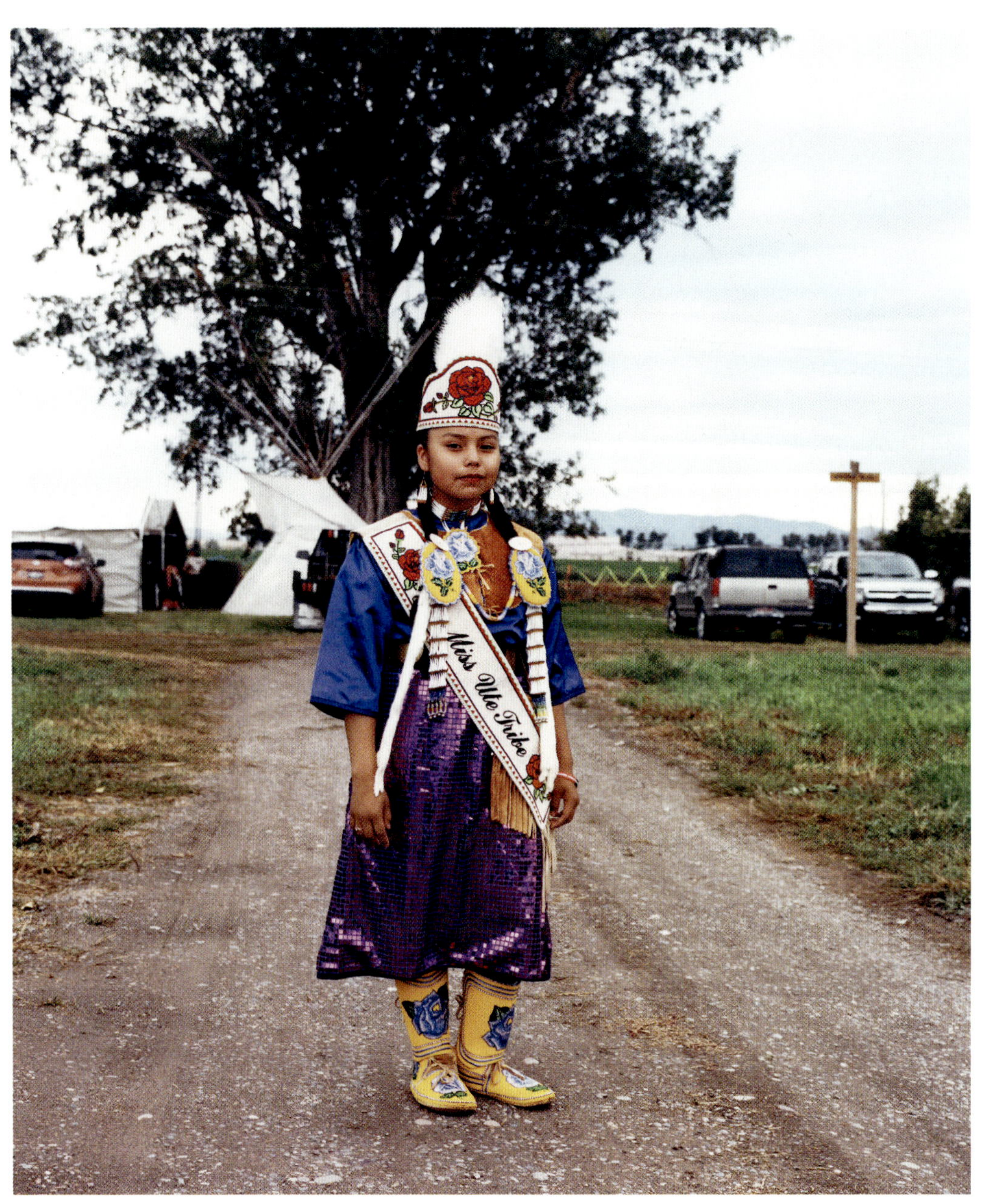
Miss Ute Tribe

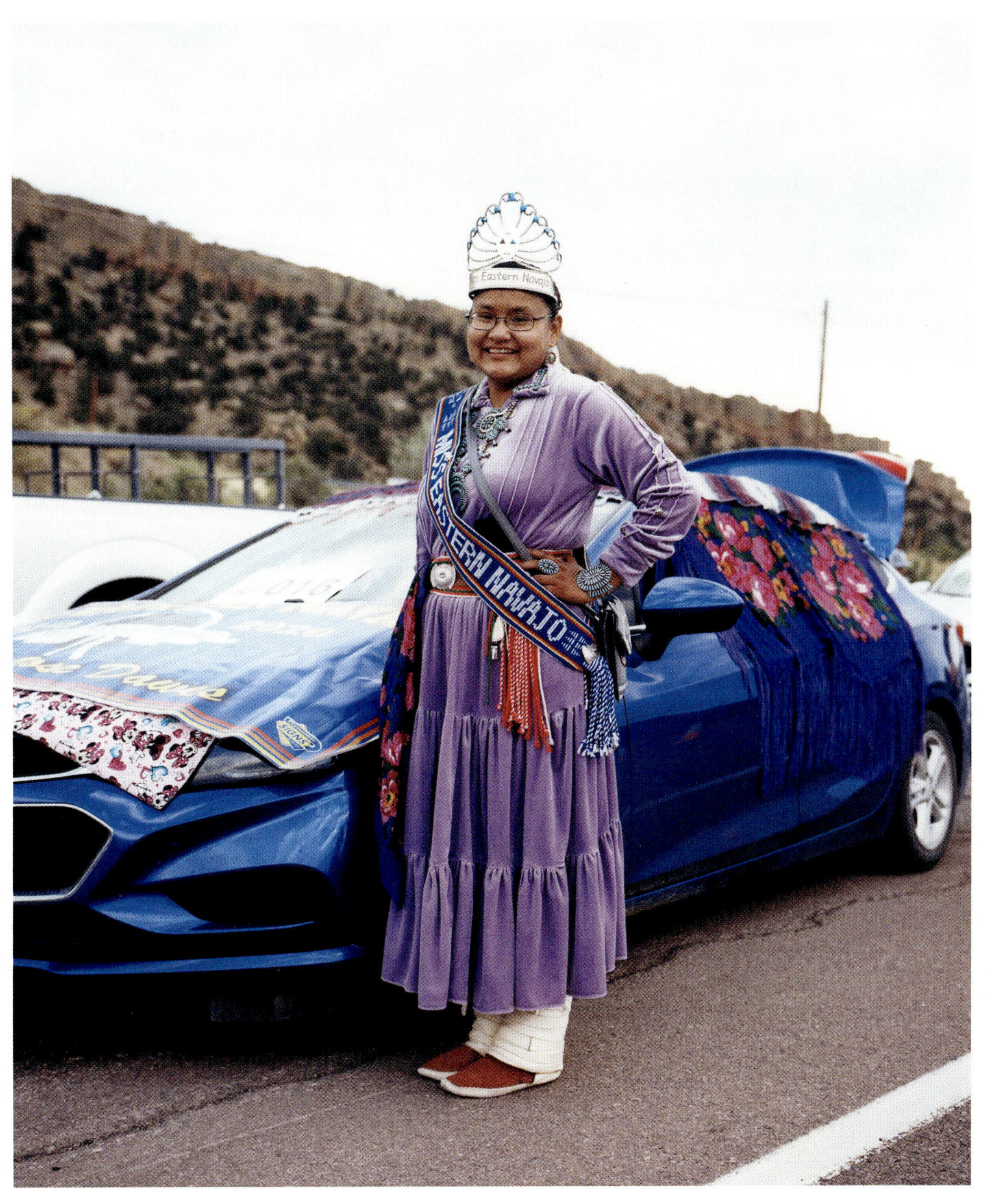
Miss Eastern Navajo
MISS EASTERN NAVAJO

"Until the 1980s, the government was sending
our children to boarding schools to erase
their Indian side. First, they had their hair cut,
then they were give Christian names. Overnight,
you were no longer 'Little Flower' but 'Melissa.'
Every time they spoke our language, the children
would get a rap on the knuckles. Today, it is time
for our way of life to return and for the newcomers
to be able to teach our languages to their parents
who have been deprived of them."

Mato Tanka,
Oglala Sioux tribe

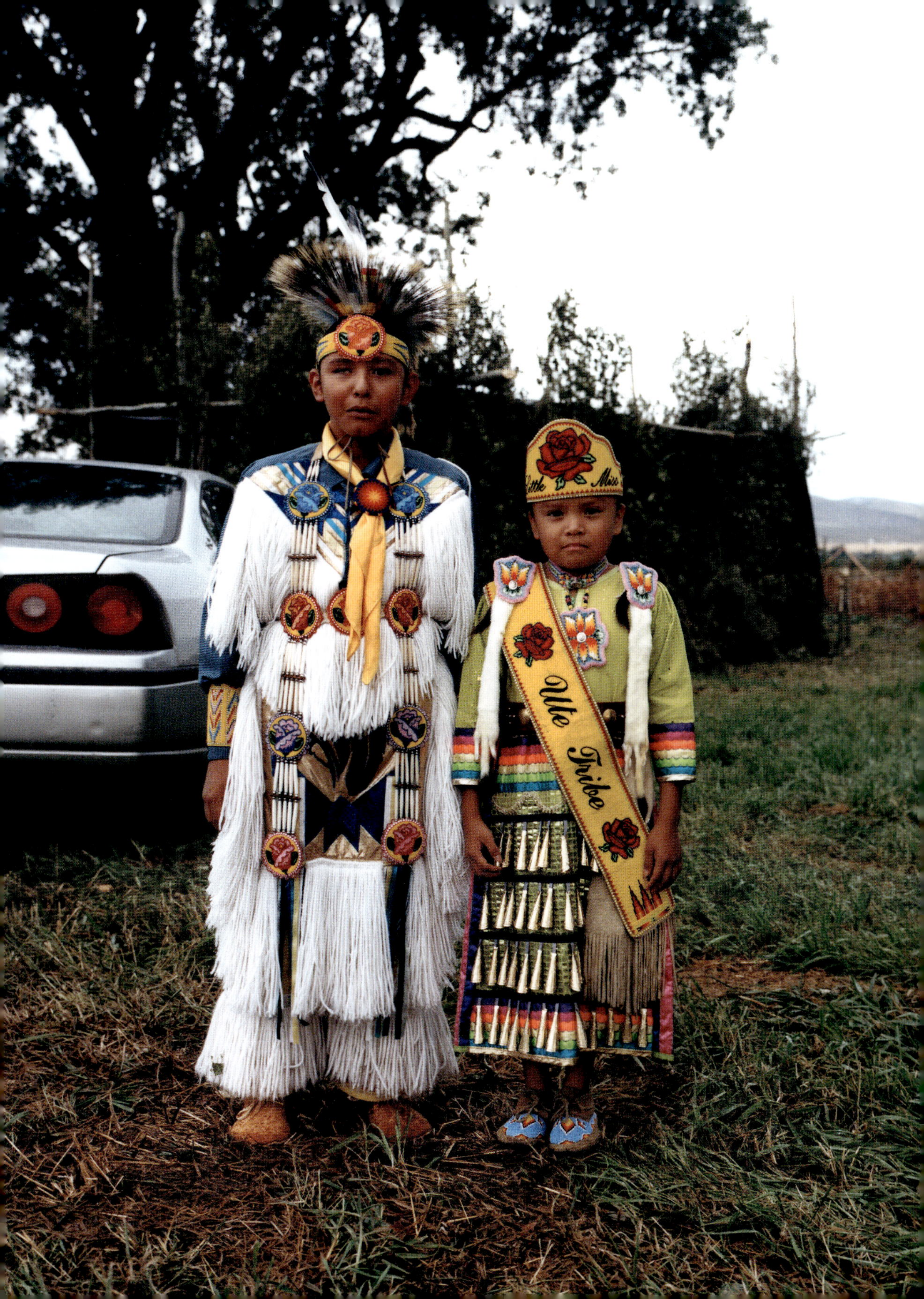
Little Miss
Ute Tribe

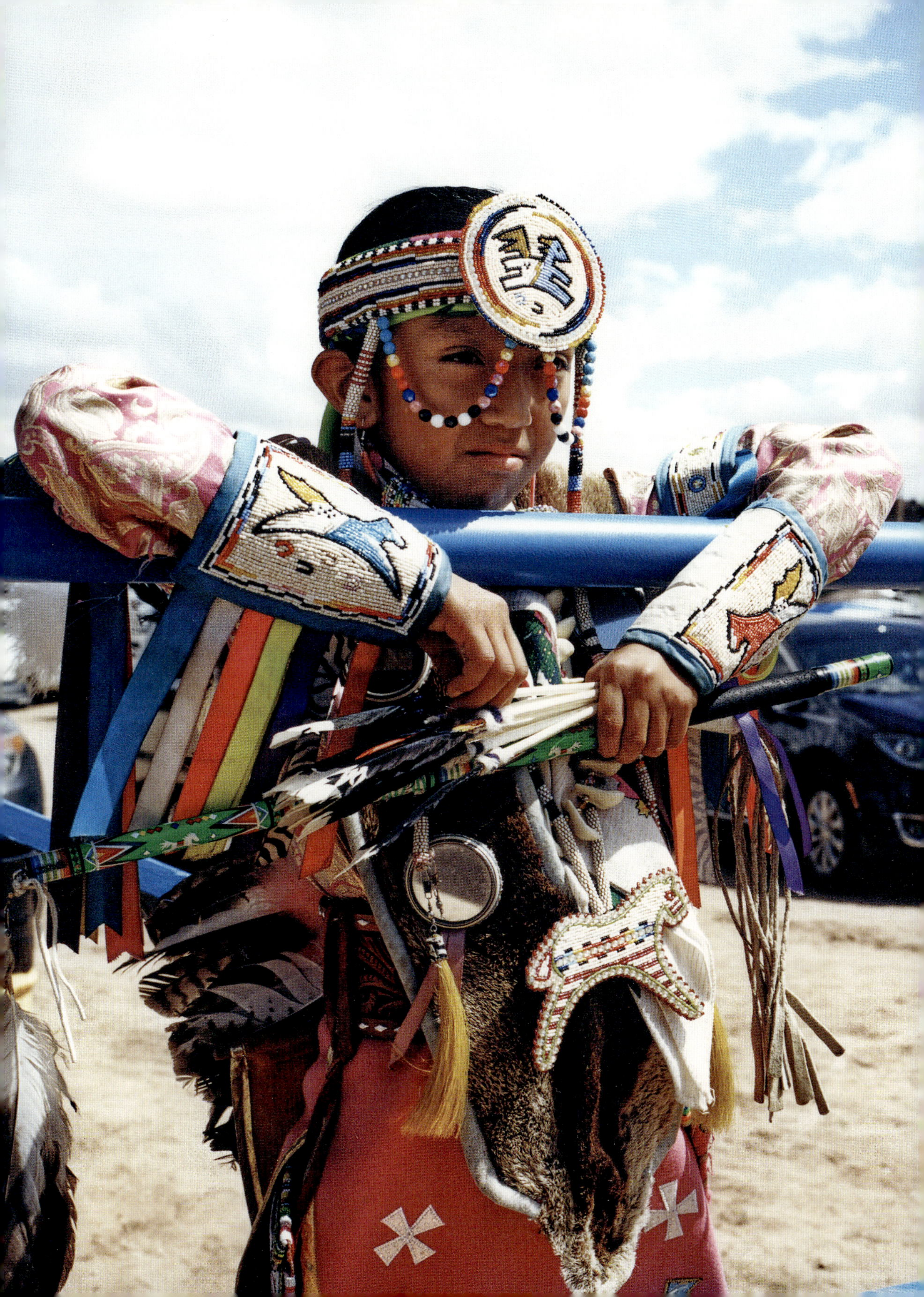

BLACK
SNAKE

"An ancient Sioux prophecy says that a black serpent will come to destroy the world at a time of great uncertainty," says Heather Water by the crackling fire. Two weeks earlier, this young mother learned on social media that a battle was raging on the plains of Dakota. Heather immediately packed her bag and took to the road with her old station wagon to come and support her tribe, threatened by the black snake. The latter is none other than a giant oil pipeline being built on the sacred lands of its ancestors. Like her, thousands of Natives from all over the United States joined the Standing Rock Indian Reservation to prevent this terrible black snake from rushing into the murky waters of the Missouri River.

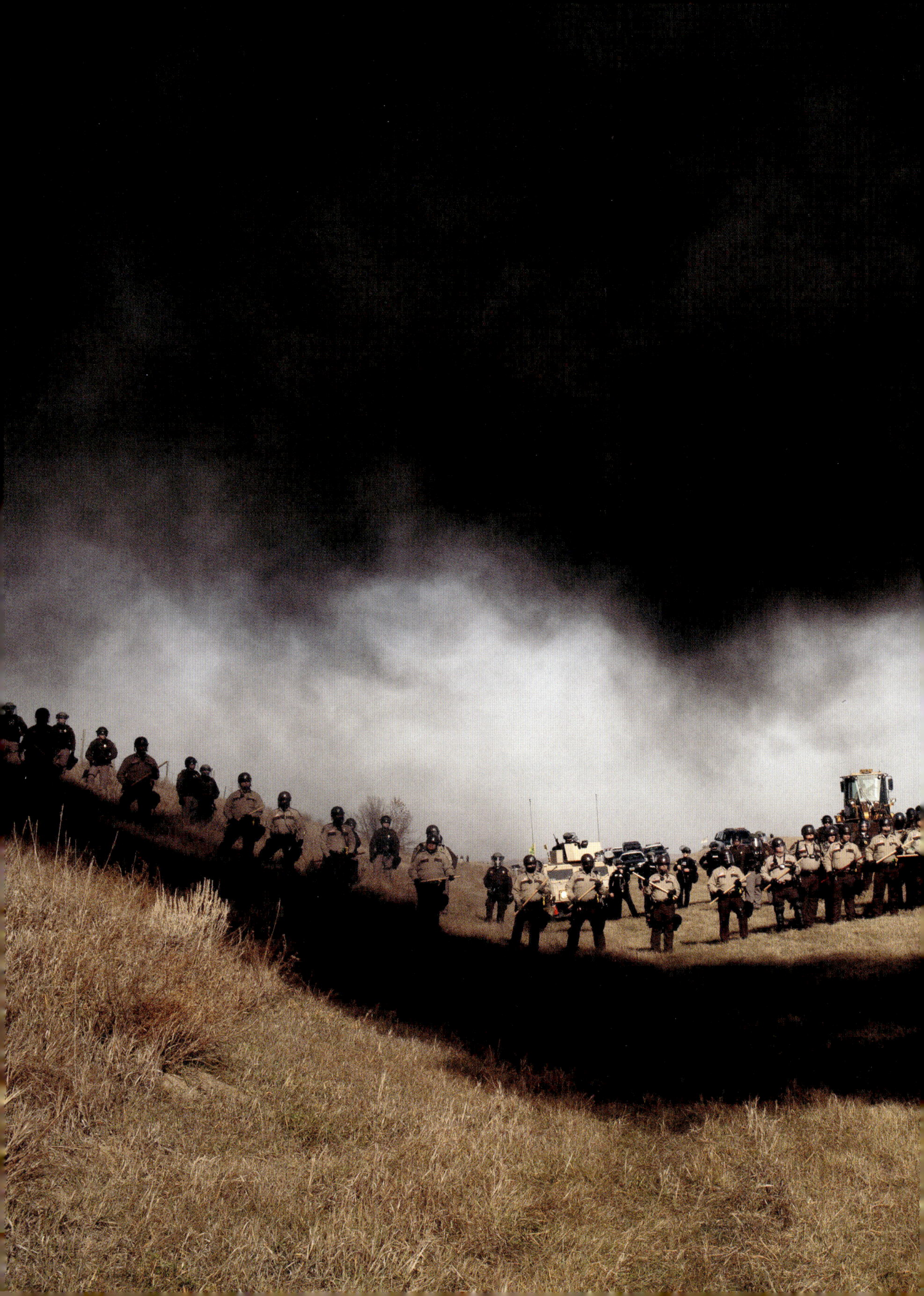

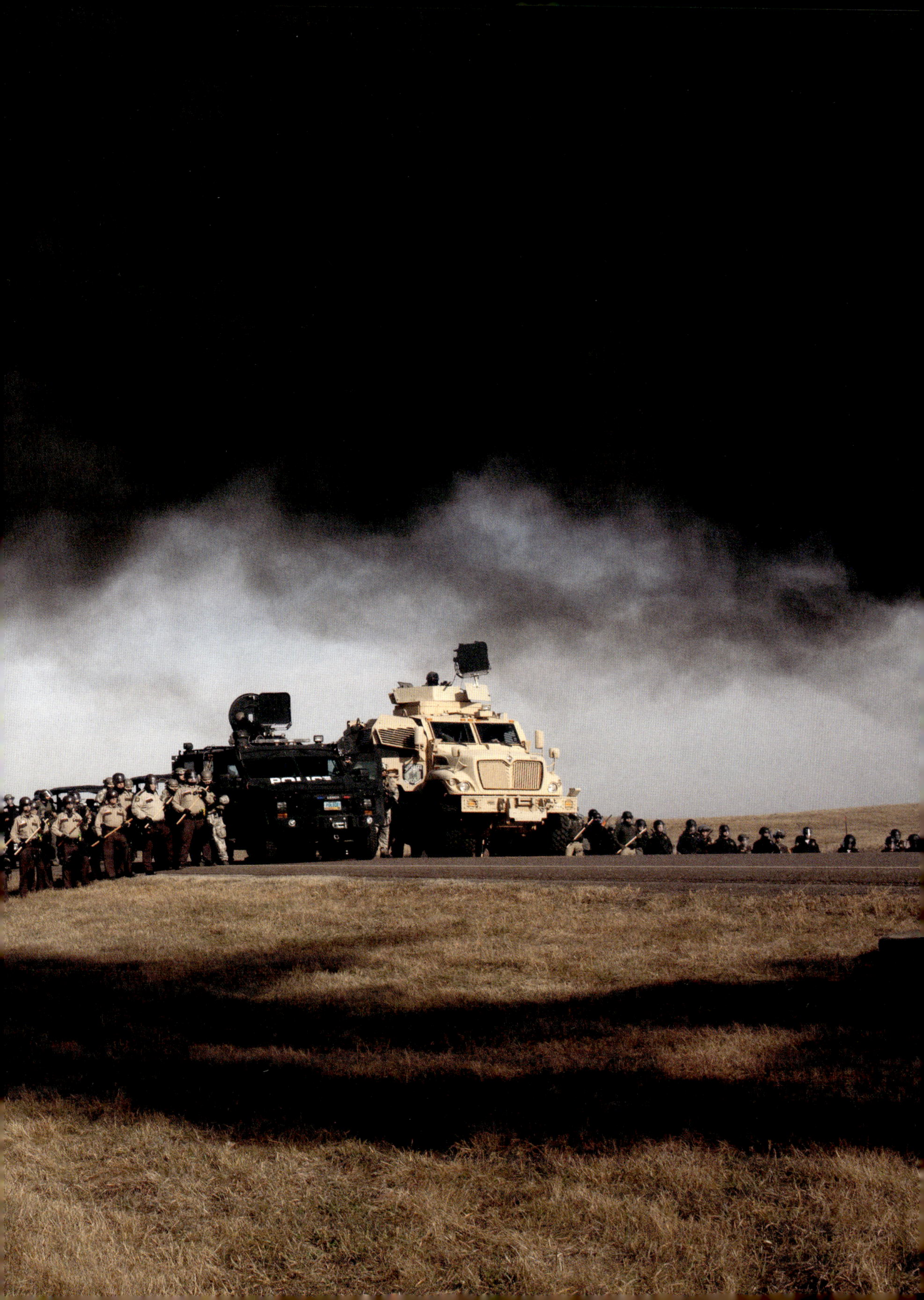

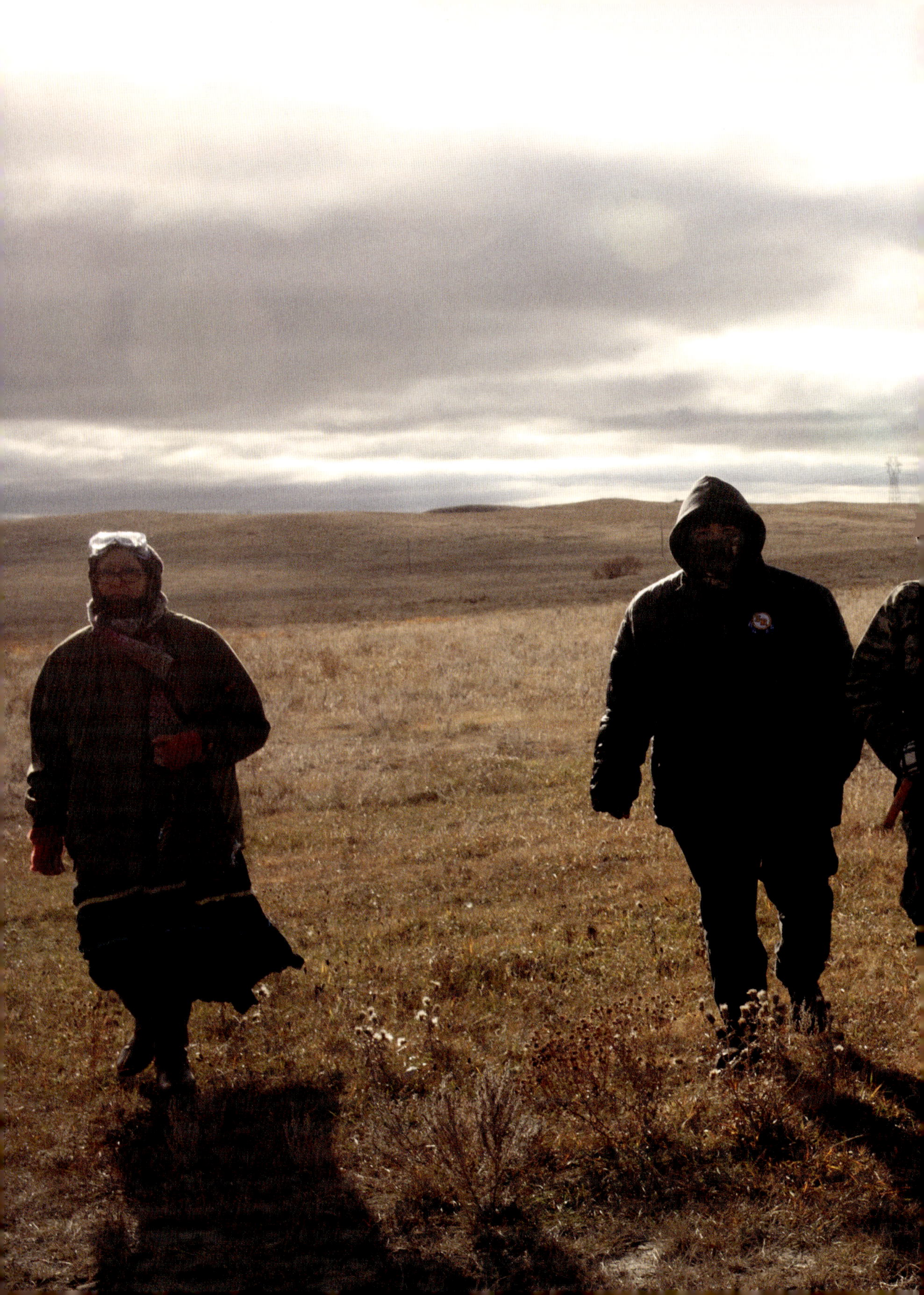

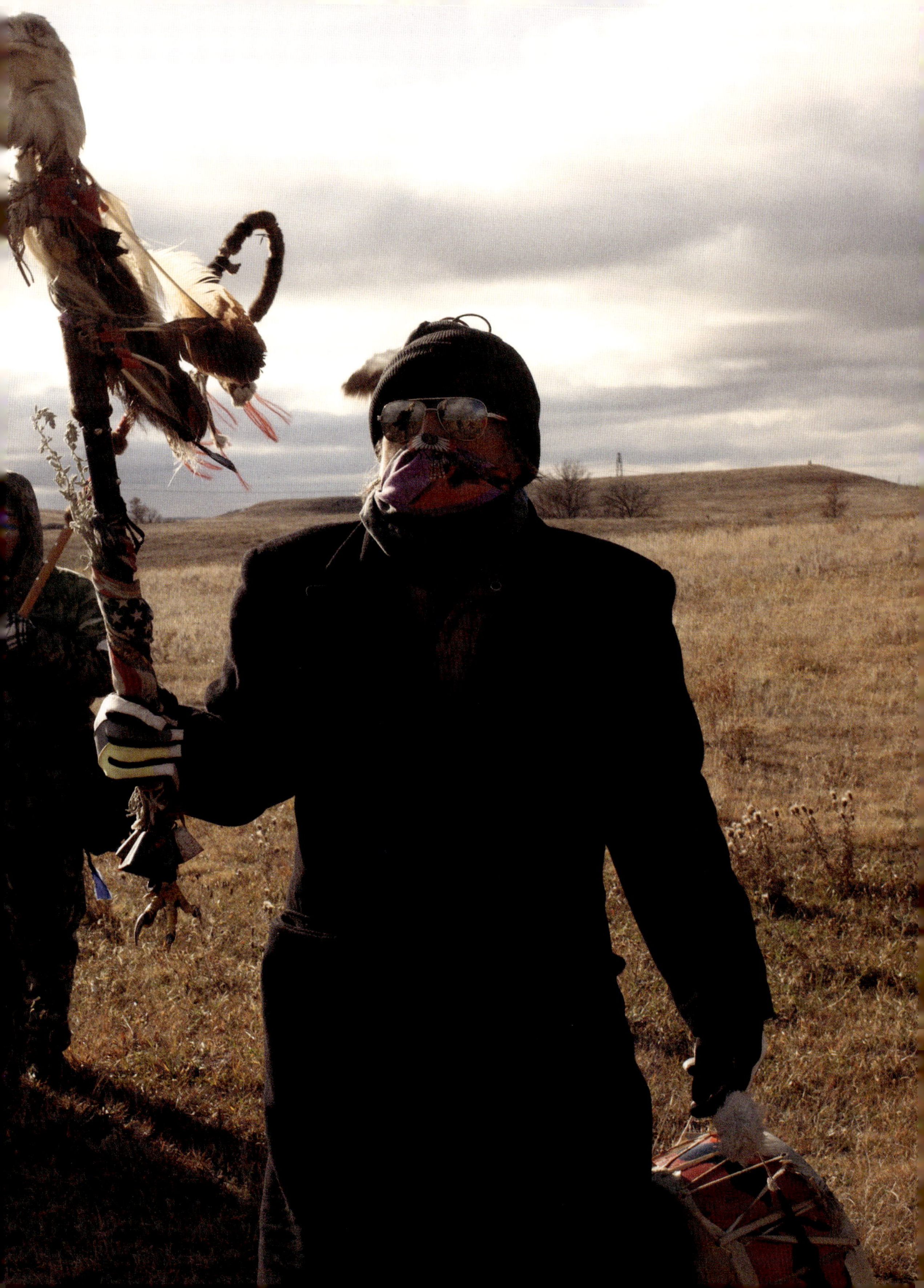

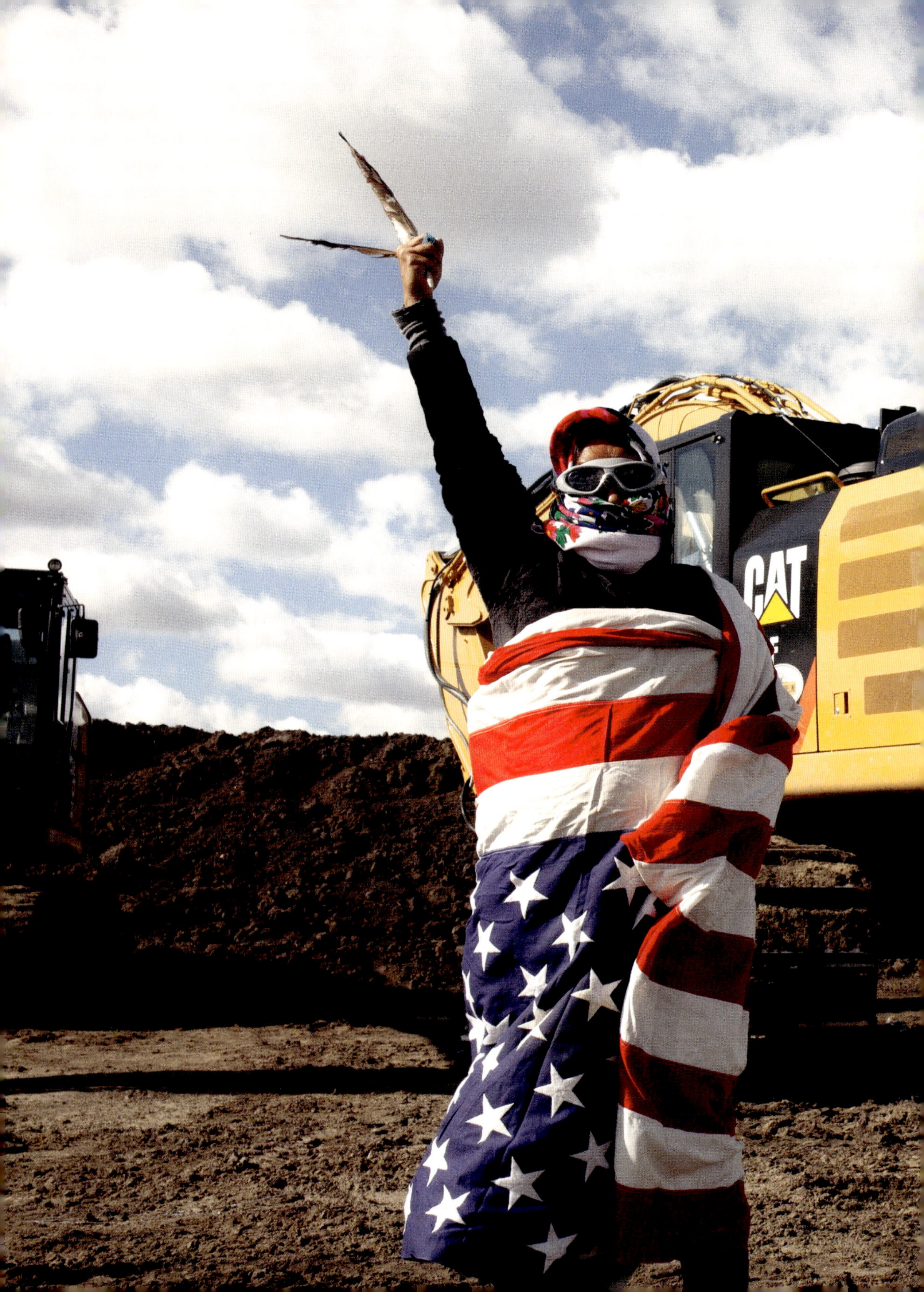

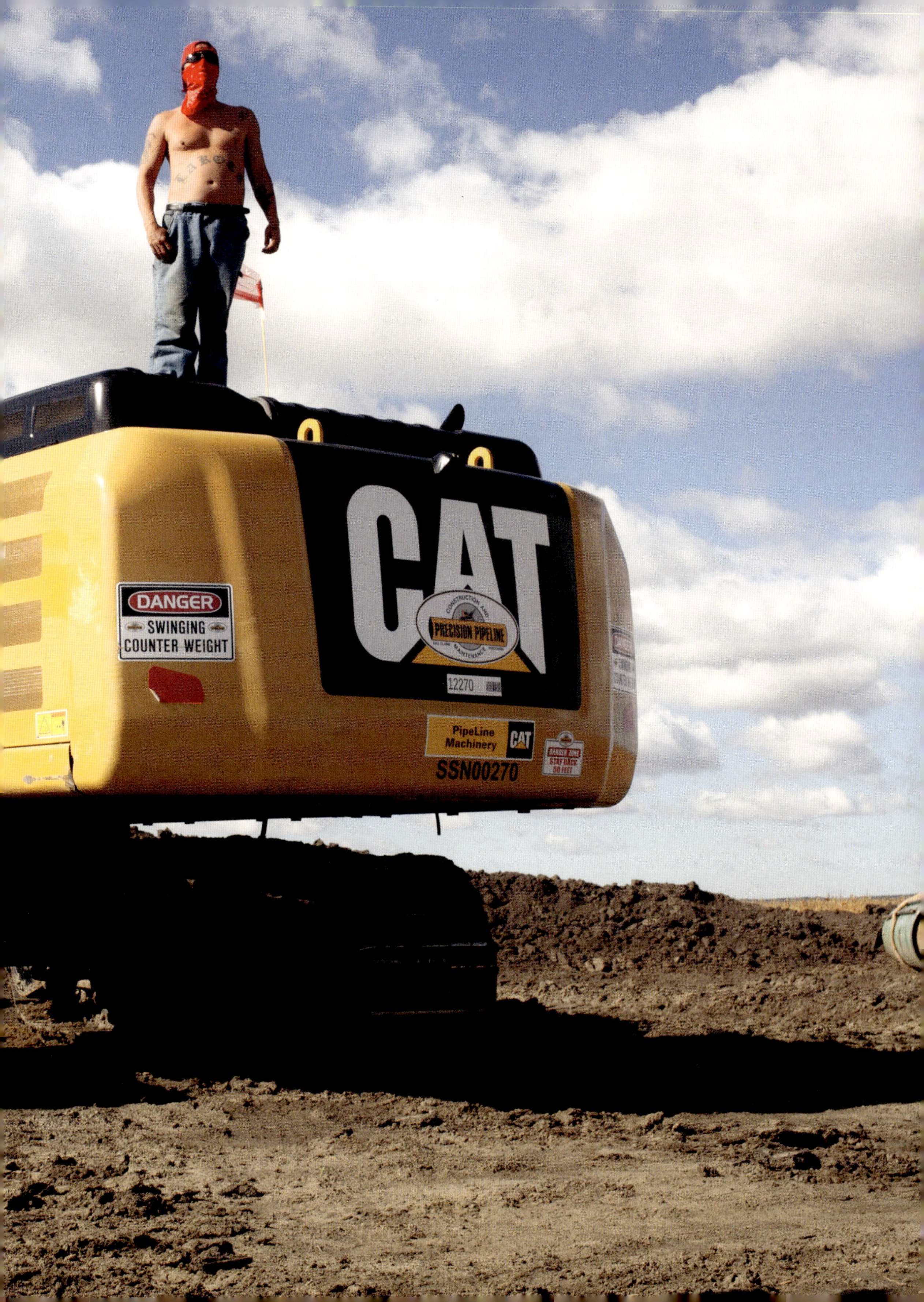
CAT
DANGER
SWINGING
COUNTER WEIGHT
PRECISION PIPELINE
CONSTRUCTION AND
MAINTENANCE
12270
PipeLine
Machinery
CAT
SSN00270
DANGER ZONE
STAY BACK
50 FEET

"The irony is that of all the Native Americans gathered at Standing Rock, many are veterans who fought in Korea, Vietnam, and Iraq for the United States. Today, they find themselves fighting against the National Guard."

Cyrus Norcross,
Navajo Nation

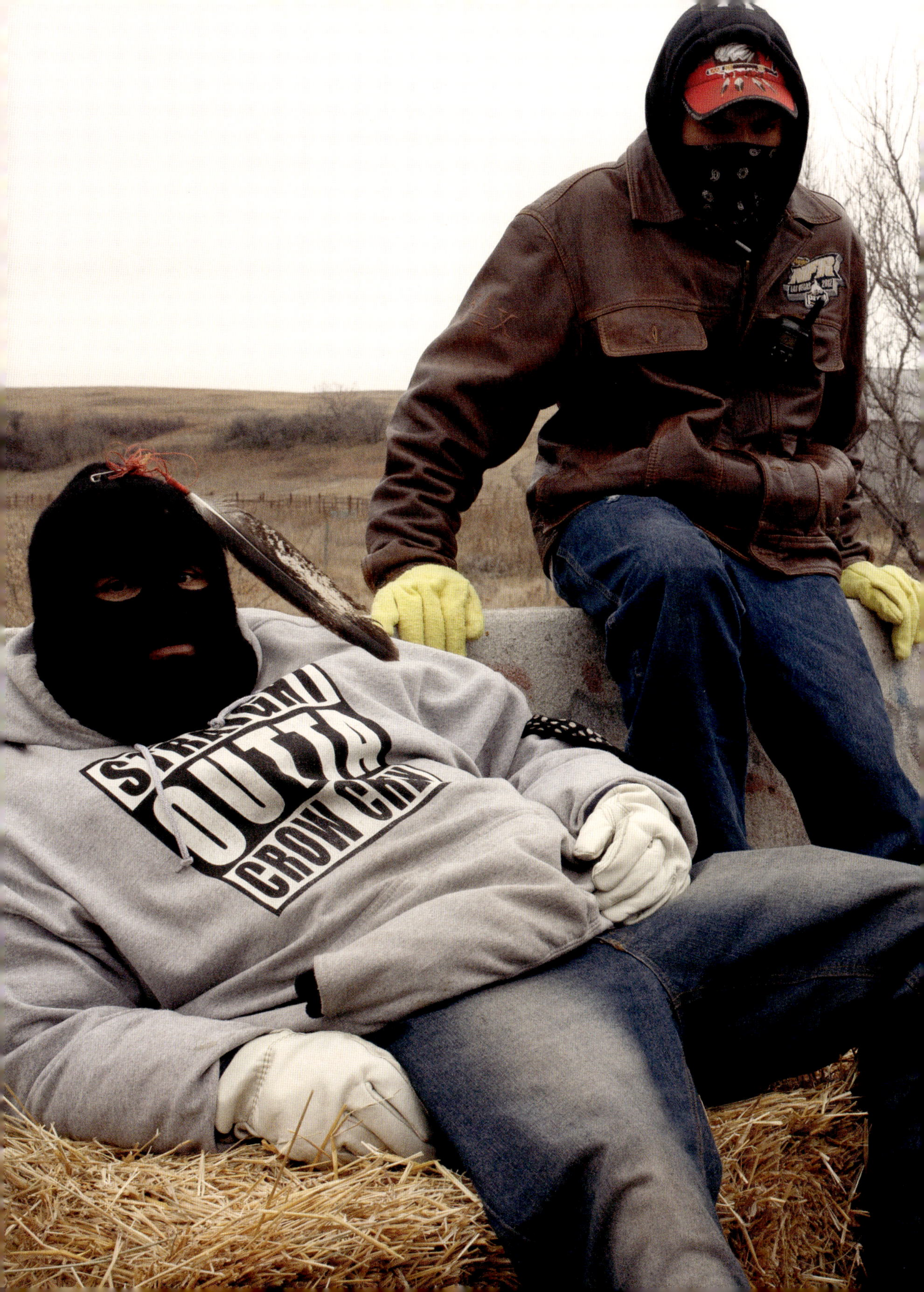

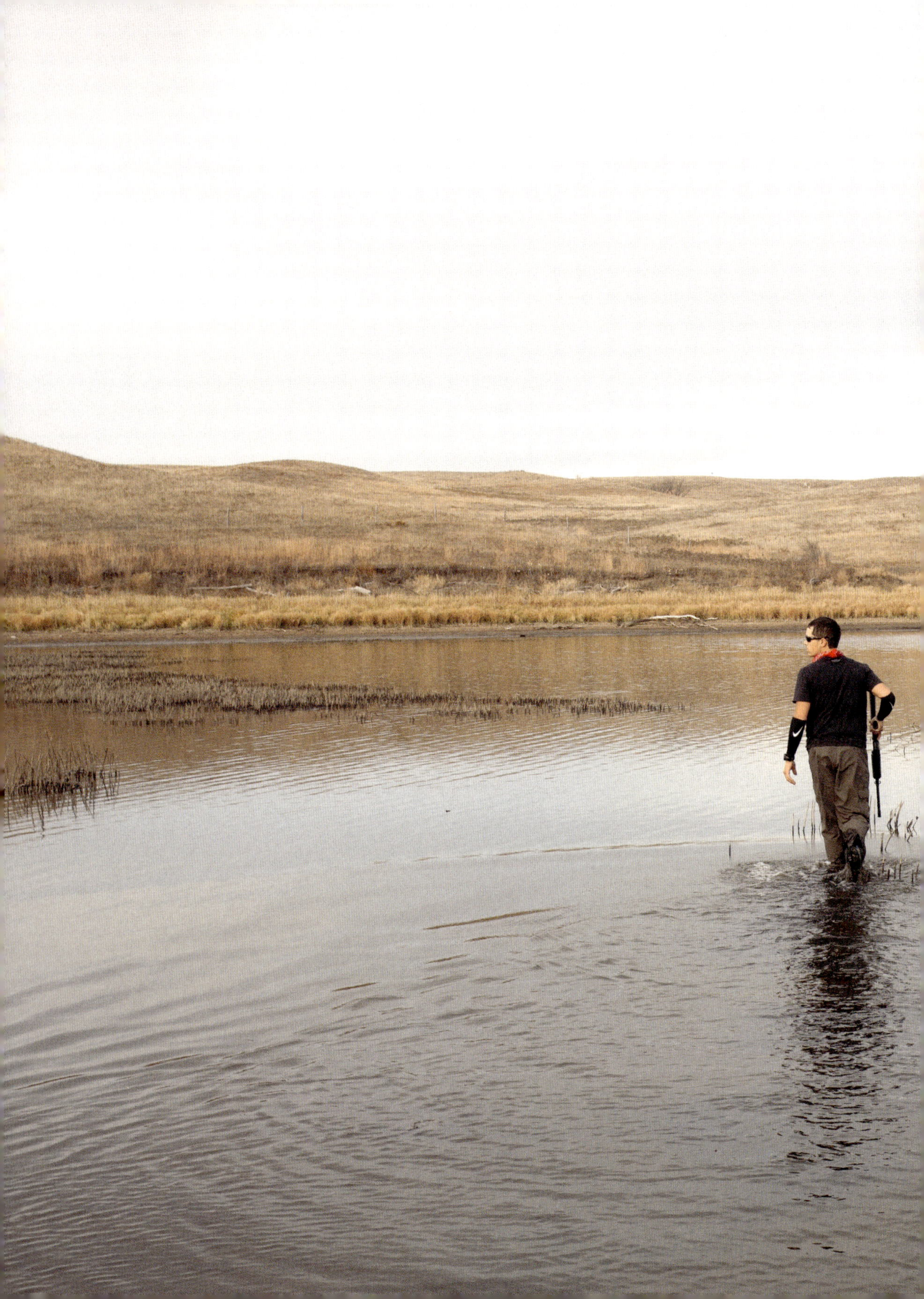

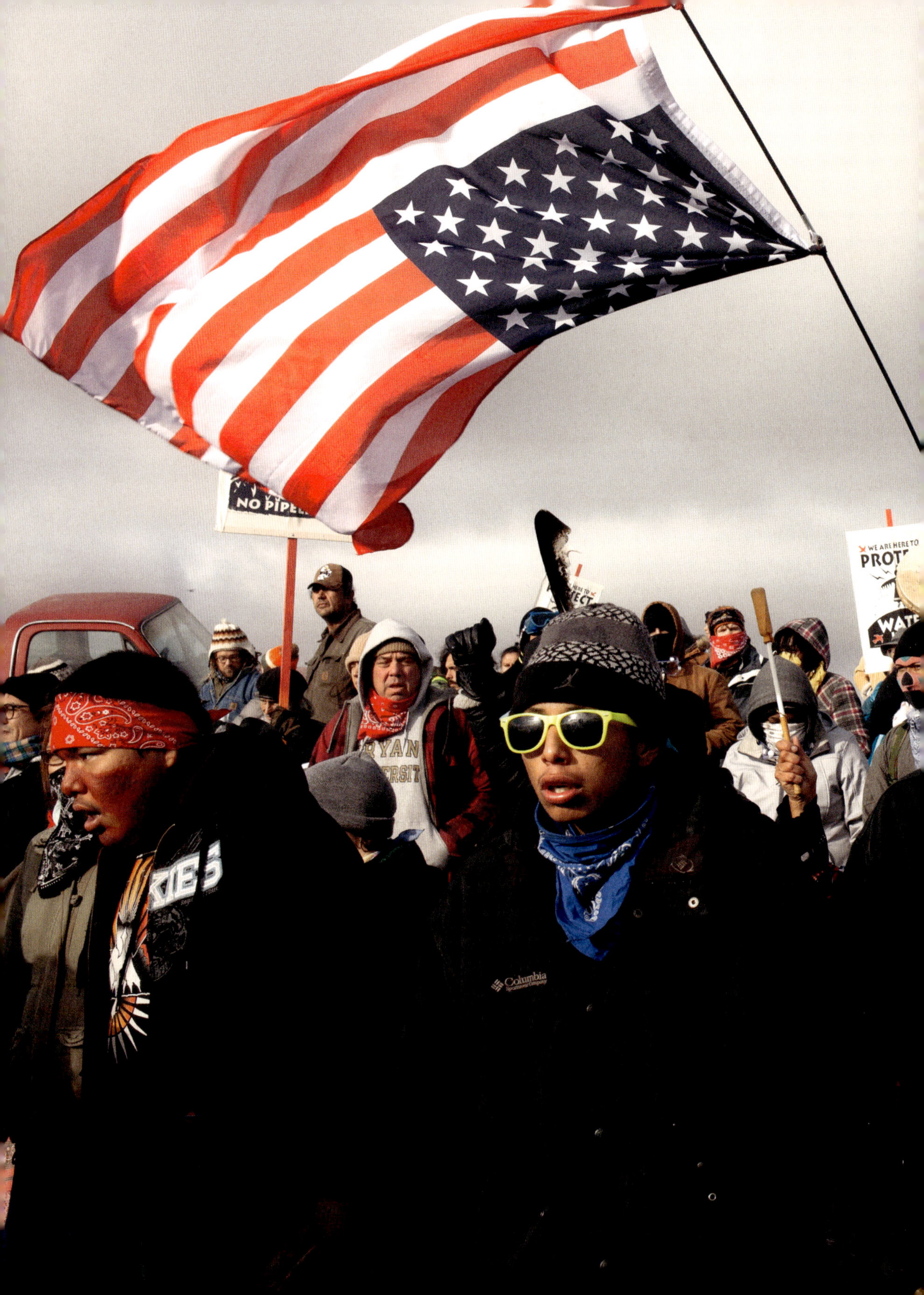

NO PIPEL
WE ARE HERE TO PROTE
WATE

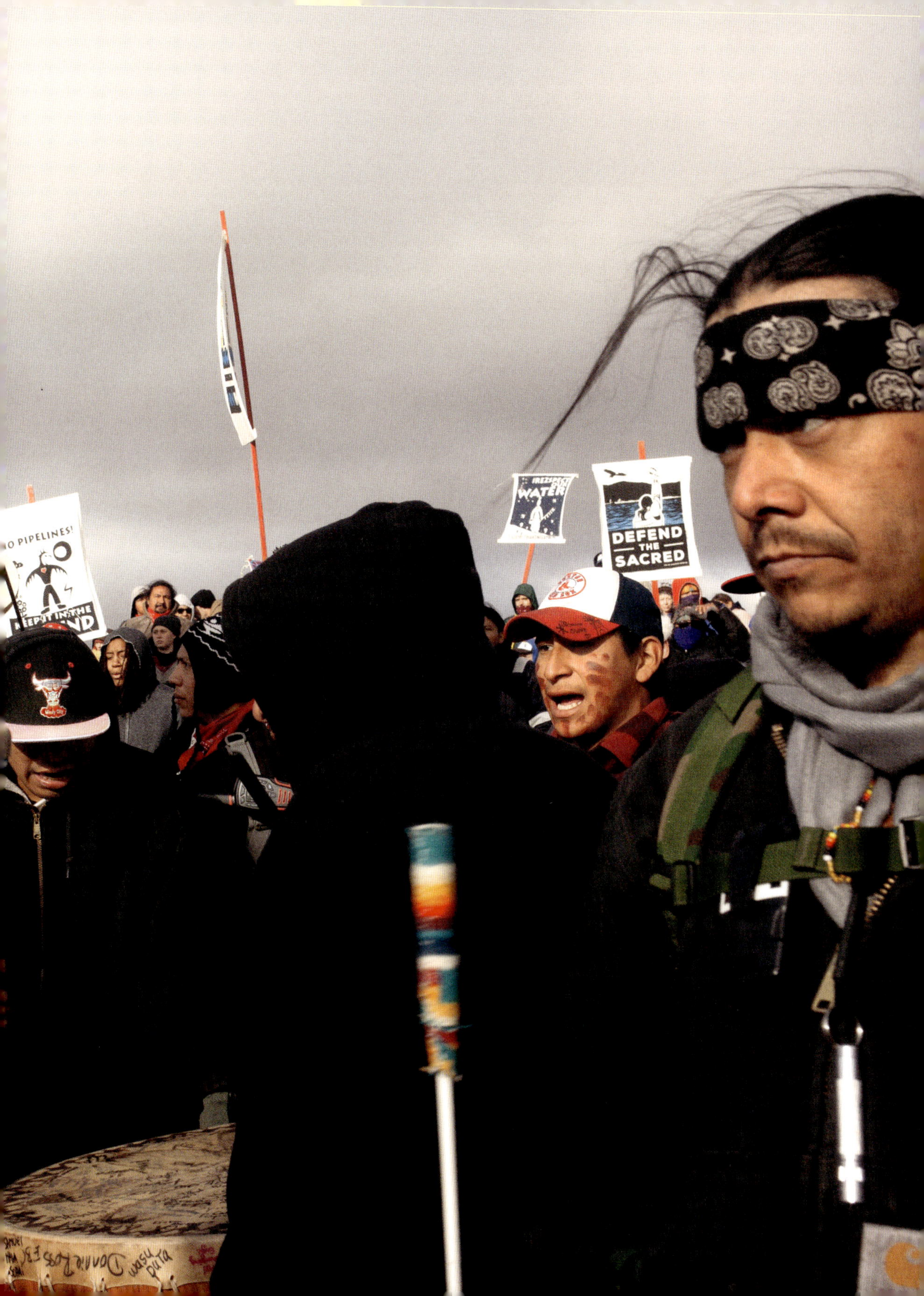
O PIPELINES!
KEEP IT IN THE
GROUND
WATER
DEFEND
THE
SACRED

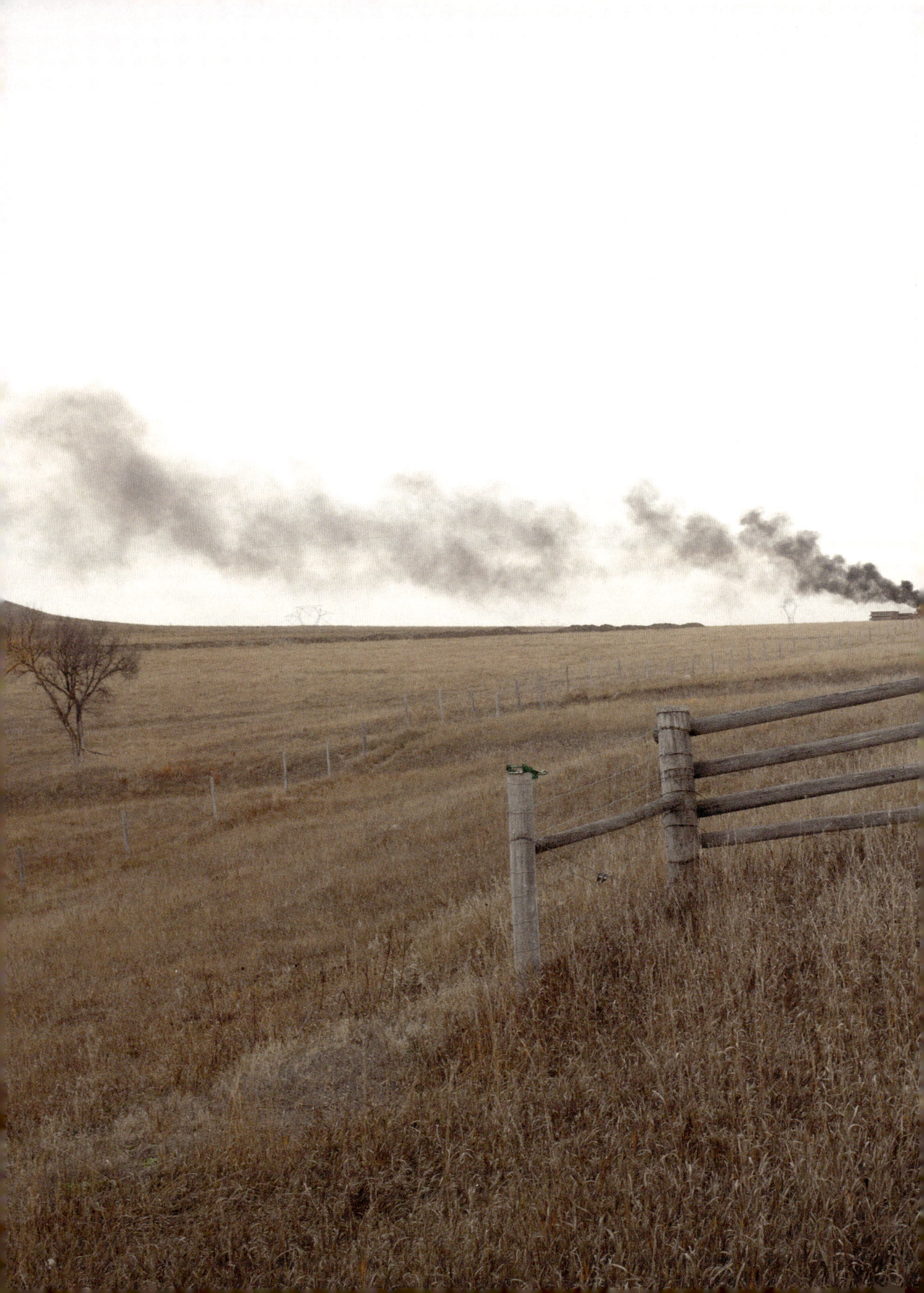

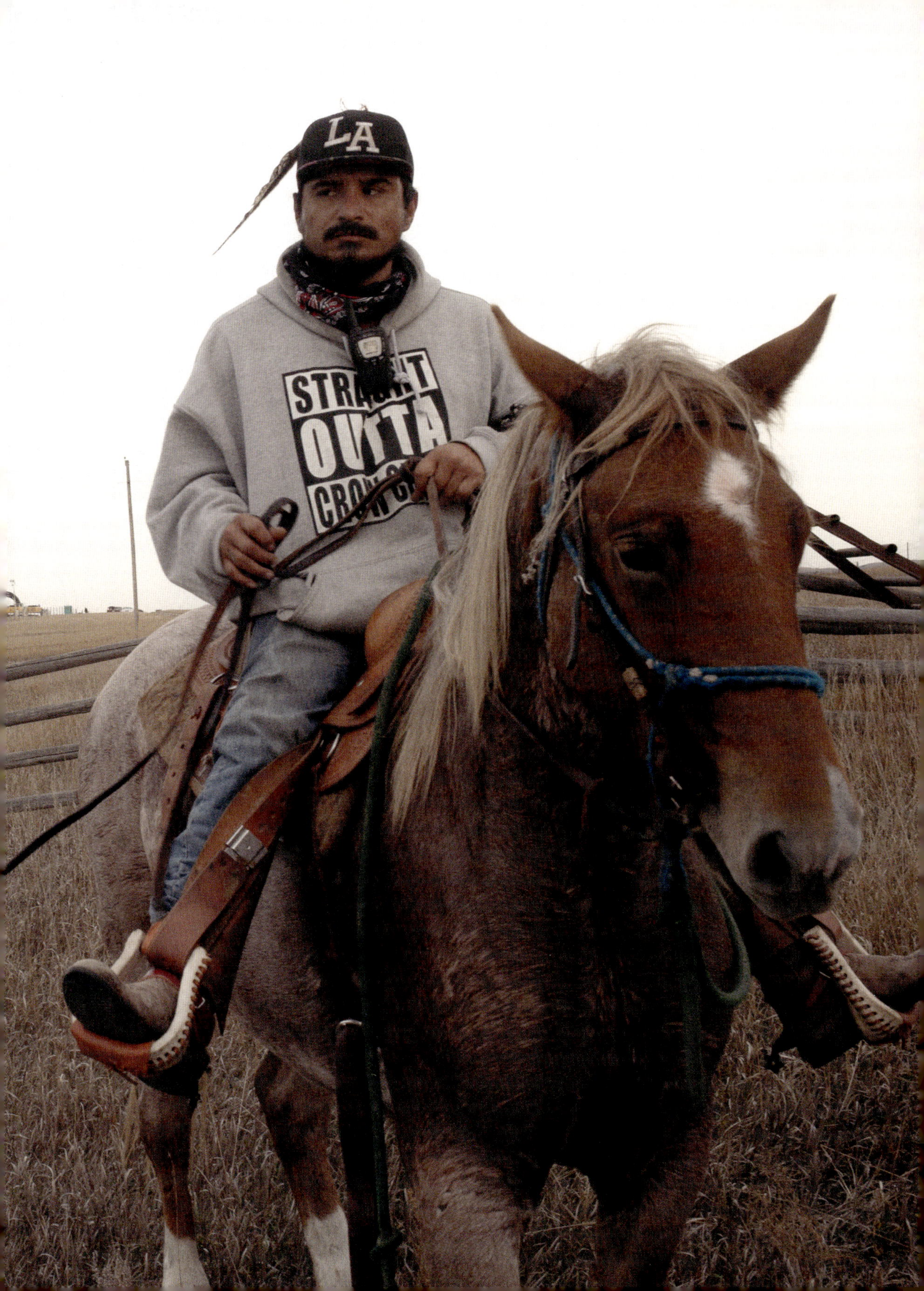

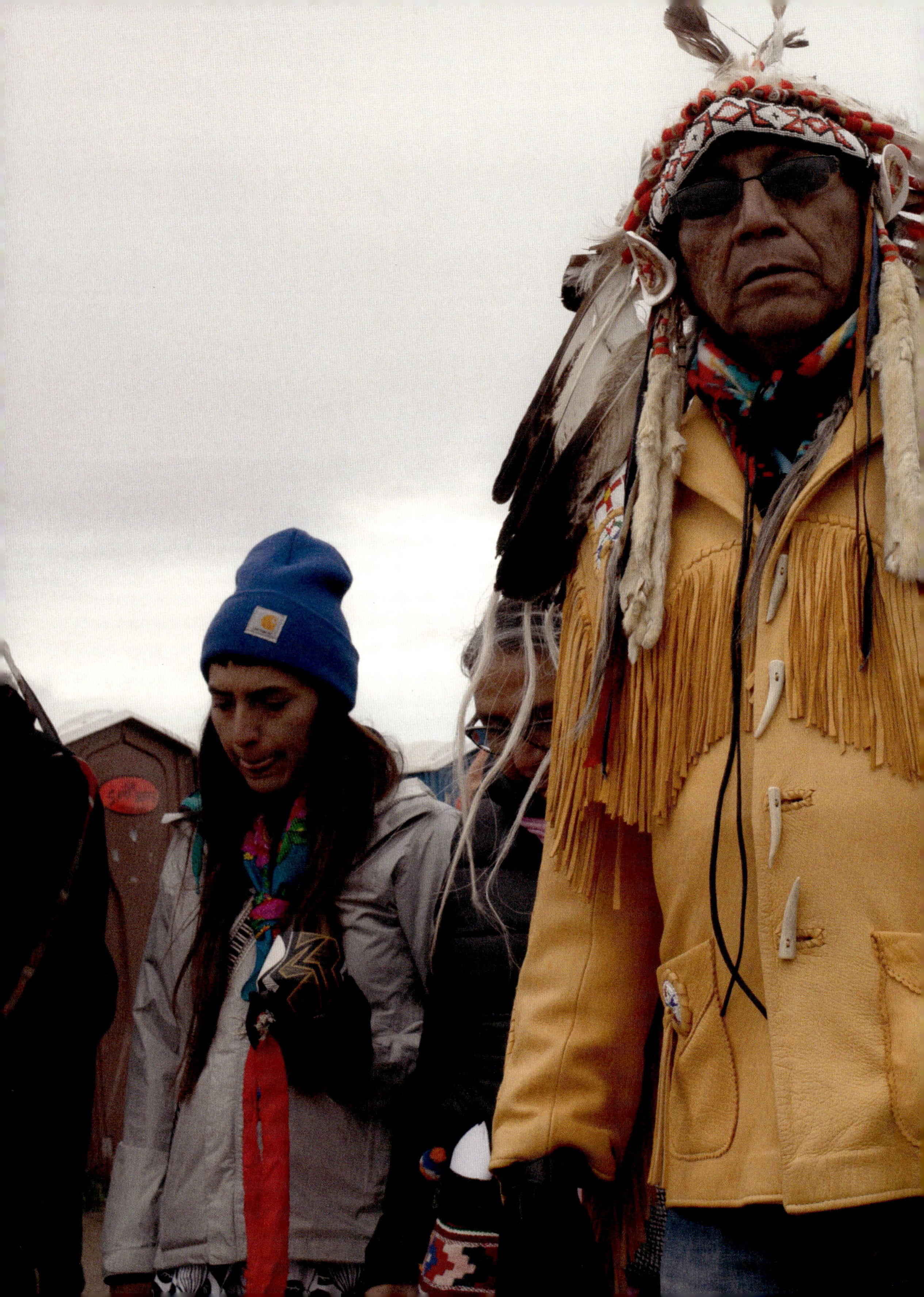

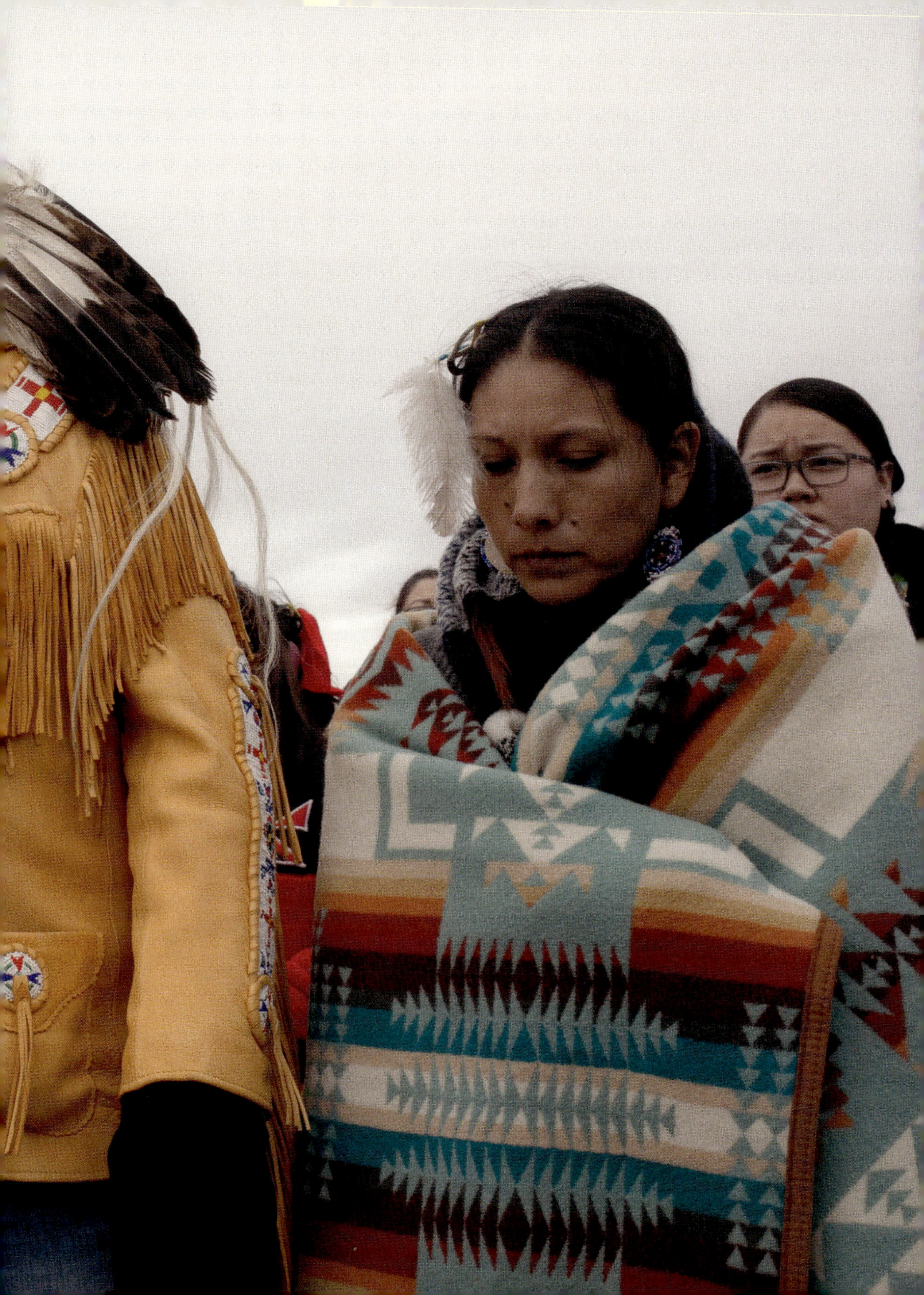

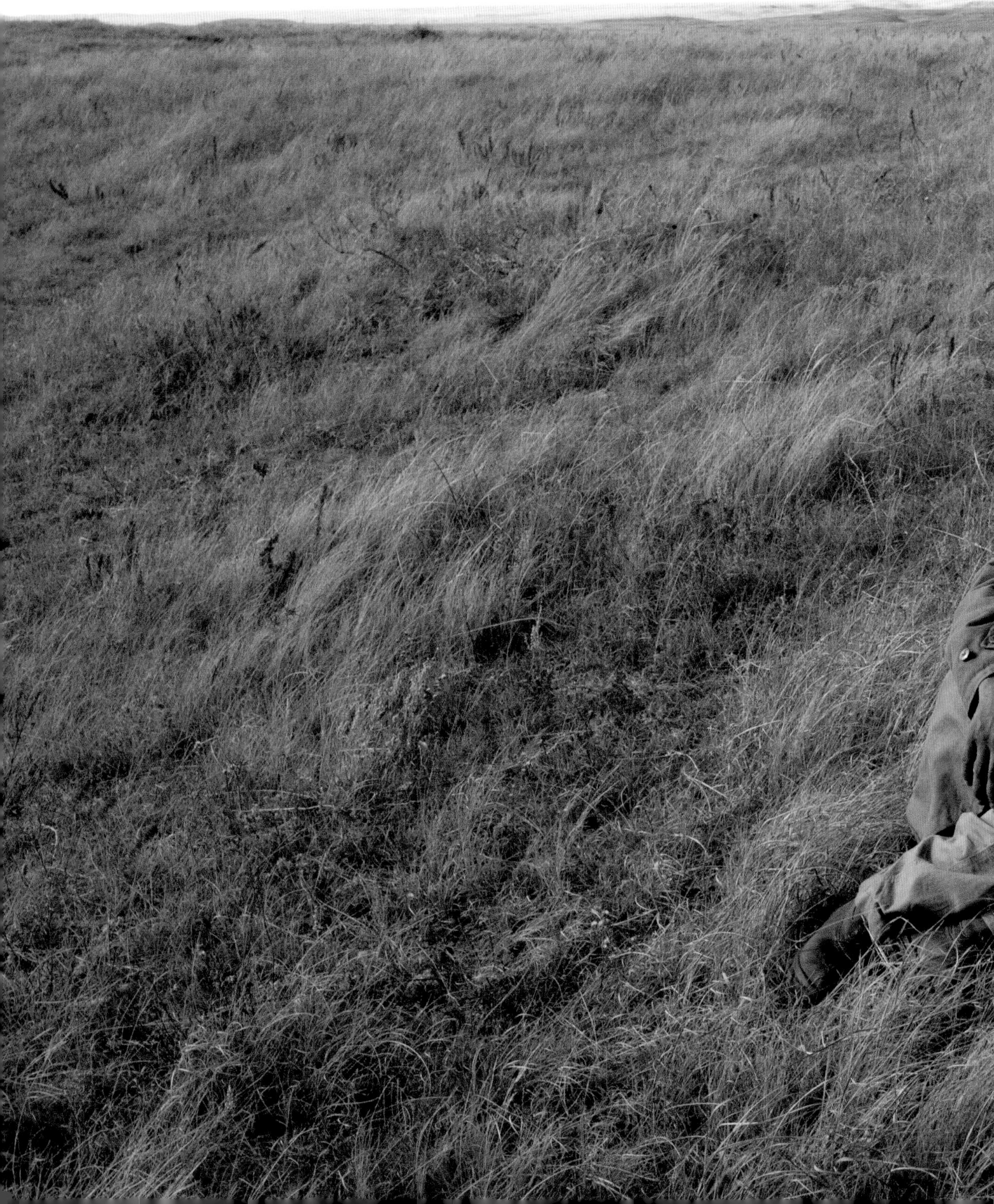

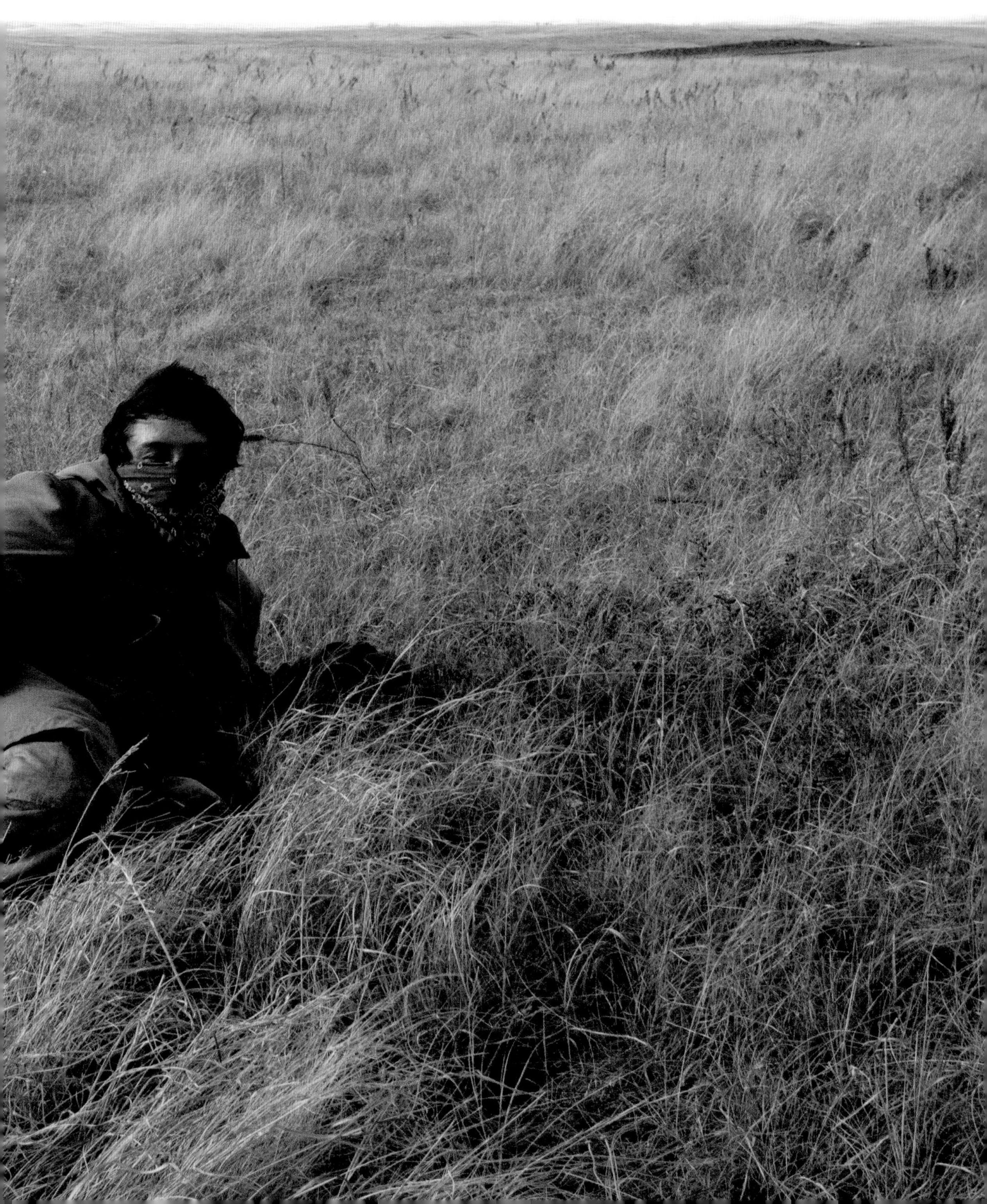

"Brothers and sisters, we have no weapons,
but we have to face men with automatic rifles.
These men are destroying Nature in the name
of Progress; it is time to open their eyes."

Amerson James,
Navajo Nation

115

A
BEAUTIFUL
DREAM

Throughout the evening, the riders sang in English around the fire. Each of them placed their bunks on the thin layer of ice, close to the flames, and some were passing a joint. Tomorrow will be a long and cold day. The hundred men will head south to Wounded Knee to pay homage to the ancestors massacred there over 130 years ago by the 7th Cavalry Regiment. Buried in the dark valleys of Wounded Knee is the heart of Crazy Horse—and with him, the beautiful dream of a people who wanted to live free.

"When we ride, they ask:
    -'It's your horse?'
    -'No, he belongs to Mother Earth of course,
    this is my brother, we have the same mother.
    When we first met, I had to beg him to let
    me ride. At first he would run and hide.
    Now he wanders where I'm at and looks for
    me. He's my best friend and it's easy to see.'"

Tate Wiedmer,
Lakota tribe

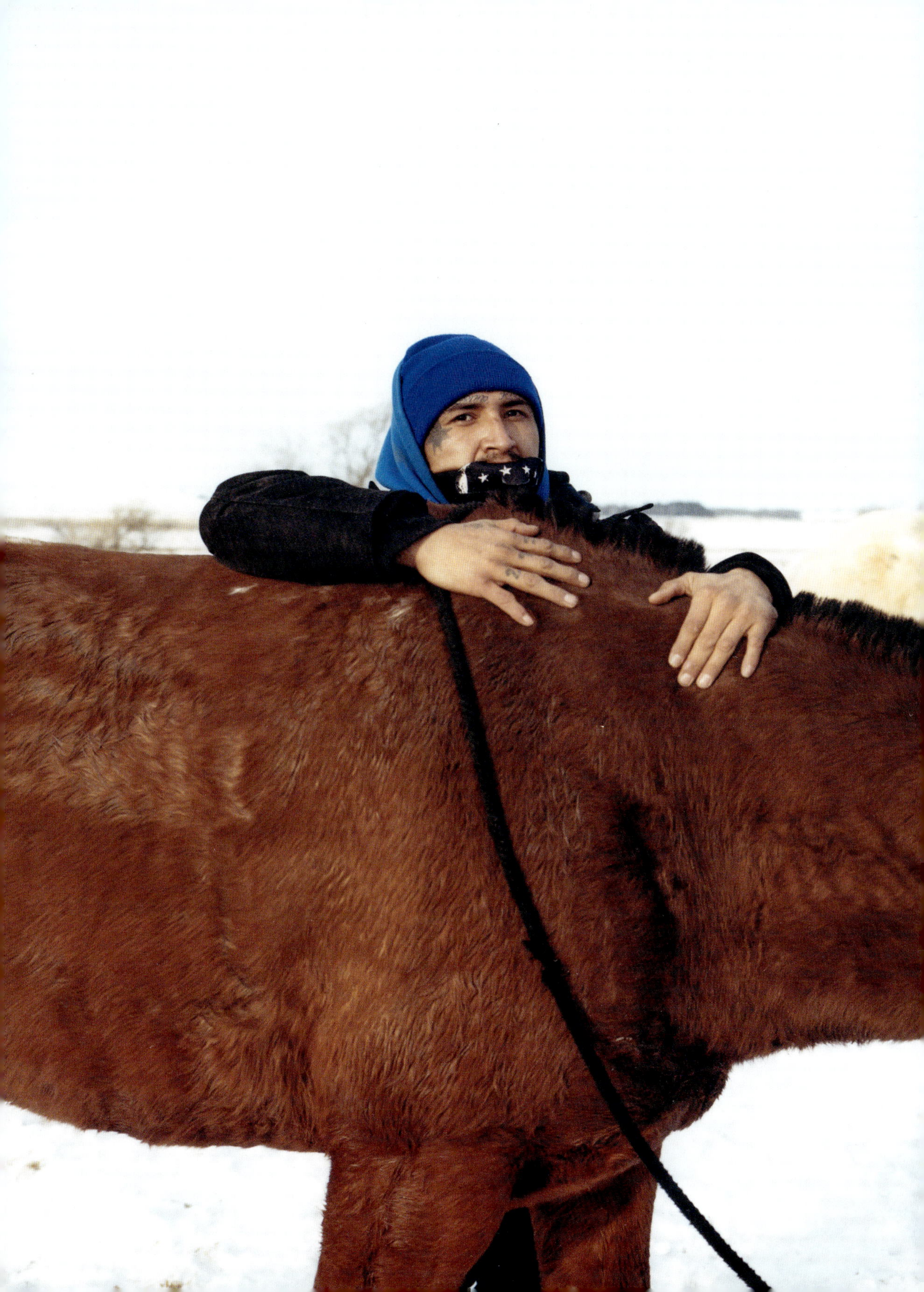

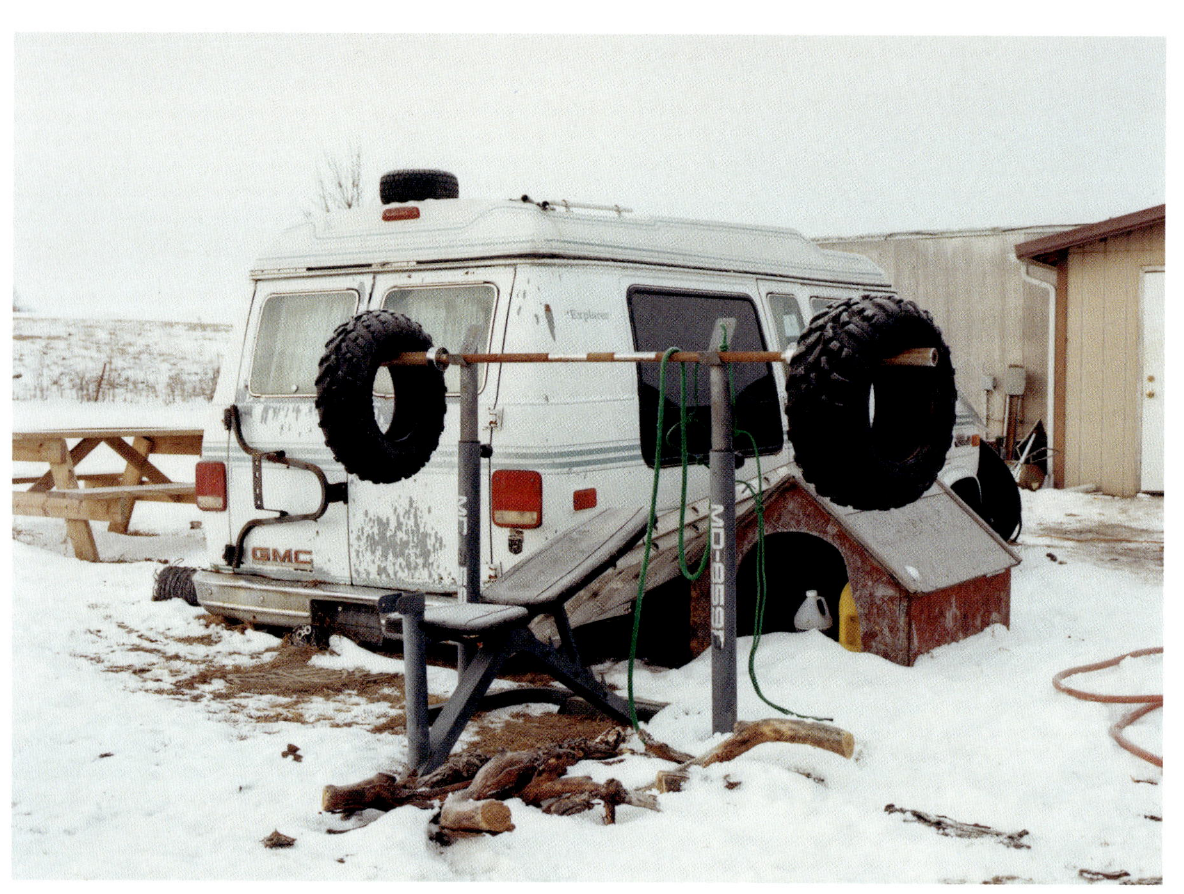

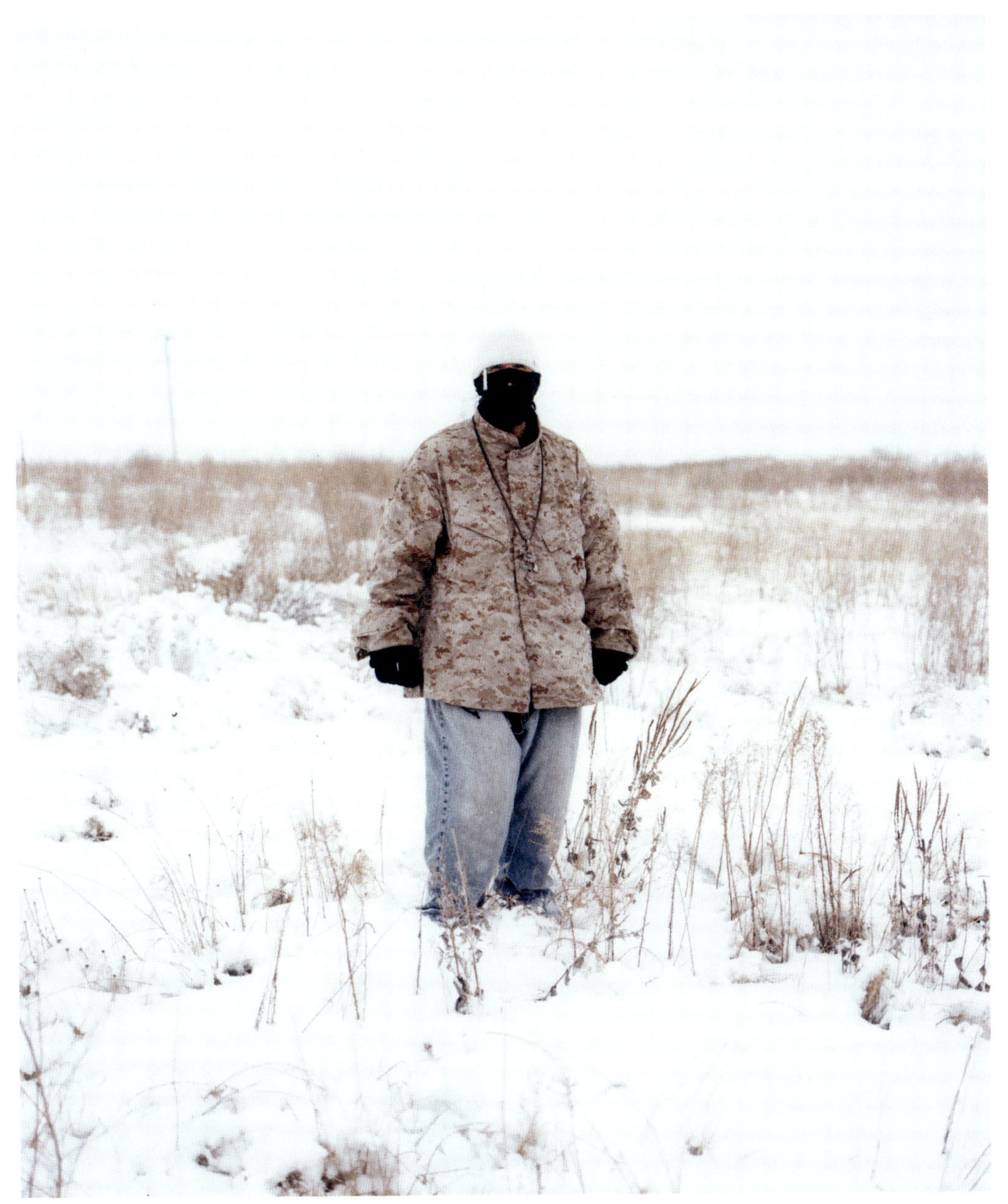

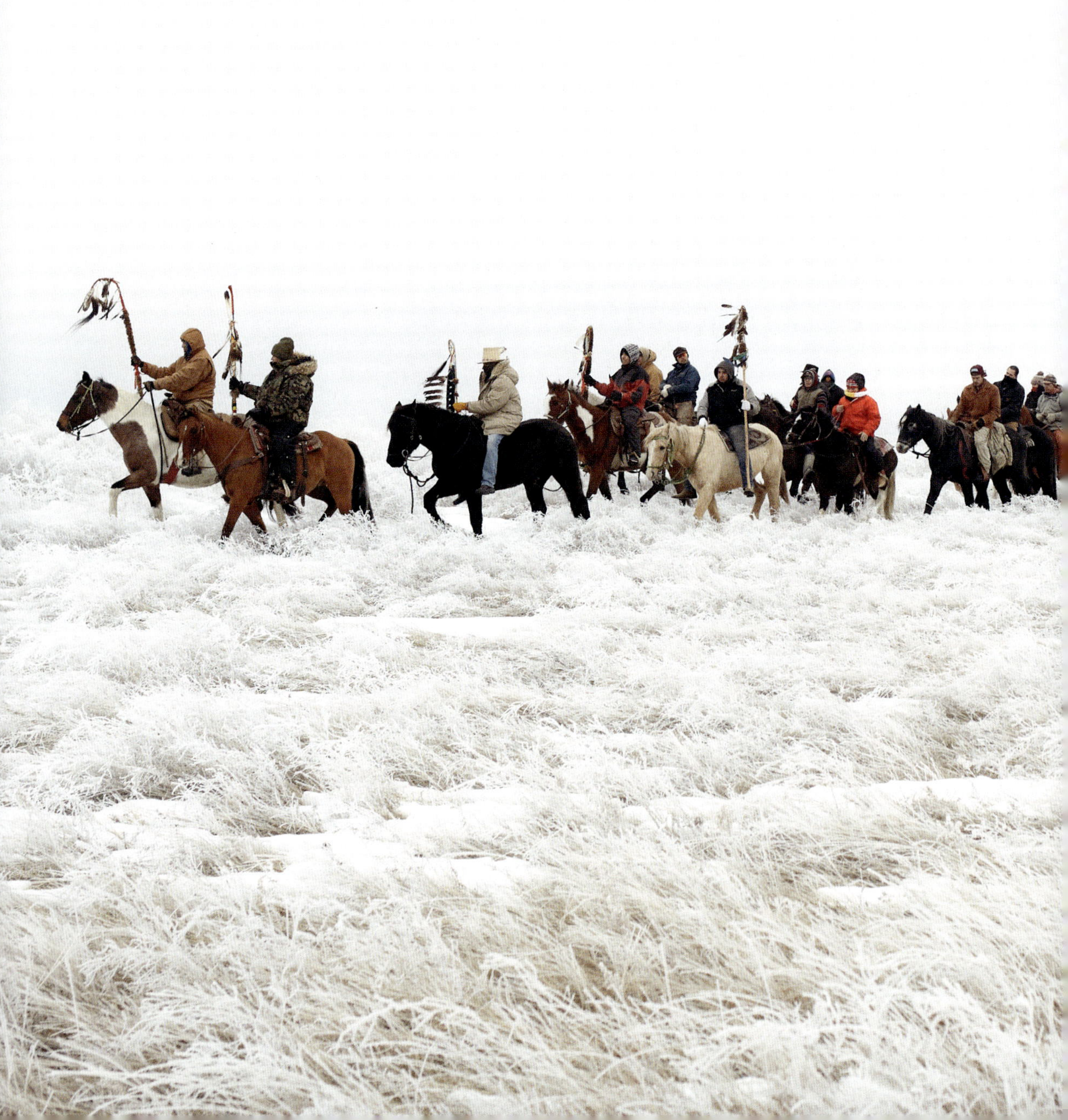

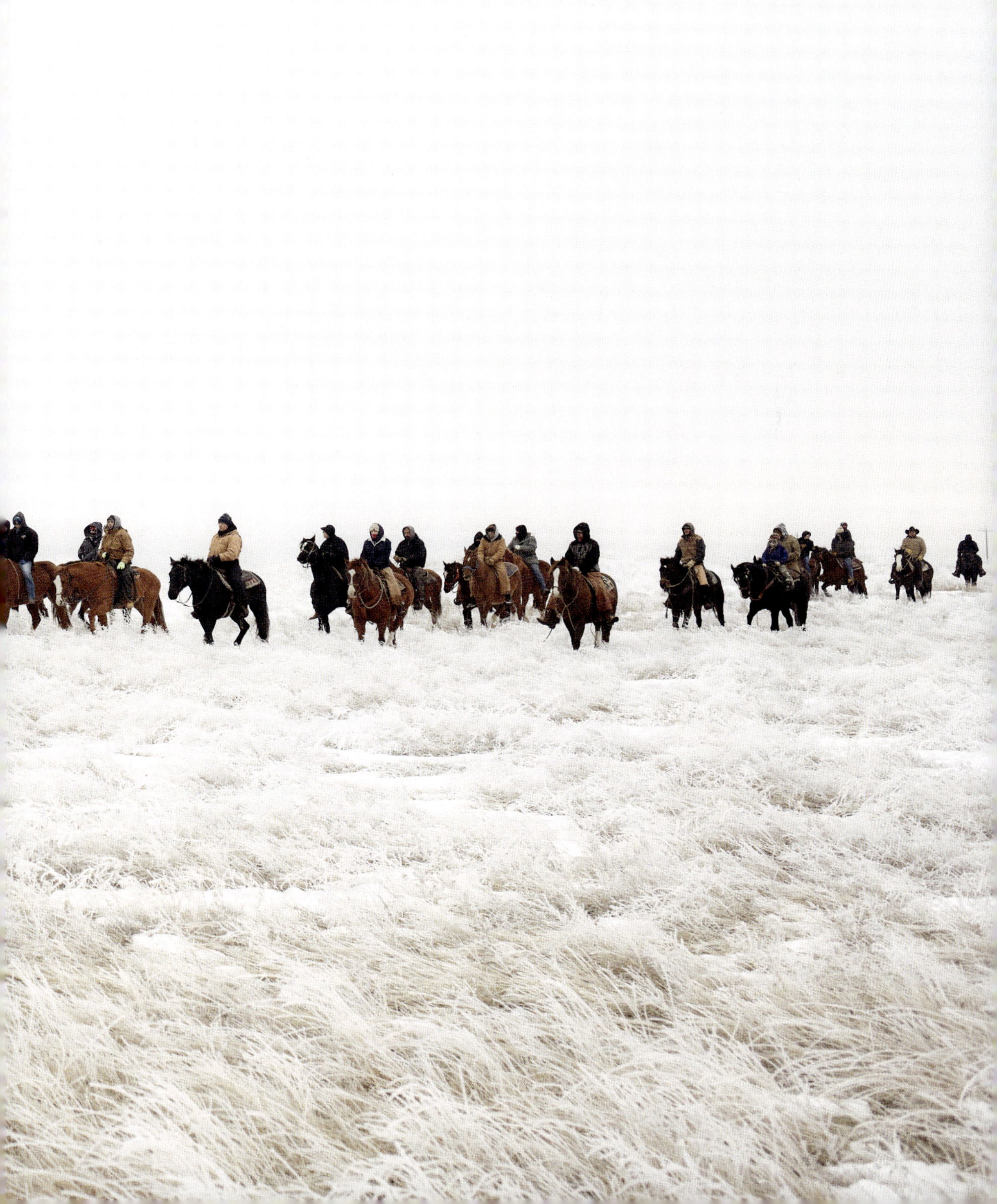

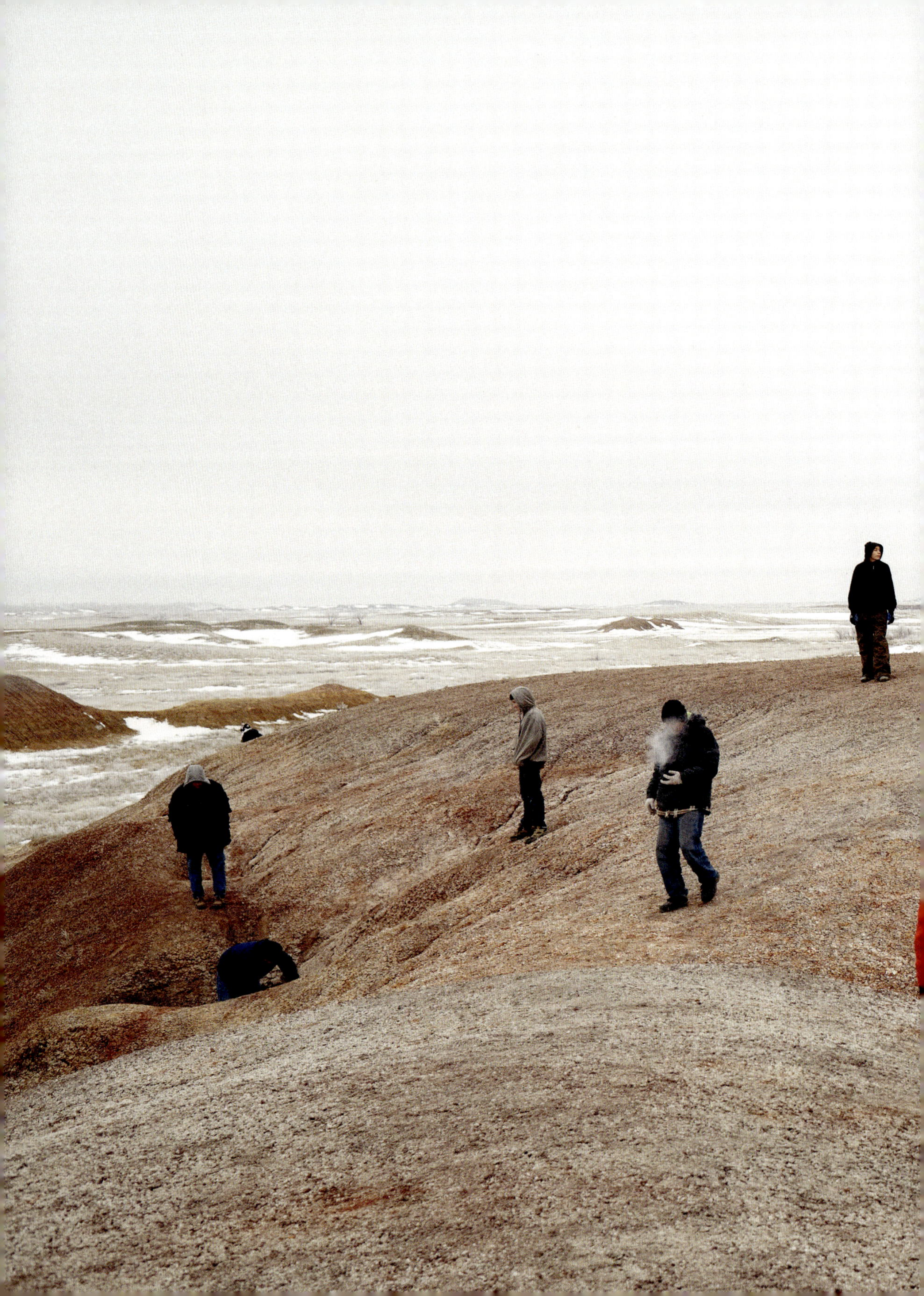

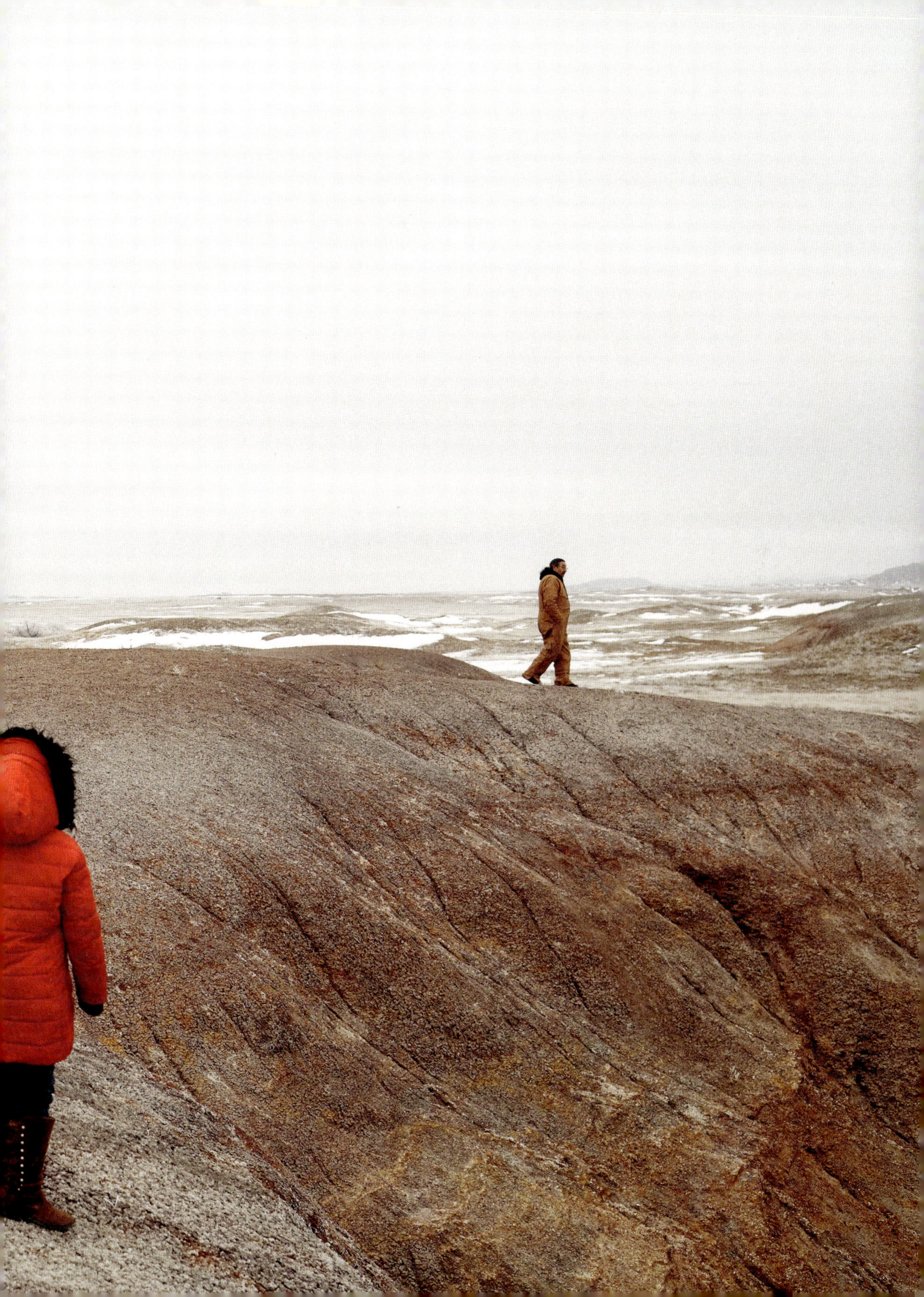

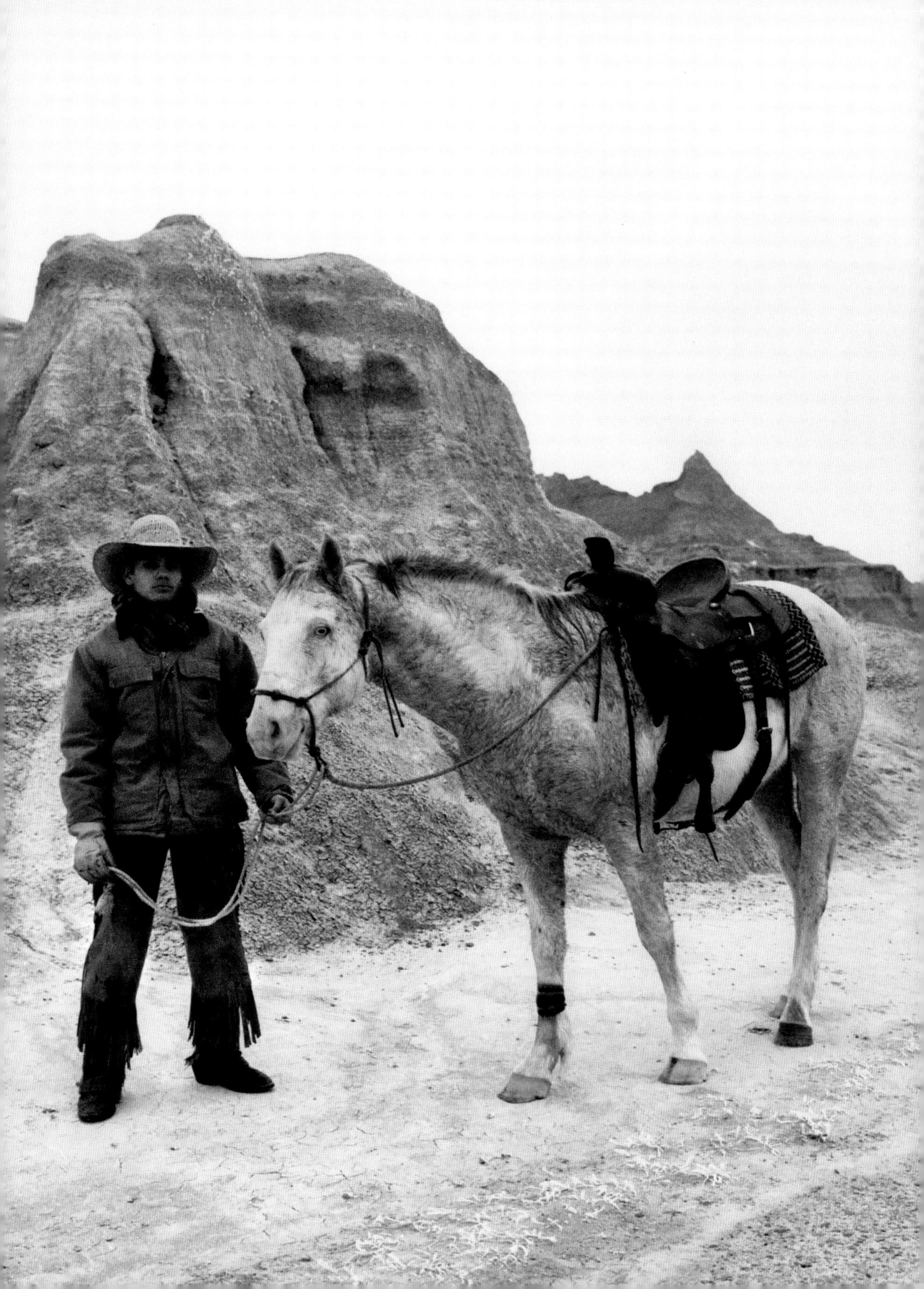

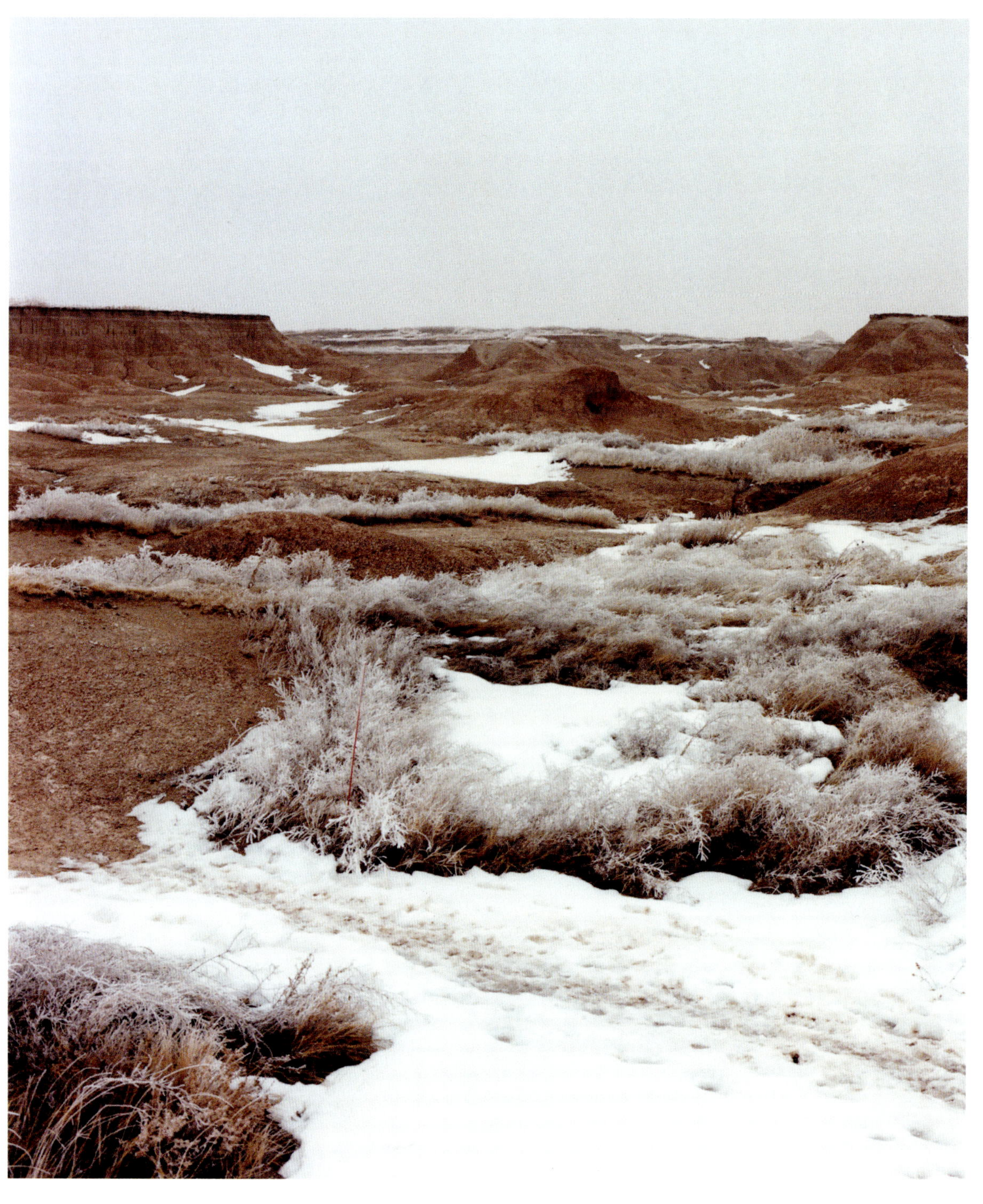

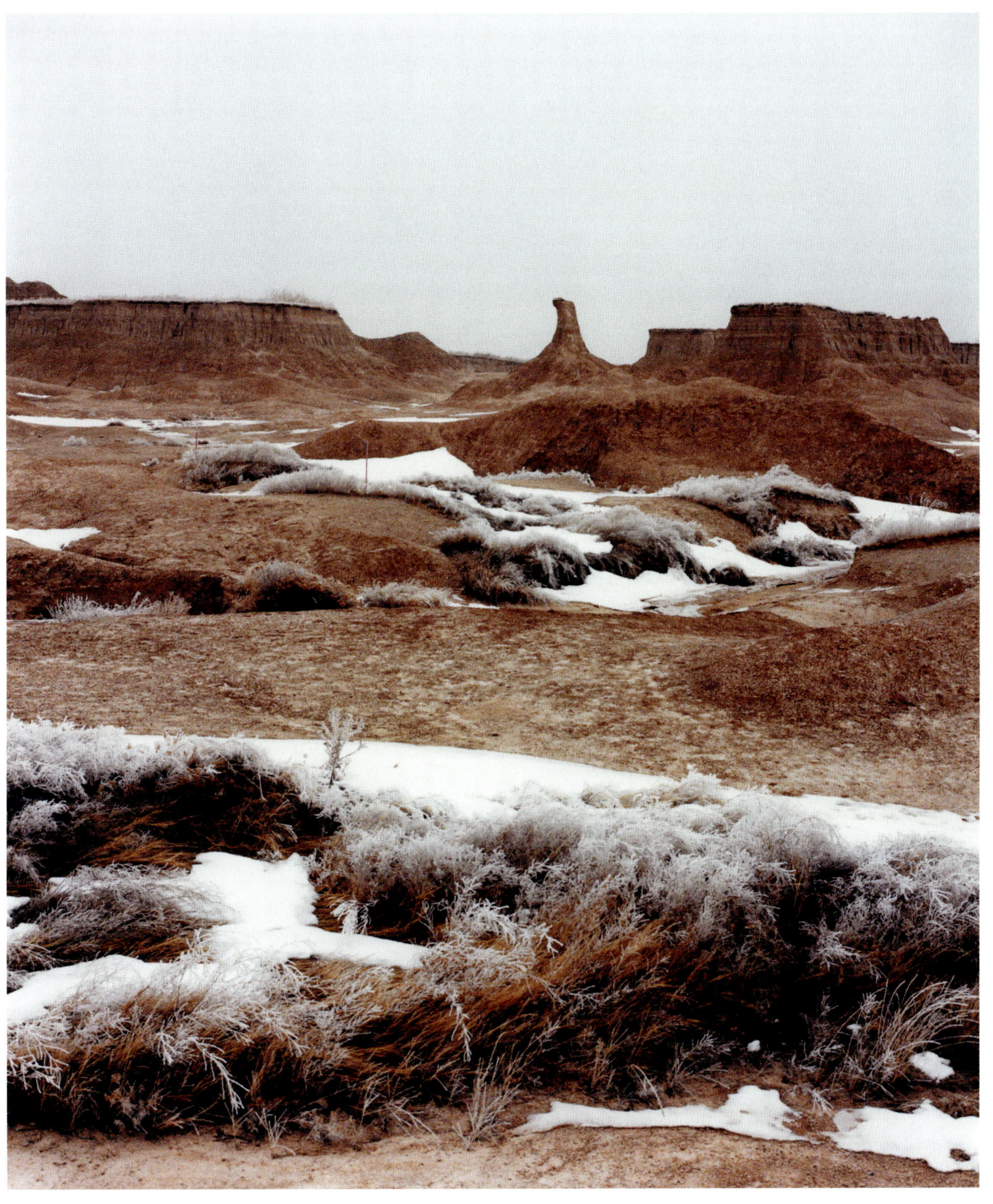

"I can see that something else died there
in the bloody mud, and was buried
in the blizzard. A people's dream died there.
It was a beautiful dream."

Black Elk,
Lakota tribe

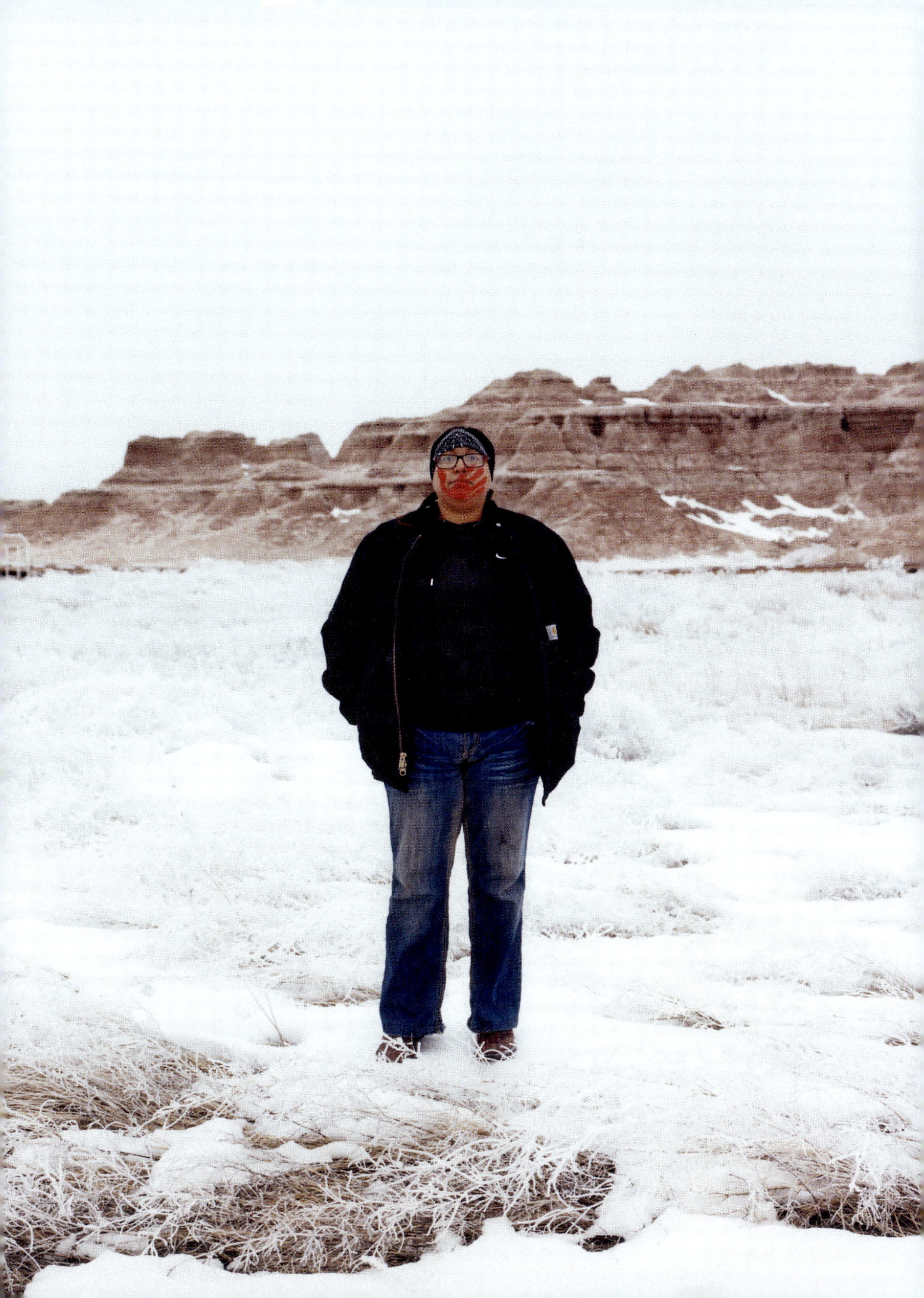

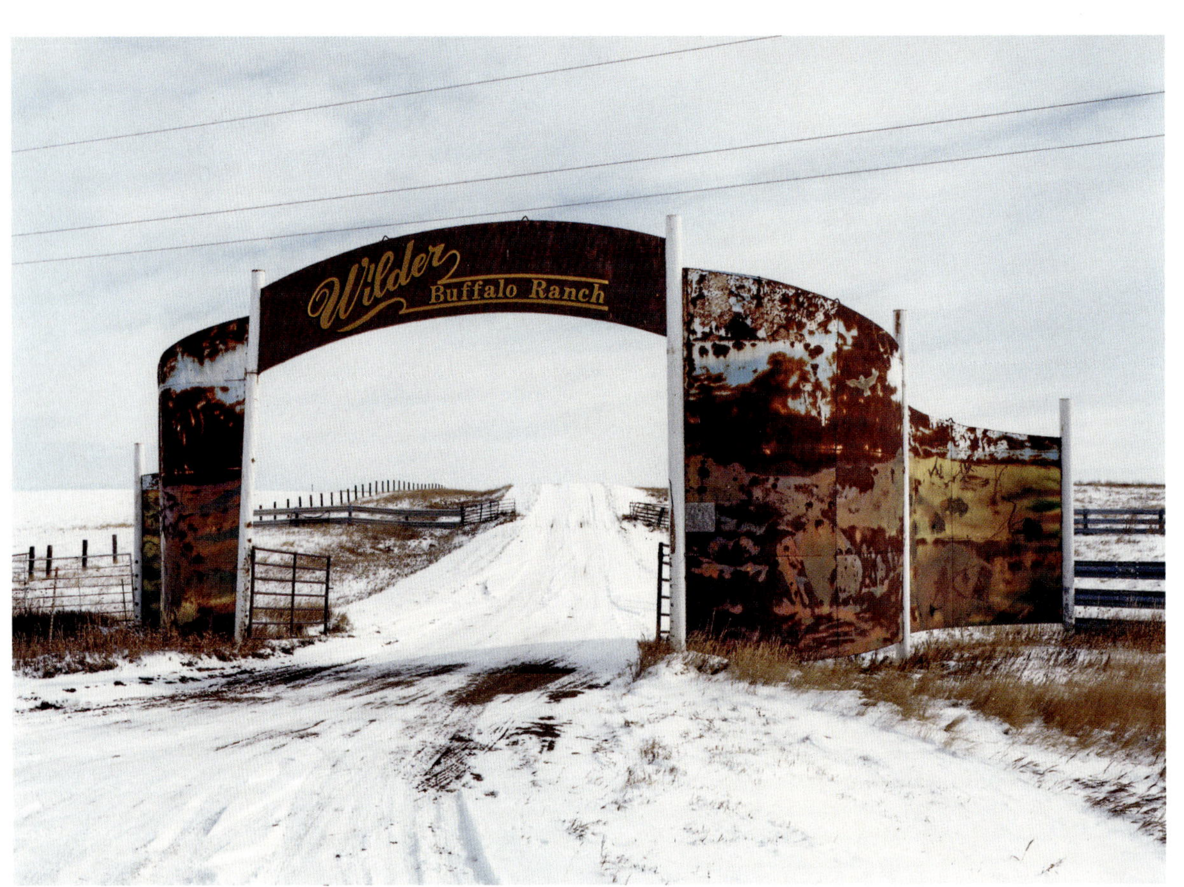

Wilder
Buffalo Ranch

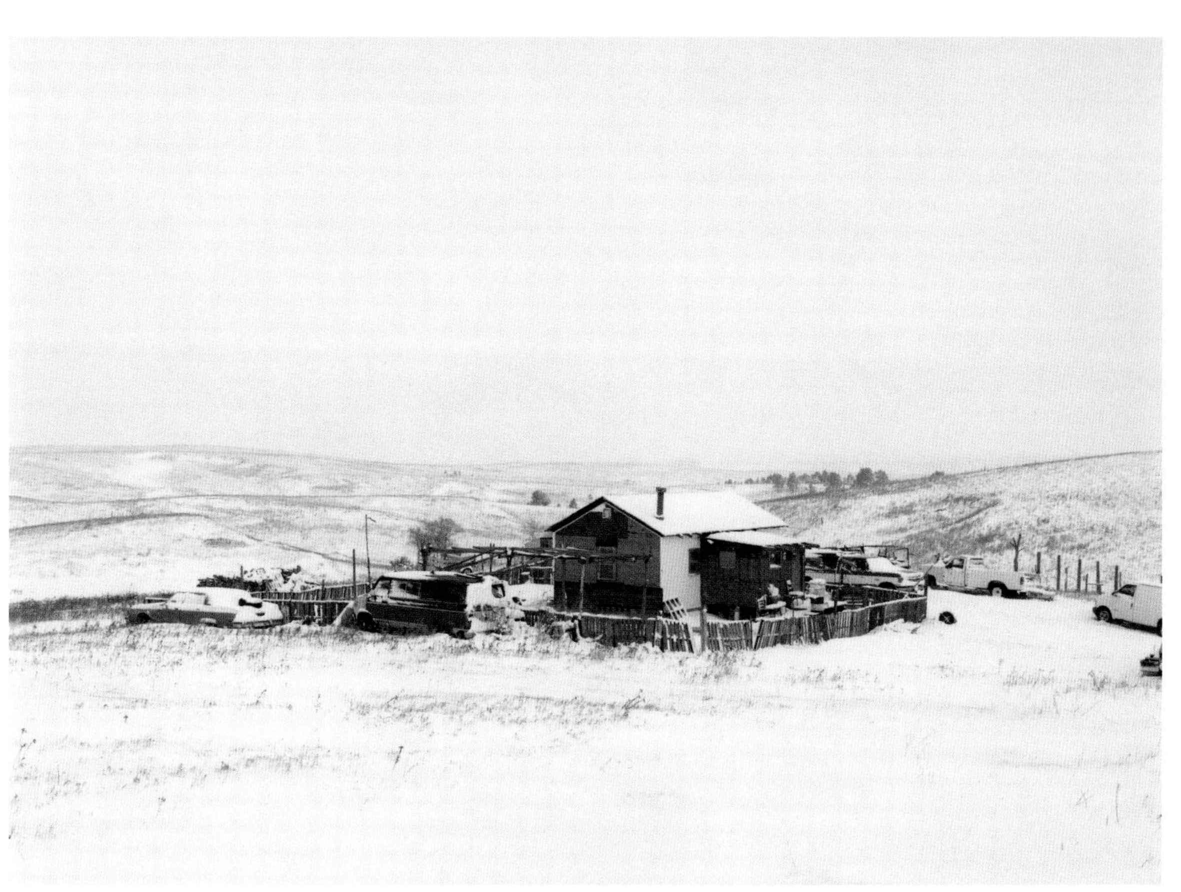

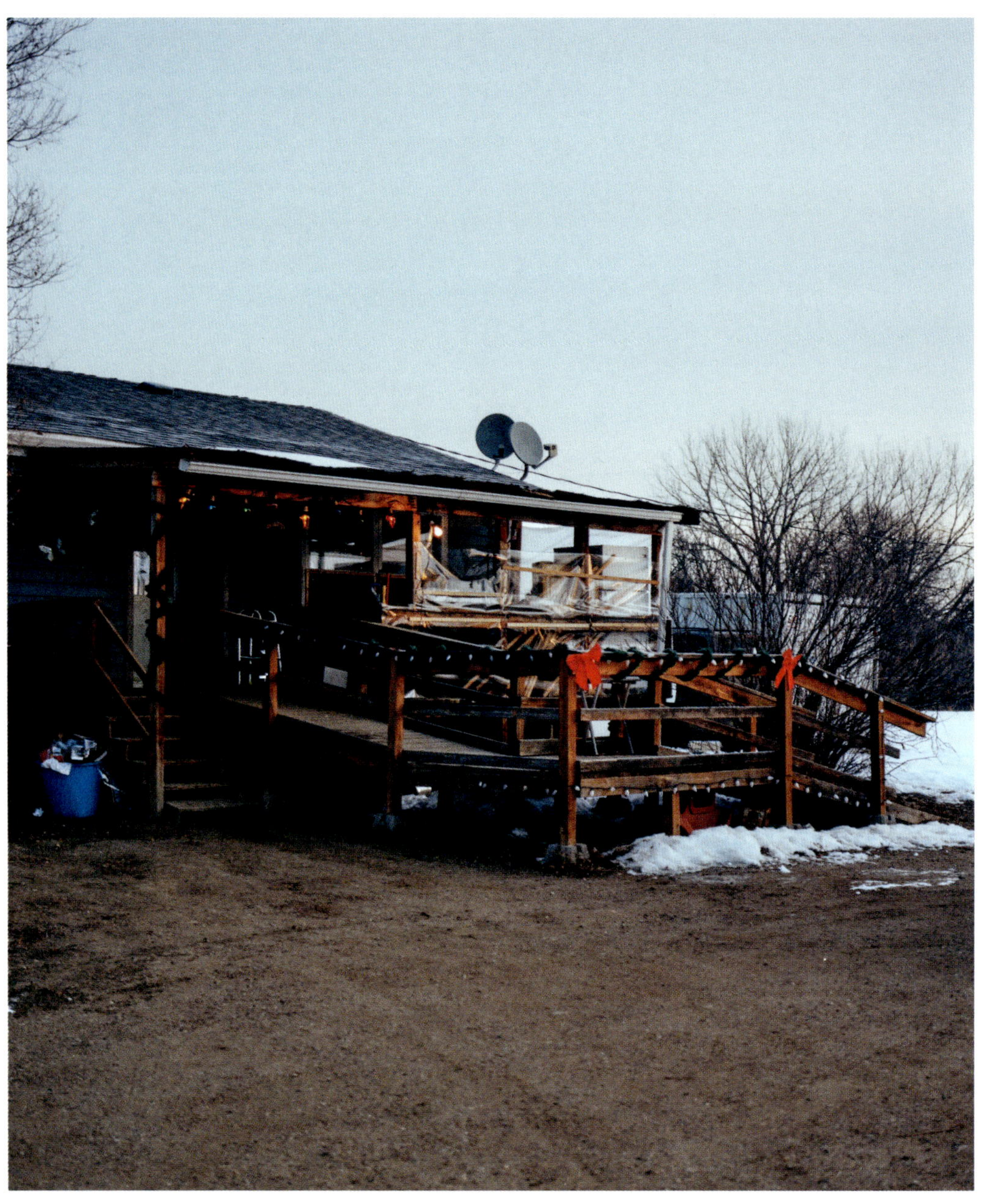

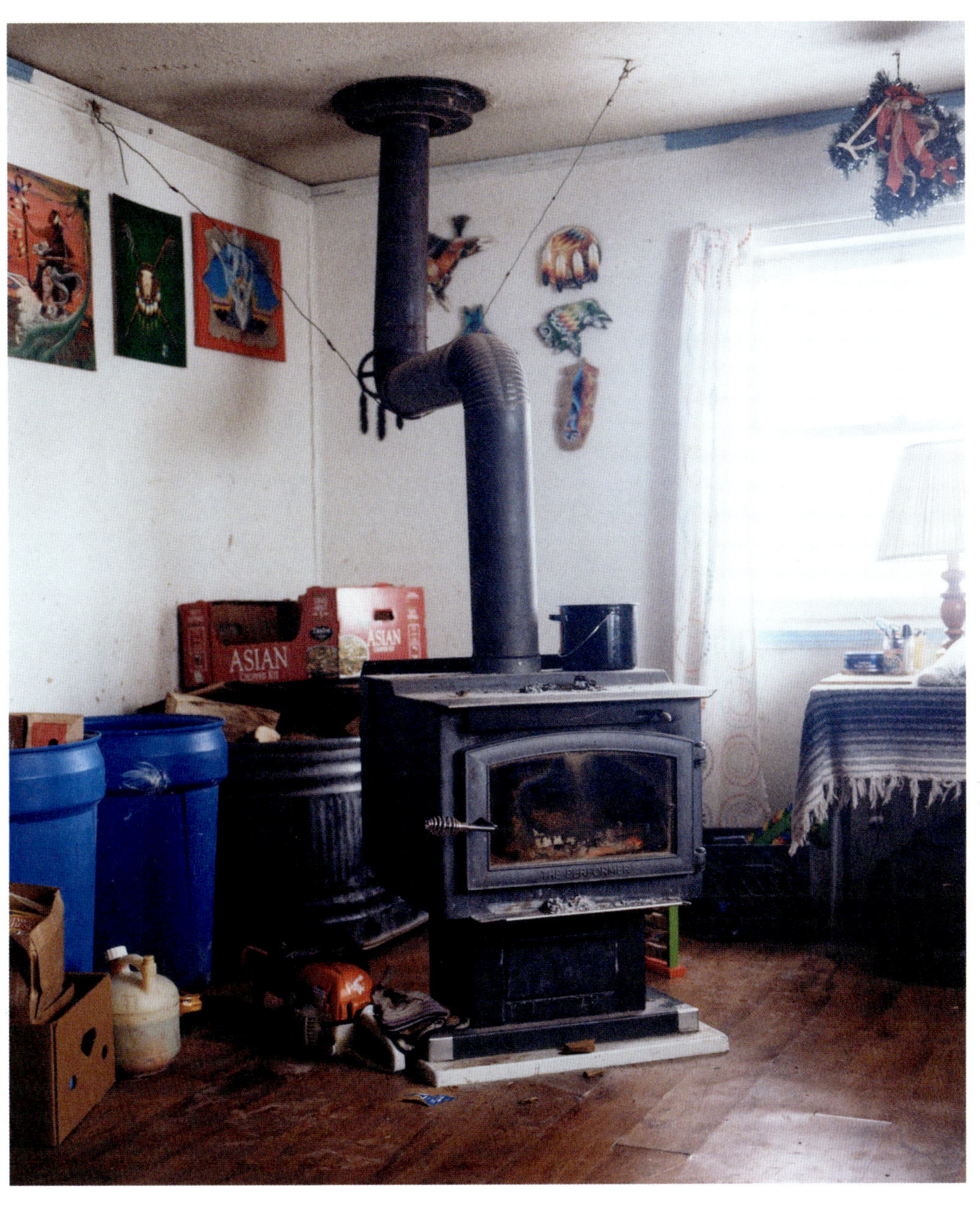

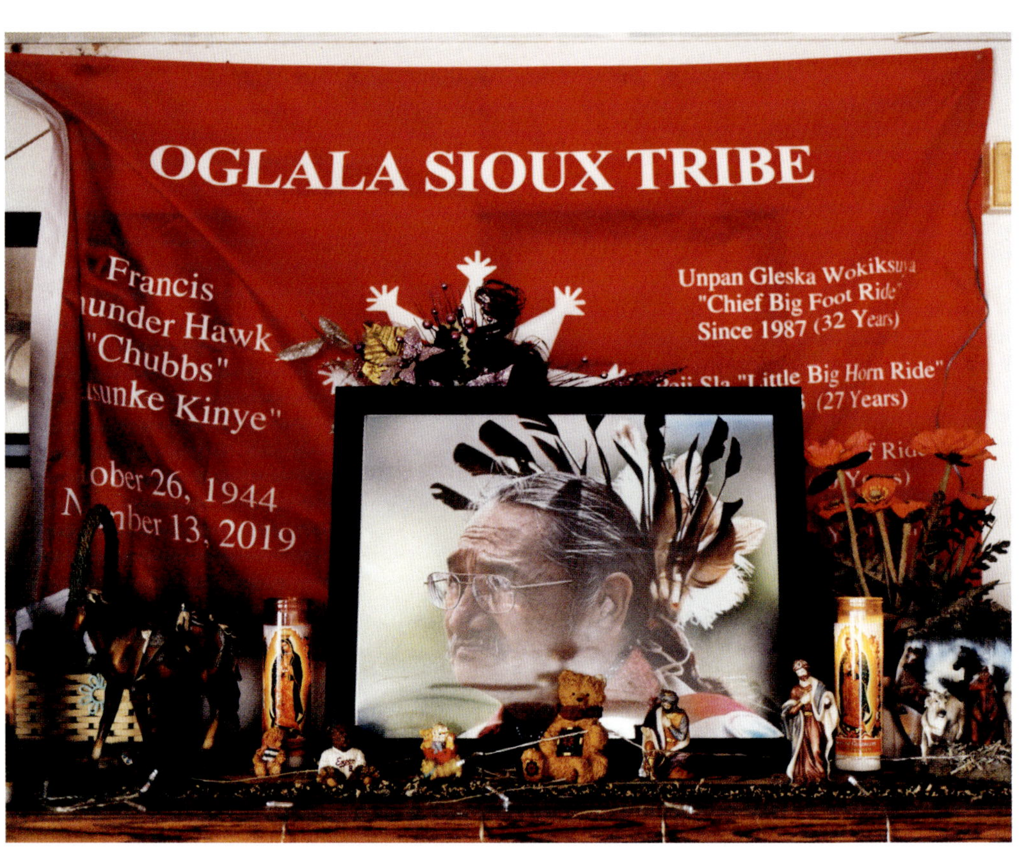
OGLALA SIOUX TRIBE
Francis
under Hawk
"Chubbs"
sunke Kinye"
ober 26, 1944
mber 13, 2019
Unpan Gleska Wokiksuya
"Chief Big Foot Ride"
Since 1987 (32 Years)
Sla "Little Big Horn Ride"
(27 Years)
Ride

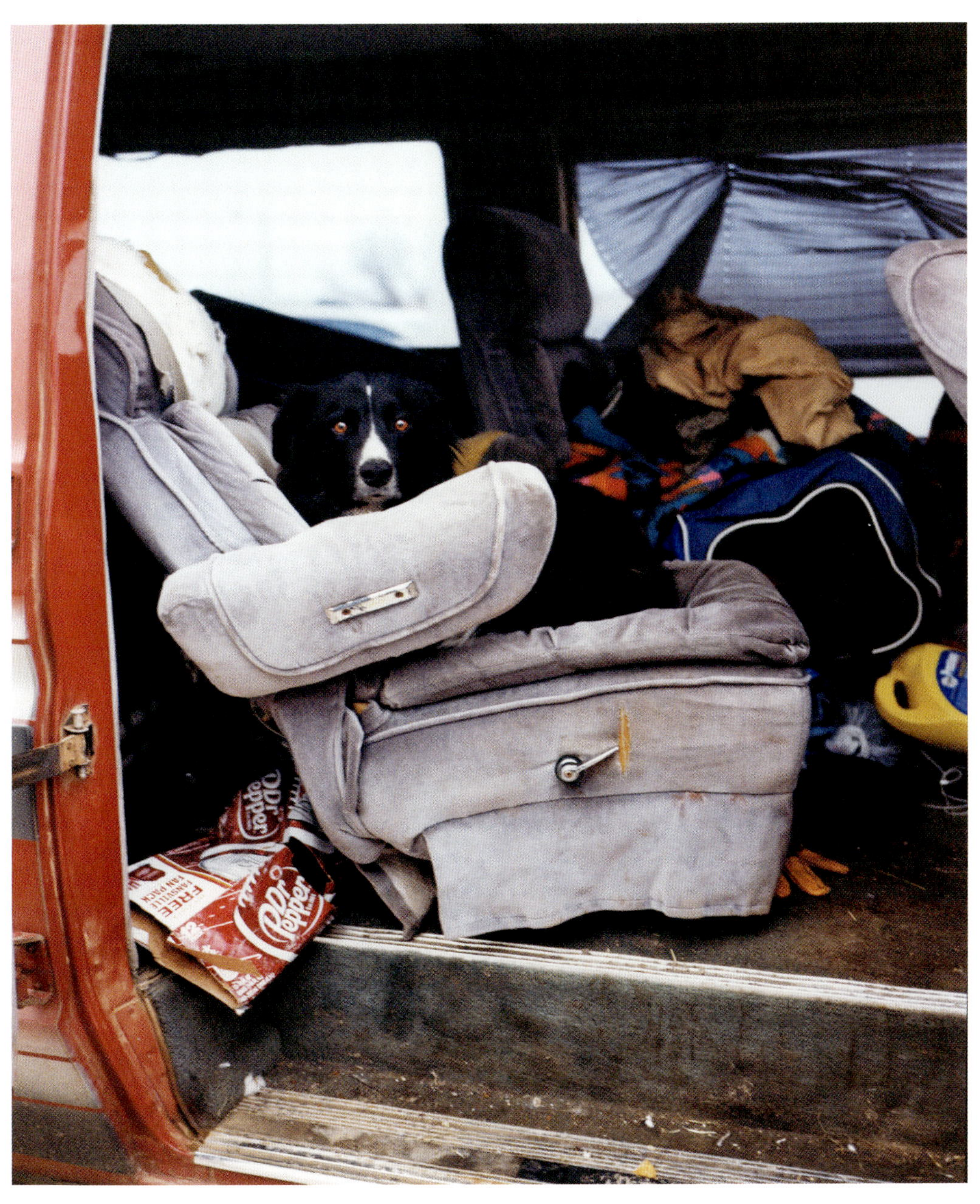

139

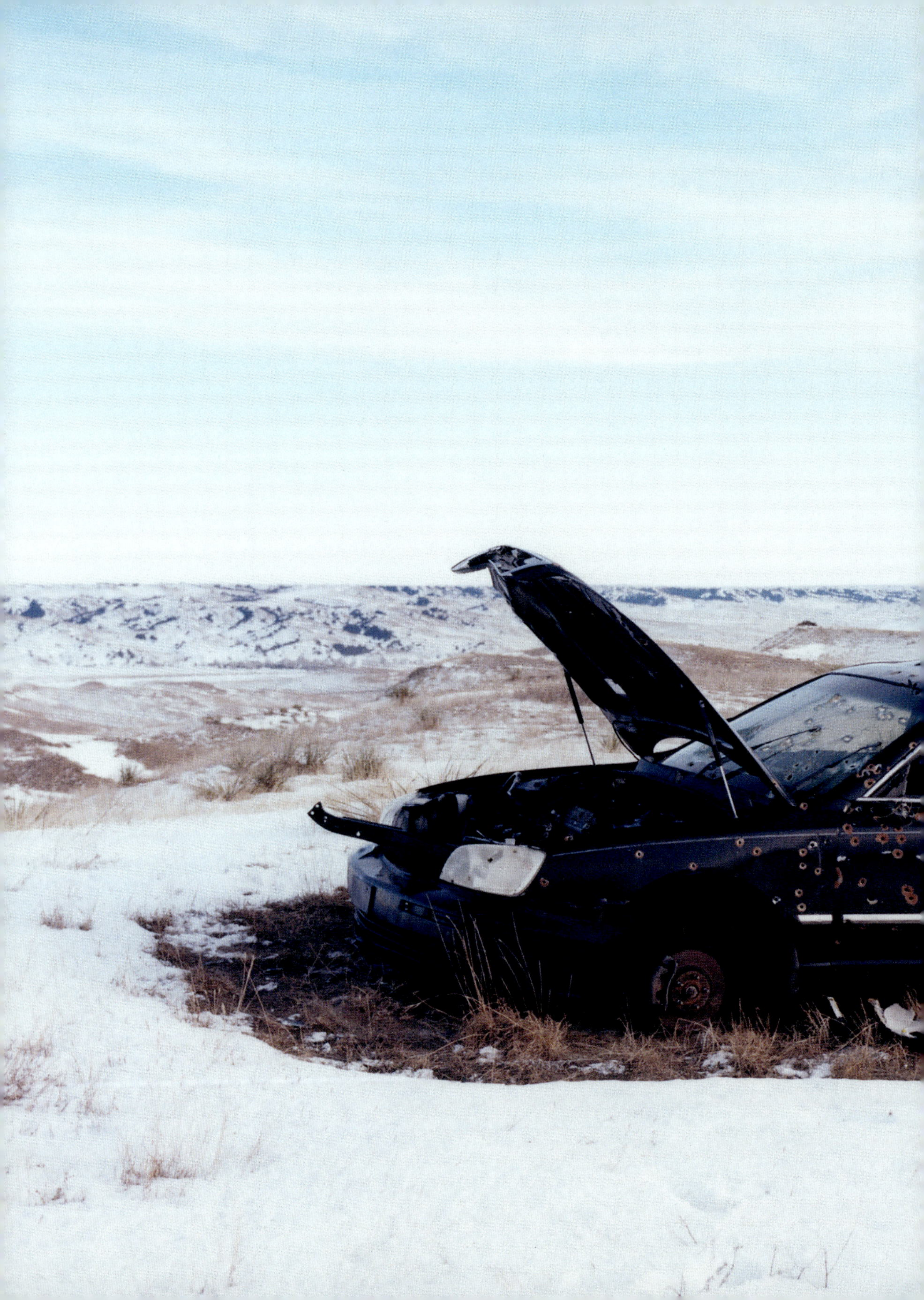

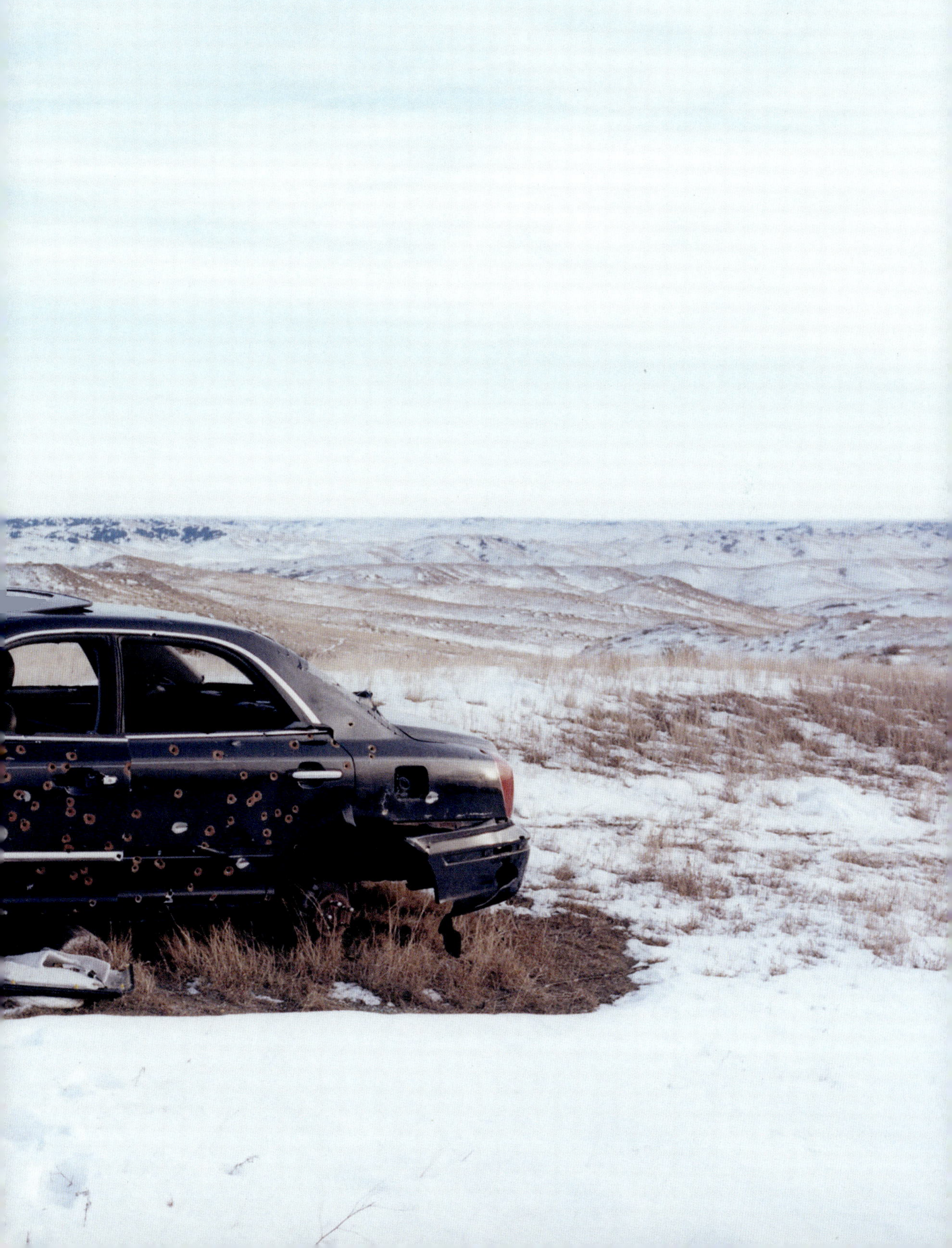

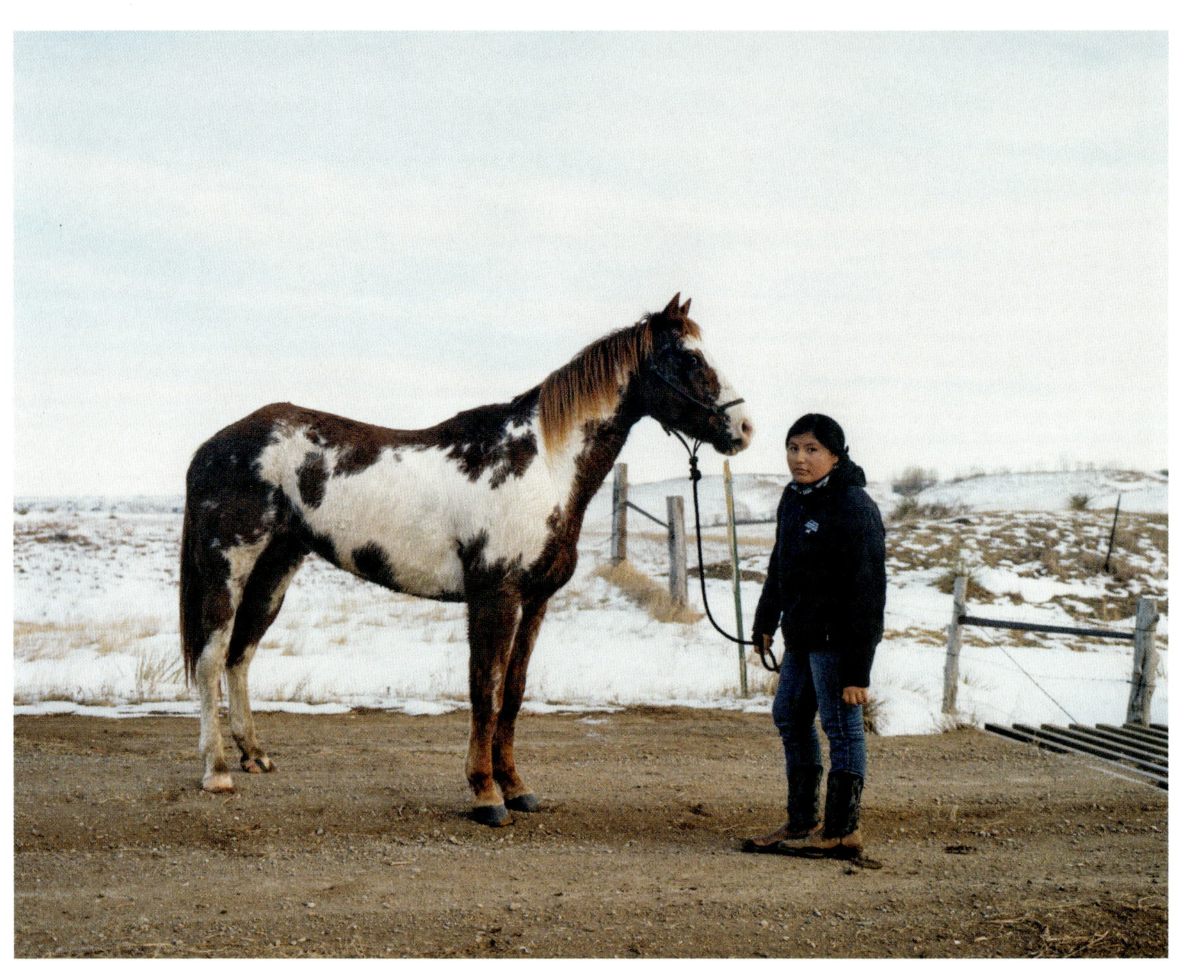

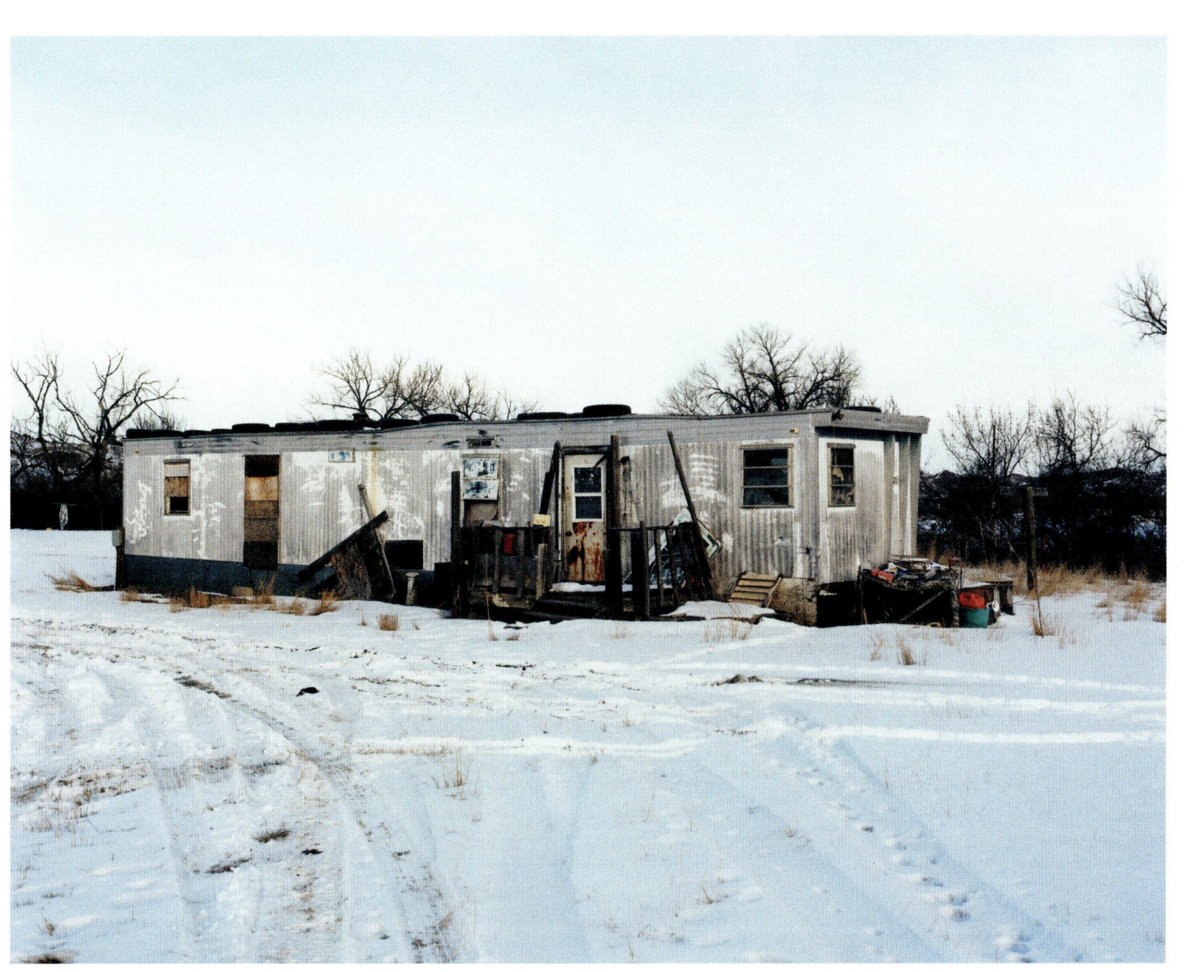

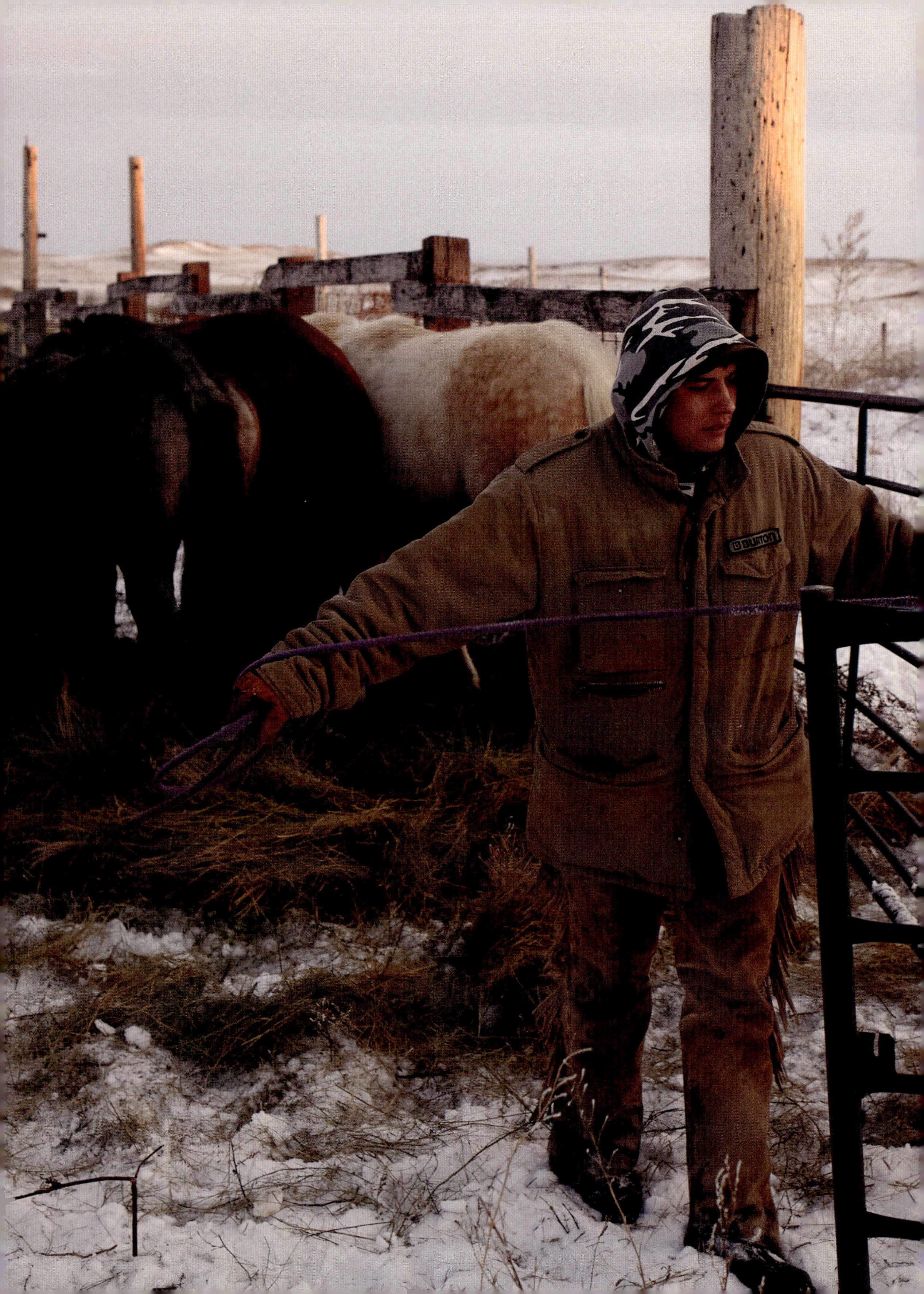

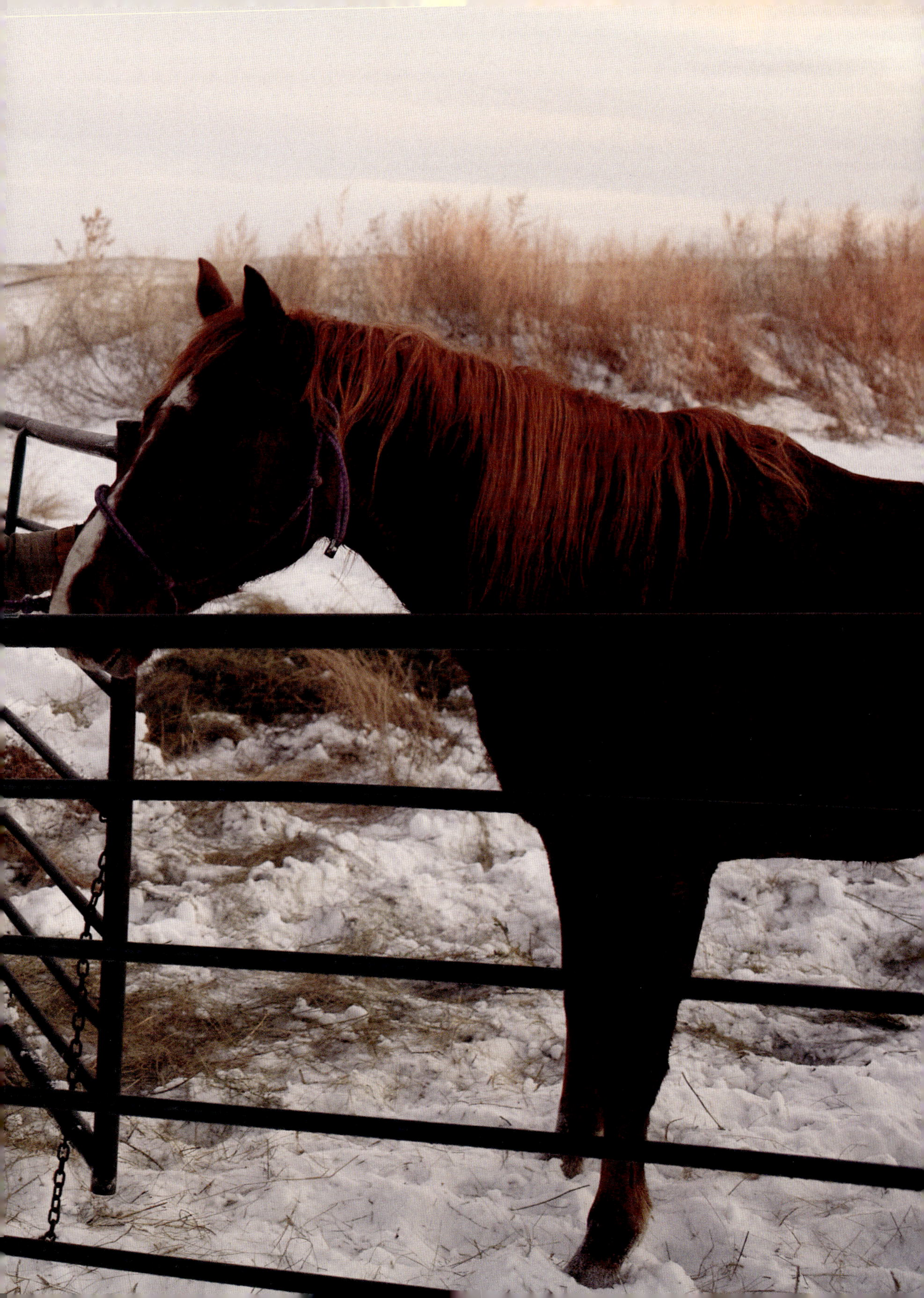

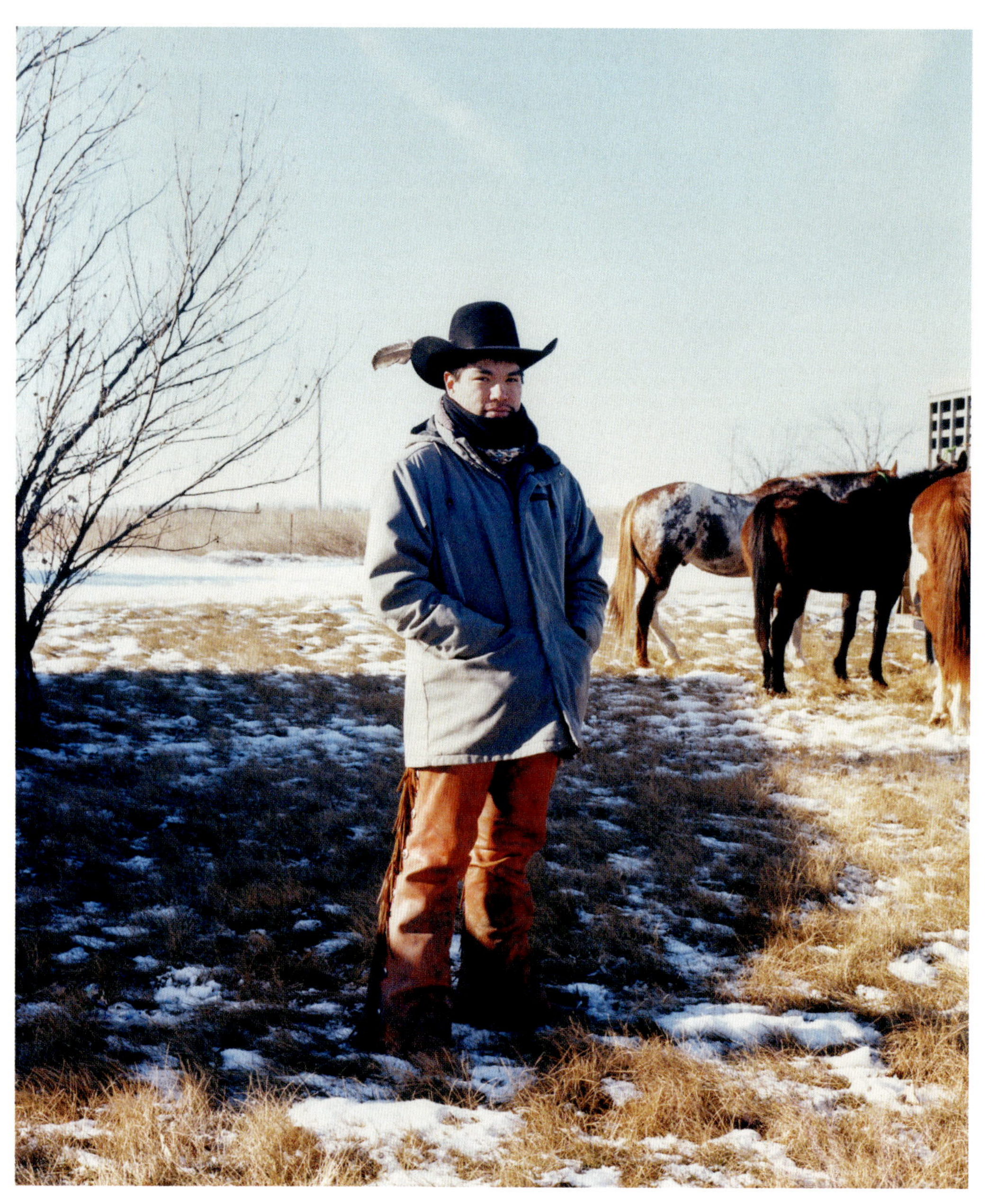

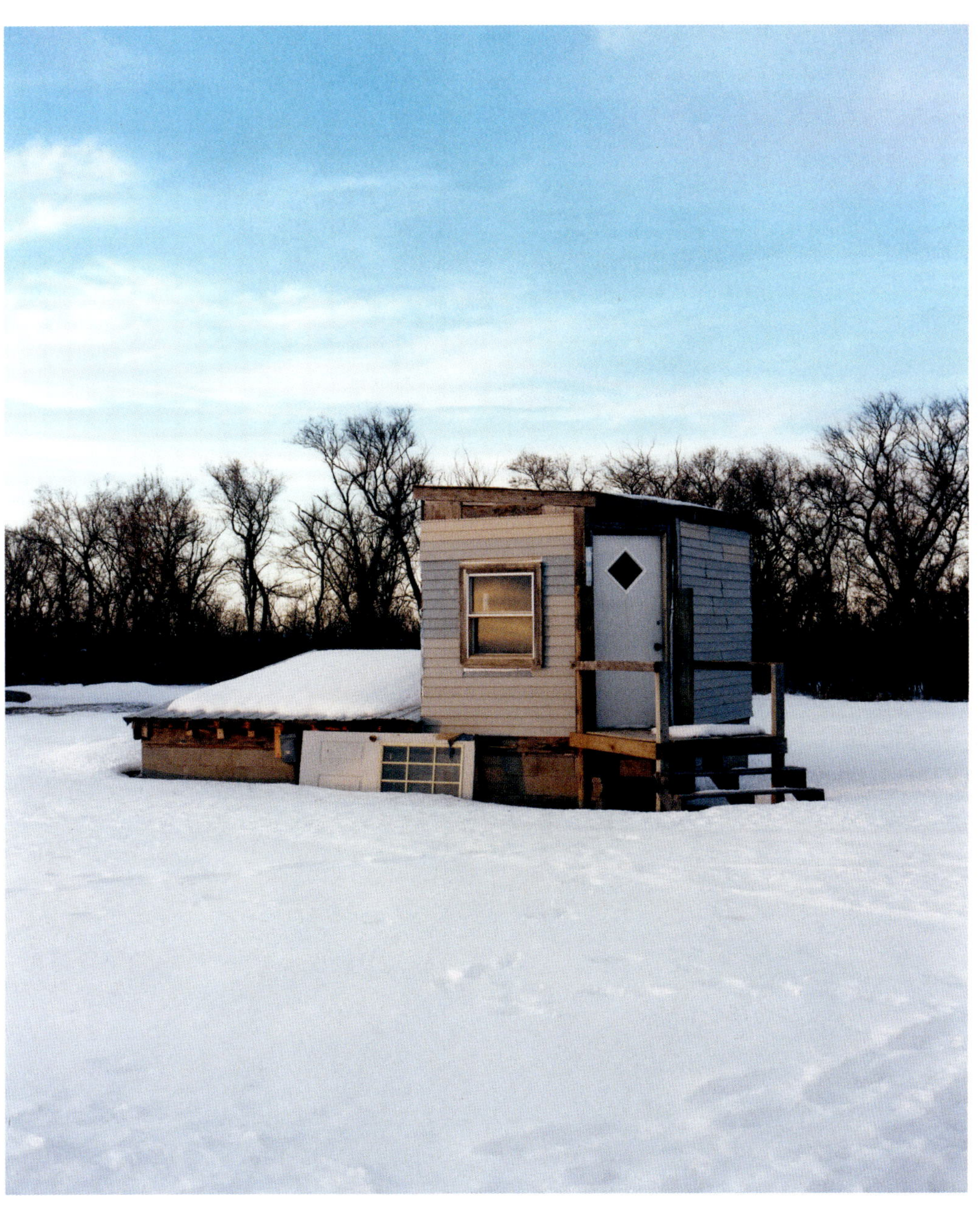

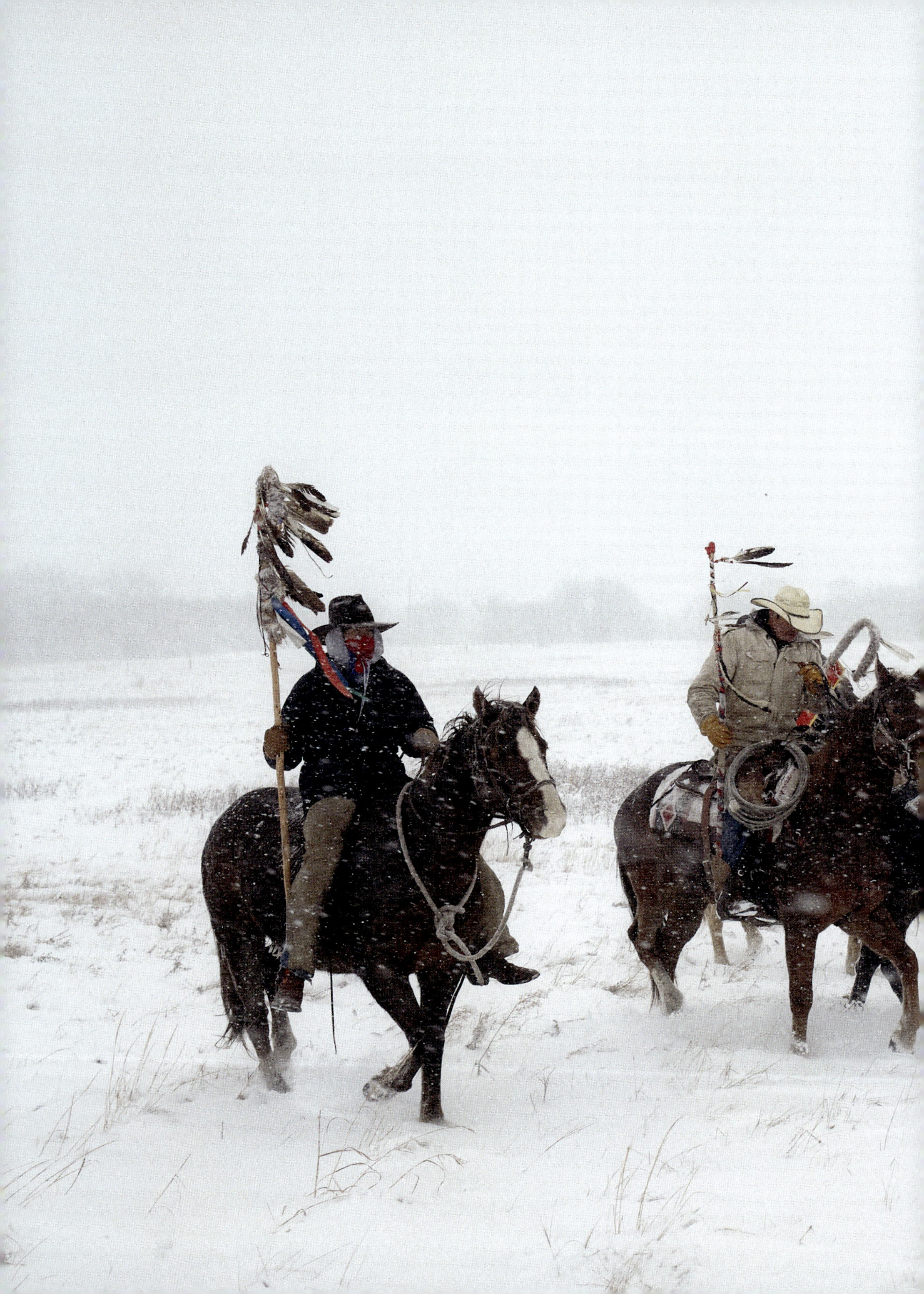

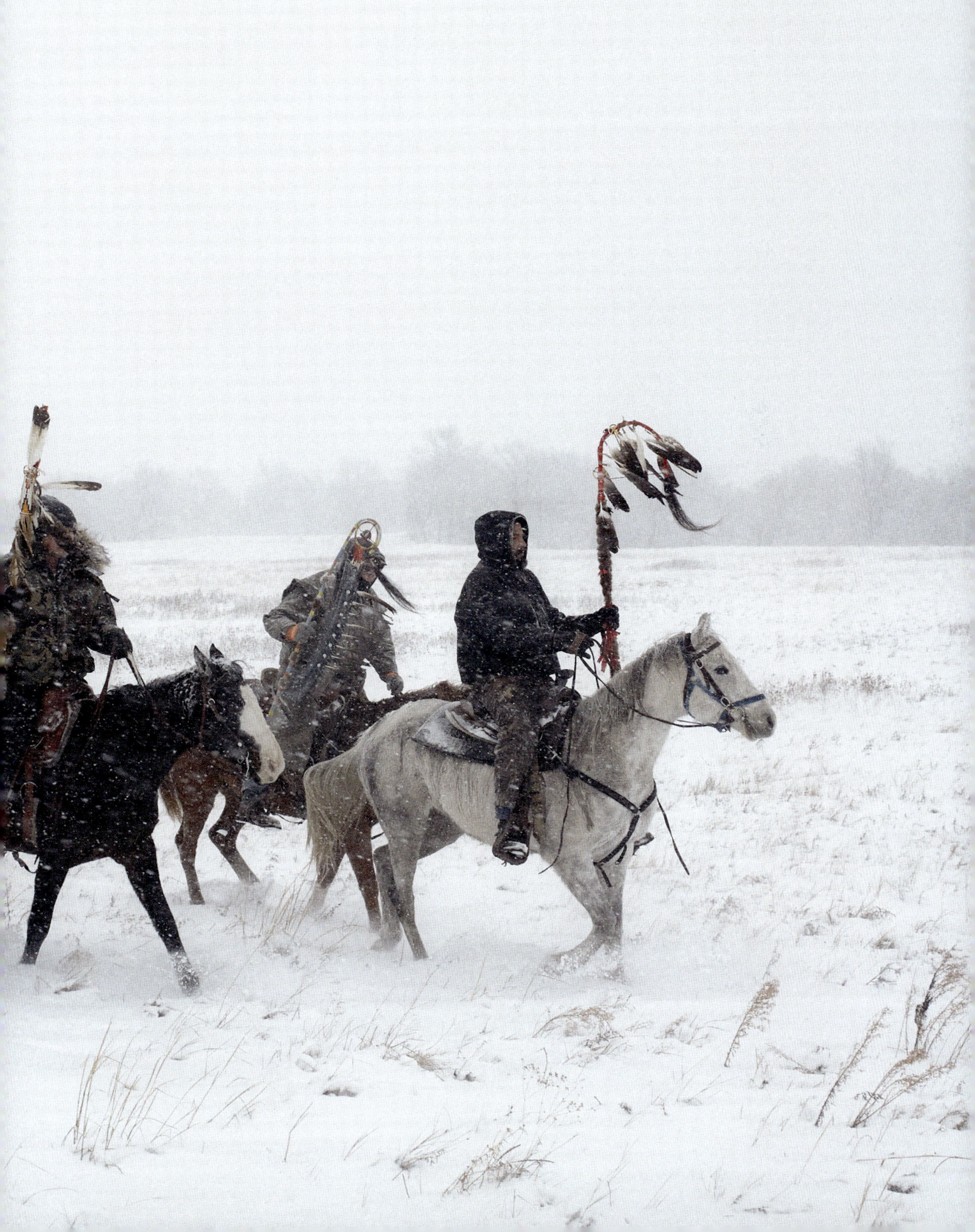

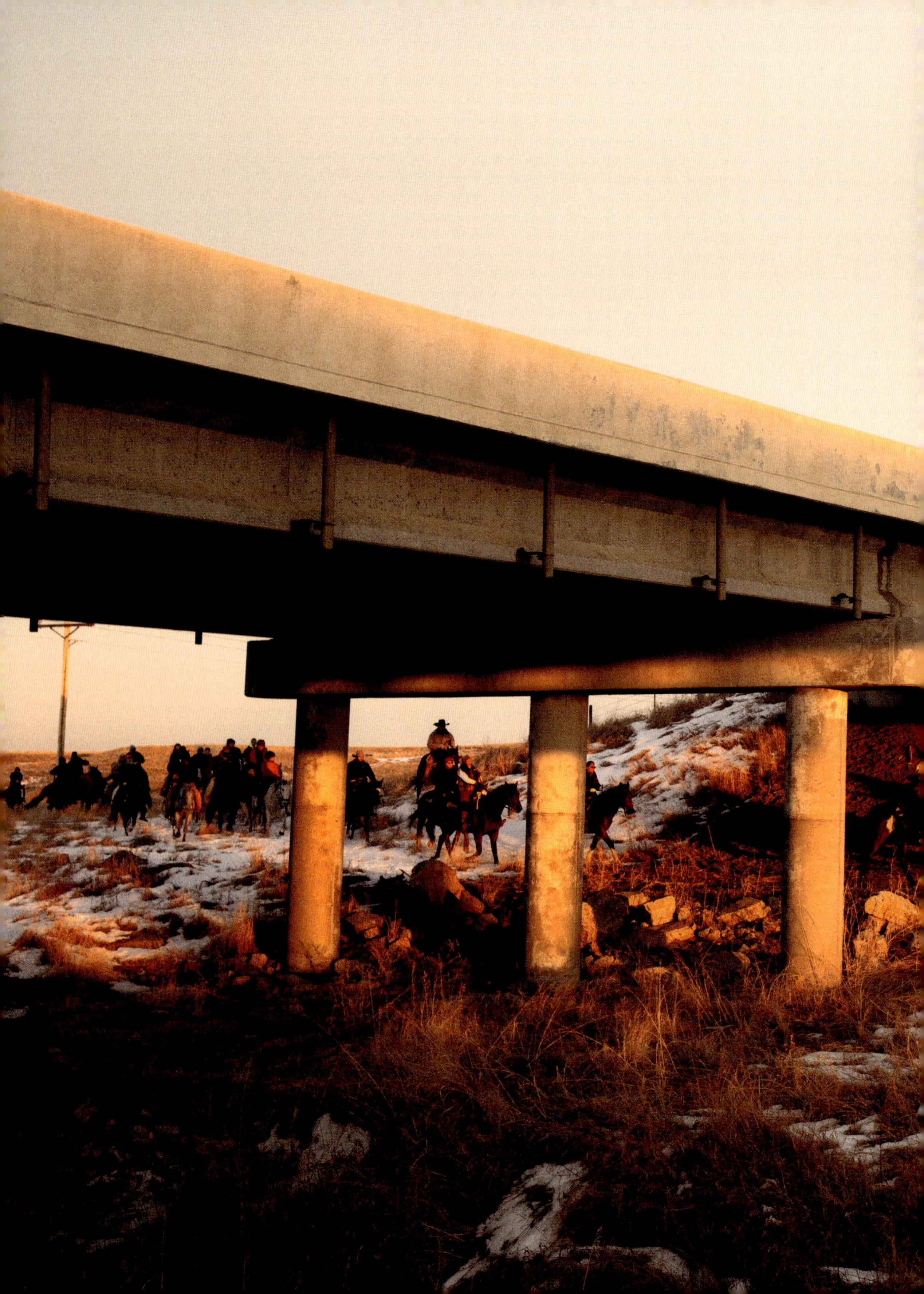

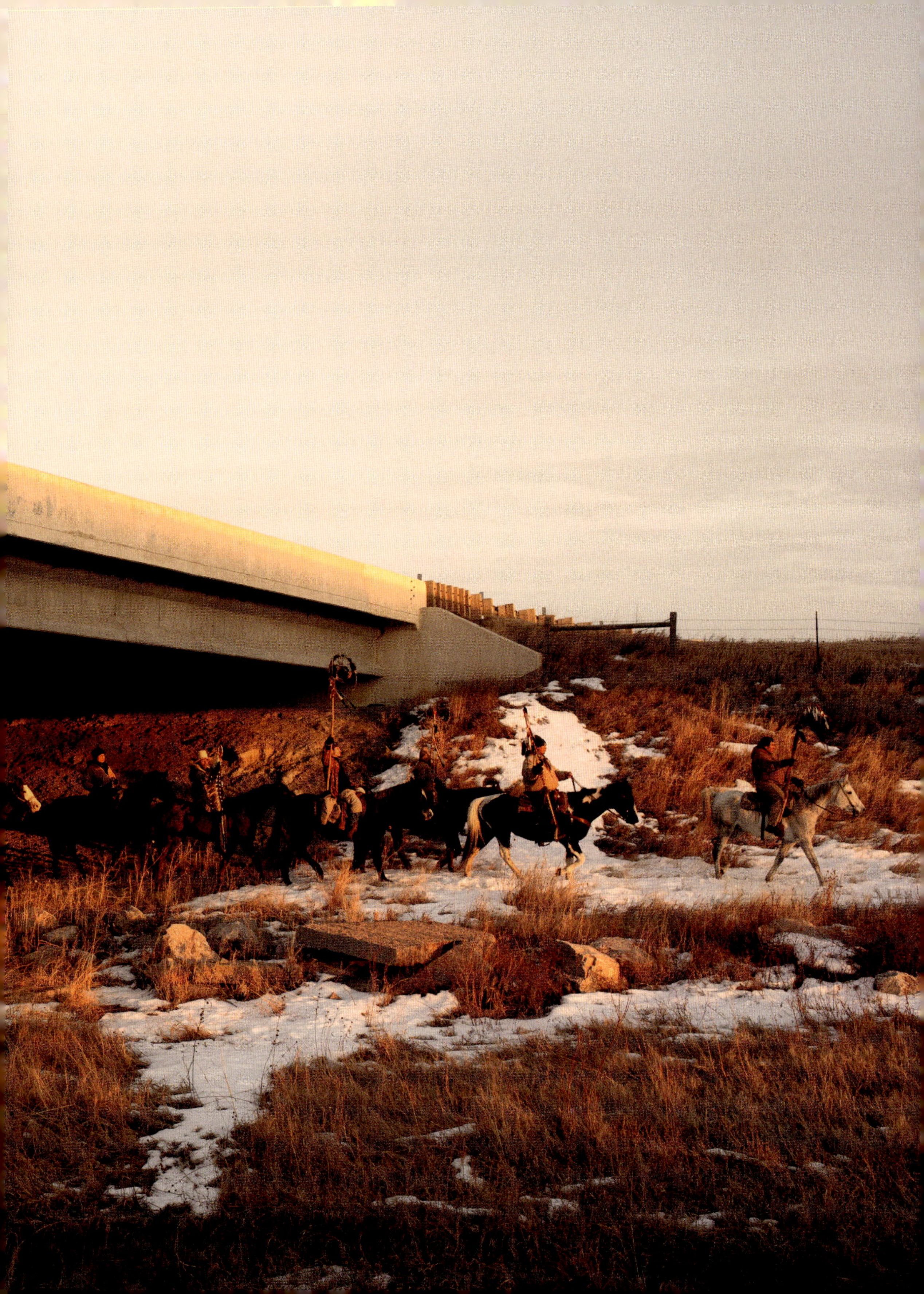

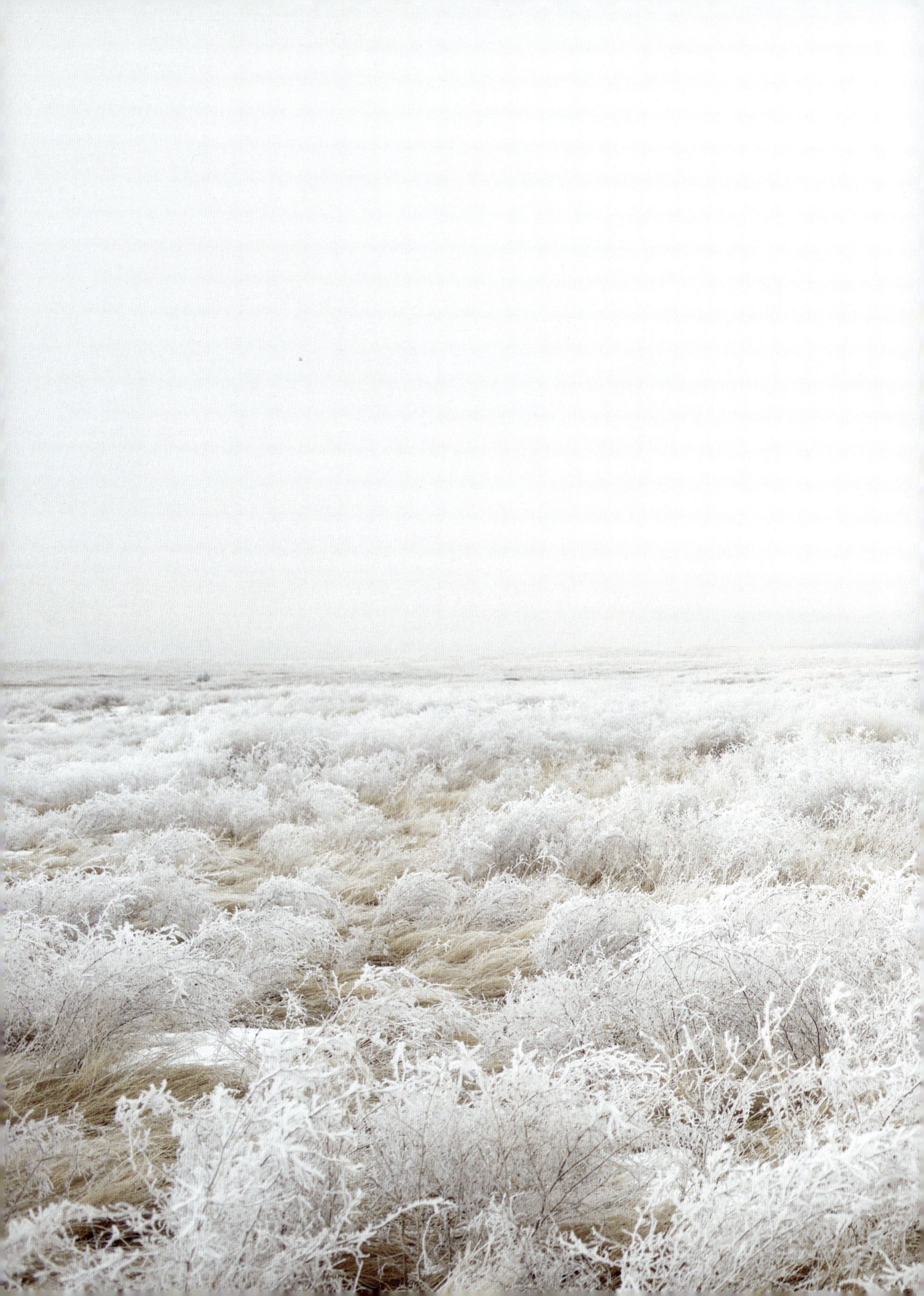

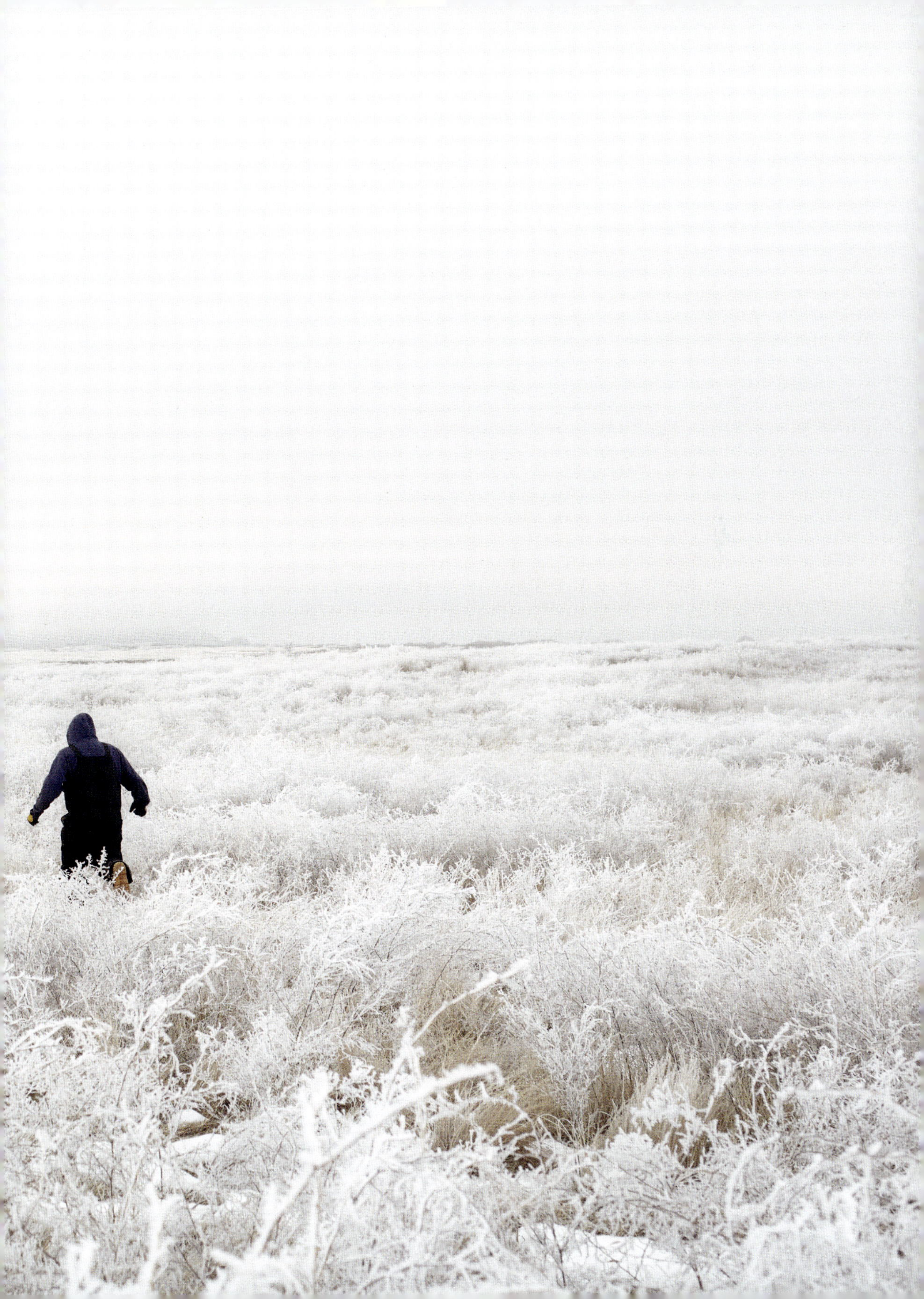

"Can you smell the sage that the east wind brings
us? Do you hear the song of that rider on the hill?
Her words in Lakota resounding by the river:
'We were free as the wind, more than a hundred
winters ago.'"

KEEPING FAITH ON THE RESERVATION

It is late April in 2020, just several months after the coronavirus first made its appearance. I arrived at the border of the Rosebud Indian Reservation at 5 a.m., still half asleep, and sipped bitter convenience-store coffee. I'd been invited to a healing ceremony run by several medicine men from my nation, the Rosebud Sioux Tribe. Several spiritual leaders had arranged a traditional Lakota ceremony in order to help the people on the reservation fight the infection, which had already devastated many Native communities.

Native Americans are no strangers to pandemics, of course. Starting in the early 1500s, European settlers brought smallpox, typhus, influenza, diphtheria, and measles to the Americas, wiping out an estimated 95 percent of the population in just over one hundred years. Entire civilizations were decimated by the diseases, the survivors left traumatized and destitute. It is no wonder that the second wave of European colonizers described the remaining Indigenous populations as abject and miserable, and the American continents as being nearly deserted.

Unfortunately, little changed for Natives during the Covid-19 plague. Many tribal communities suffered extremely high per capita infection rates, worsened by substandard and overcrowded housing, a shortage of adequate medical facilities, and even a lack of running water in many reservation homes. The Navajo Nation was hit especially hard, with large numbers of Covid-19 cases and one of the highest per capita death rates in the country.

My own nation, the Rosebud Sioux Tribe in South Dakota, was also badly affected by the virus, with thousands of cases and many deaths. Tribal officials required that people wear masks and strongly encouraged vaccinations. But traditional Native spirituality was also utilized in the fight against the virus. When the infection first began to spread, a community elder told me, "Our people are going back to their home sweat lodges and communities and using our medicines." She invited me to a healing ceremony, and I decided to attend, despite the freezing cold.

Two days later, I arrived on the reservation, which felt deserted. There were no people walking on the side of the road and very few cars. Three deer stood silently, waiting for me to pass. I drove by the Rosebud Casino, the digital billboard announcing, "We are temporarily CLOSED until further notice." I entered the Adam Bordeaux Memorial Arena, a circular space about the size of a soccer field. A handful of people were outside in the bitter cold, one woman in a ribbon skirt already praying. I helped build the fire and waited.

An hour later, the medicine man arrived. He set up his altar, spoke briefly in Lakota and English, and then began the silent prayer ceremony, facing each of the four directions in turn. We stood there for a long time; I felt bitterly cold and began to regret my decision to attend. But after a while, I no longer noticed the chill as I focused upon my prayers. I prayed for my grandparents and great-grandparents, buried just a few miles away, and I prayed for my *tiospaye*—my larger family—and for the *oyate*, the Lakota people, as well as for all of those fighting the virus and those who were gone. I repeated the words to myself, over and over, and I began to feel some solace, some comfort, some hope.

Looking at the photographs in Zen Lefort's remarkable book, I'm filled with the same sense of hopefulness and optimism. Lefort shows—with incredible artistry—the beauty, joy, and resilience of Native people. Whether it's the battle against the Keystone XL pipeline, dancers at a powwow, or a young man riding a horse—these photos depict Native life in all of its fullness. The dazzling pictures are a testament to the fact that Indigenous people endure, despite centuries of disease, genocide, and governmental neglect.

Perhaps we have contained the coronavirus by now, or perhaps the virus will continue to plague us. No matter. Native people have survived countless cataclysms, and this book is a testament to our endurance, our persistence, and our strength. *Wopila*, Zen Lefort, for sharing these beautiful photographs with the world.

David Heska Wanbli Weiden

CAPTIONS

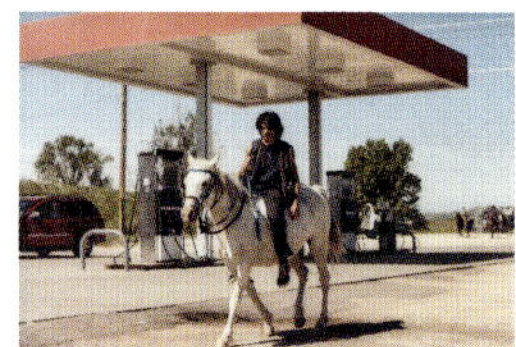

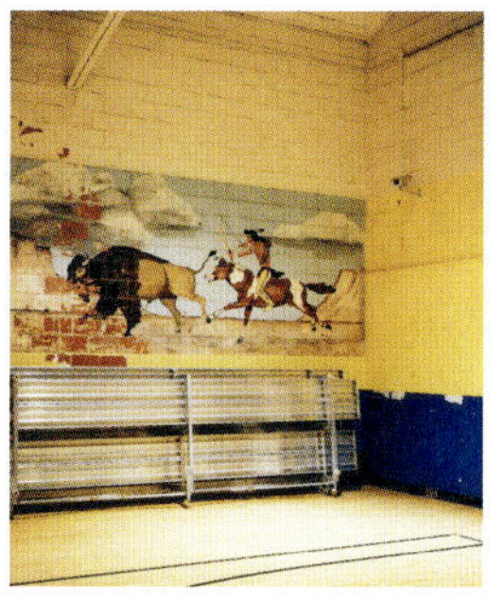

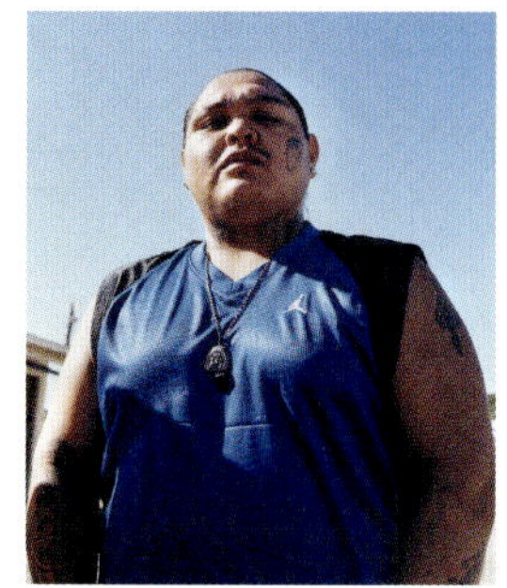

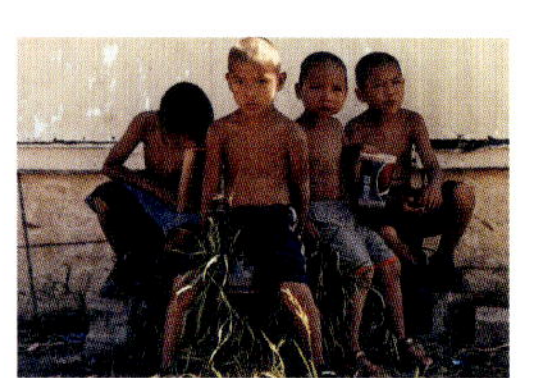

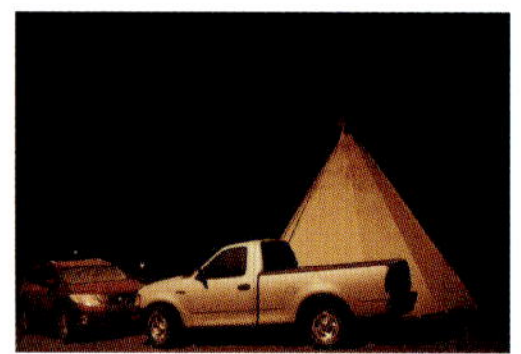

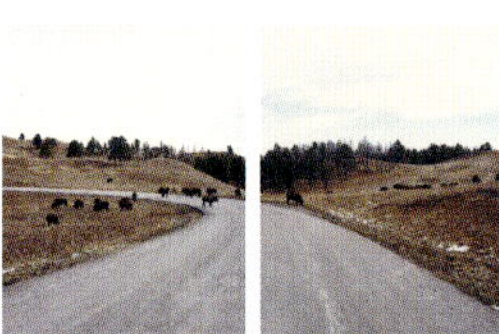

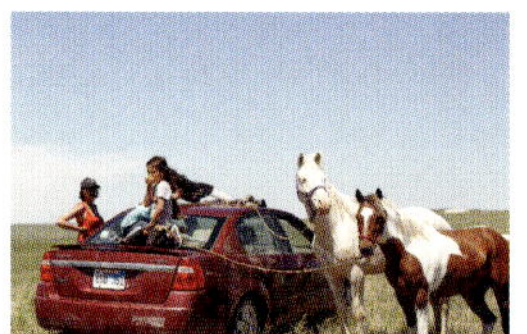

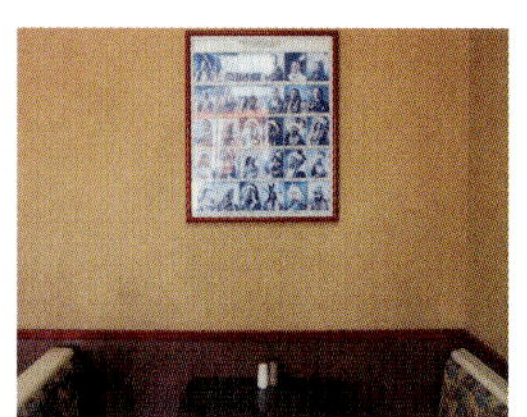

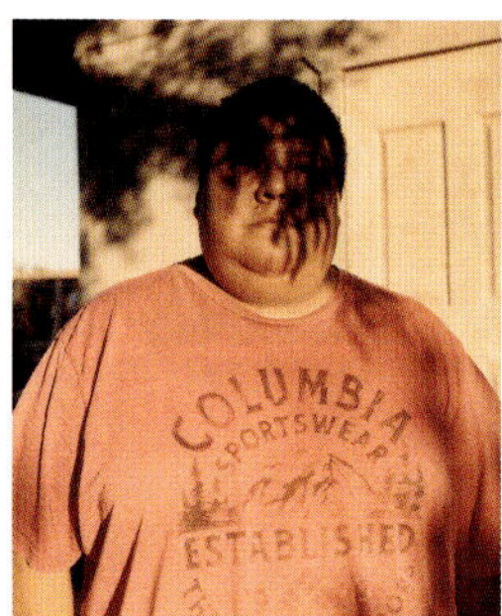

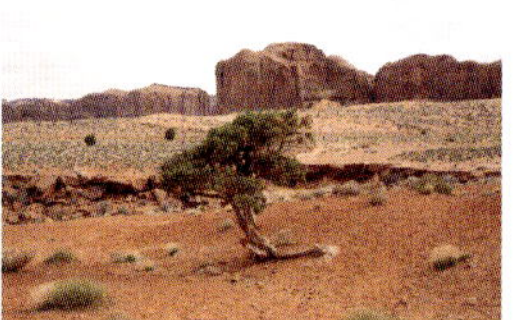

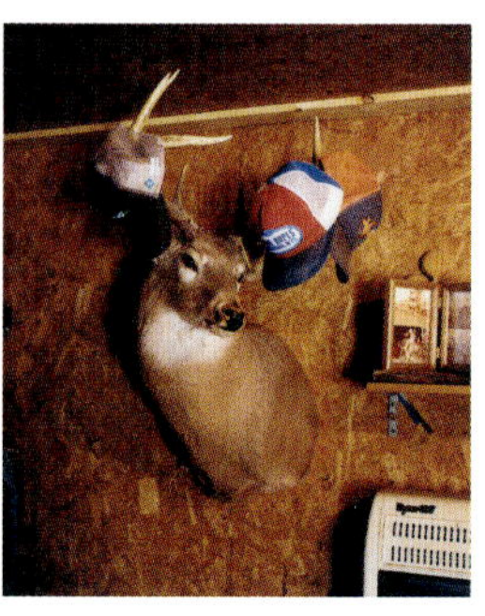

37

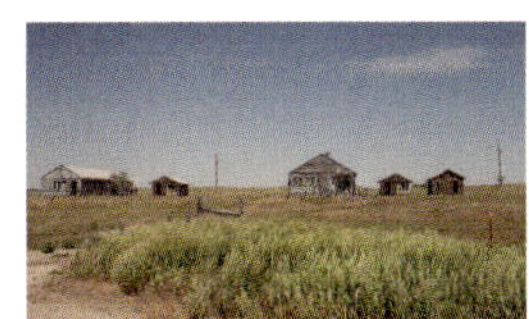

Navajo Nation,
Arizona,
2019

38

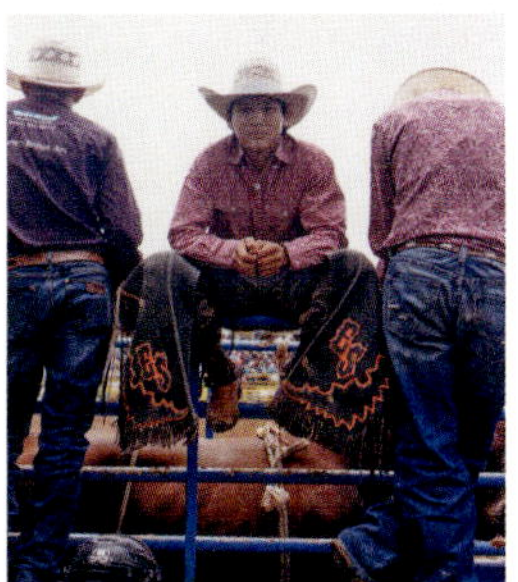

Pine Ridge Indian Reservation,
South Dakota,
2016

41

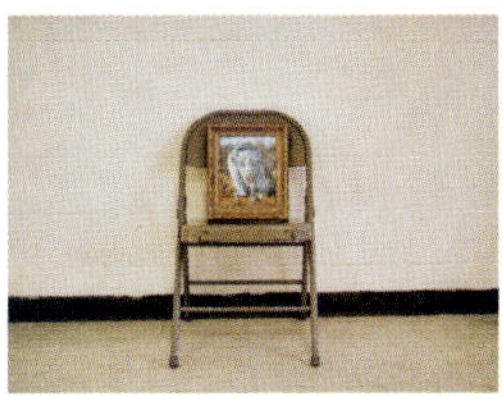

Navajo Nation,
Arizona,
2019

43

Cheyenne River Indian Reservation,
South Dakota,
2019

44

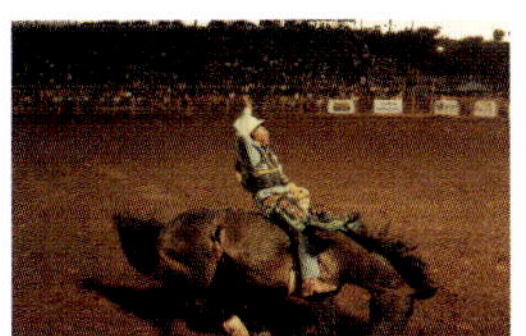

Navajo Nation,
Arizona,
2019

46

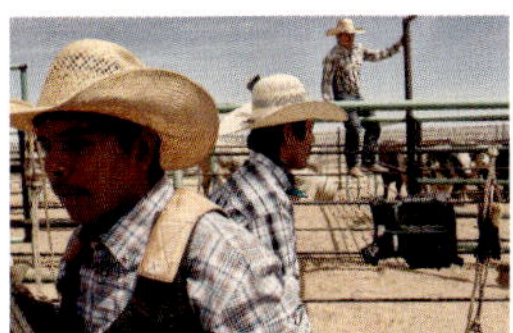

Navajo Nation,
New Mexico,
2017

49

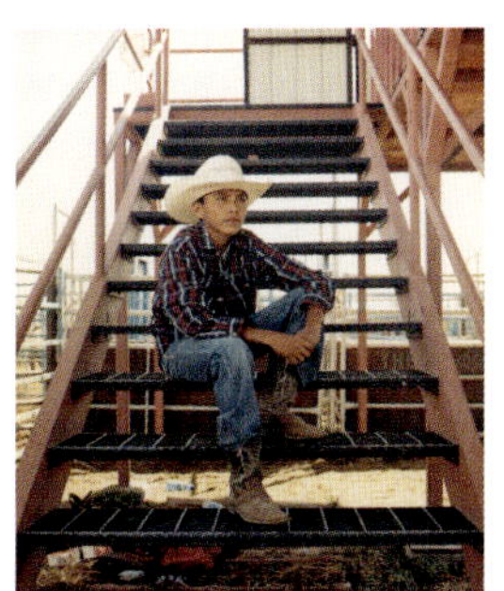

Navajo Nation,
Arizona,
2019

51

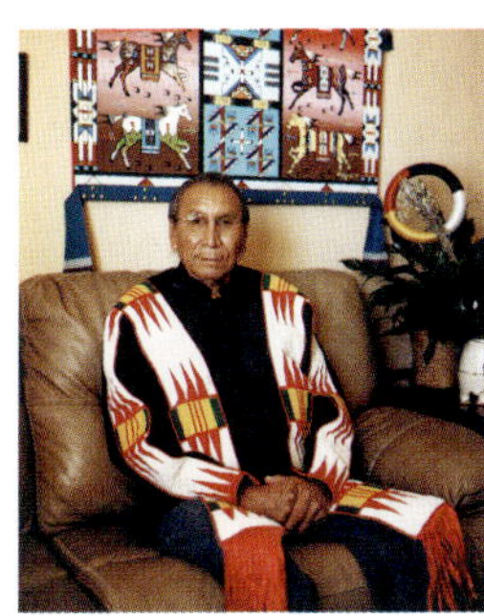

Lake Traverse Indian Reservation,
South Dakota,
2020

52

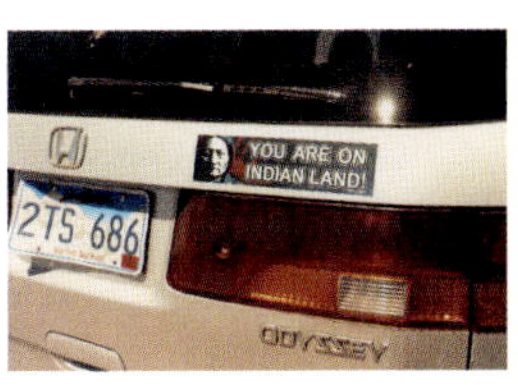

Fort Robinson,
Nebraska,
2016

53

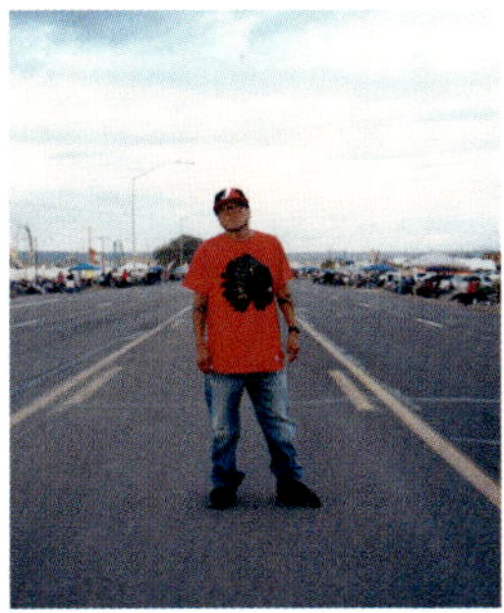

Navajo Nation,
Arizona,
2019

54

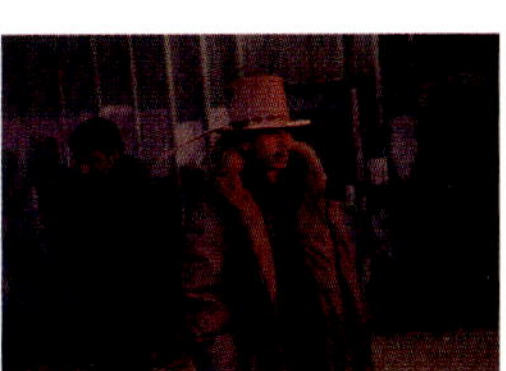

Cheyenne River Indian Reservation,
South Dakota,
2019

57

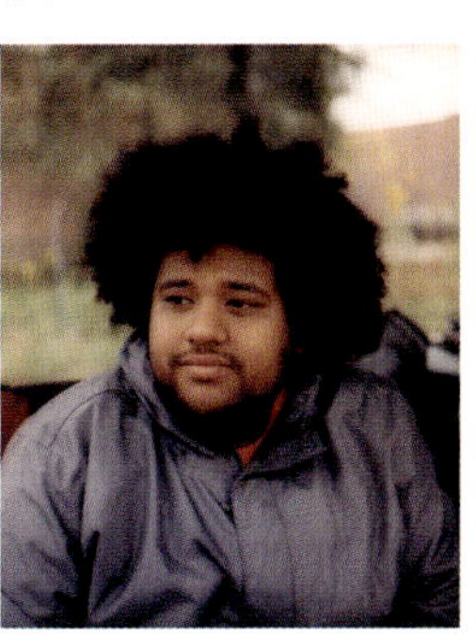

Chicago,
Illinois,
2020

58

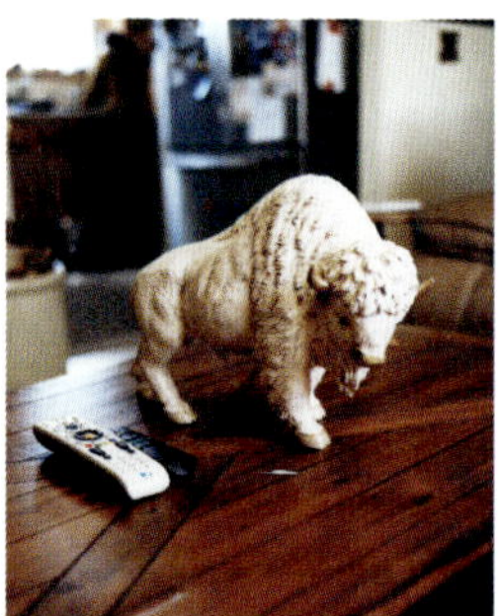

Lake Traverse Indian Reservation,
South Dakota,
2020

60

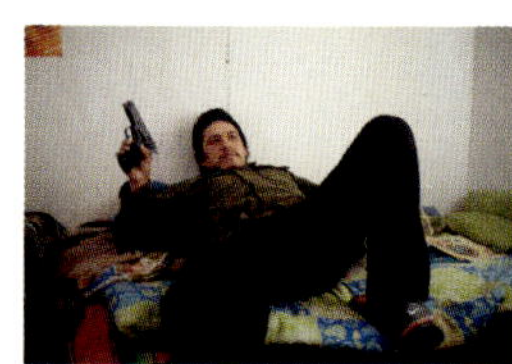

Navajo Nation,
Arizona,
2017

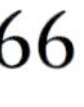

66

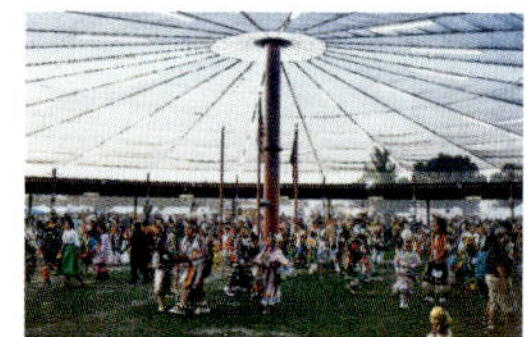

Fort Hall Indian Reservation,
Idaho,
2019

69

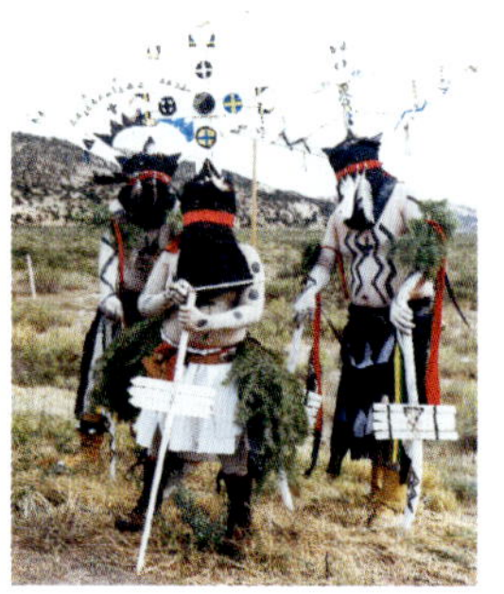

Navajo Nation,
Arizona,
2019

70

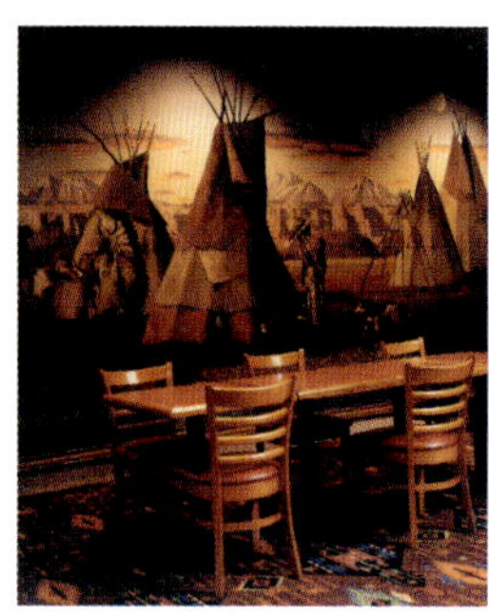

Standing Rock Indian Reservation,
North Dakota,
2020

73

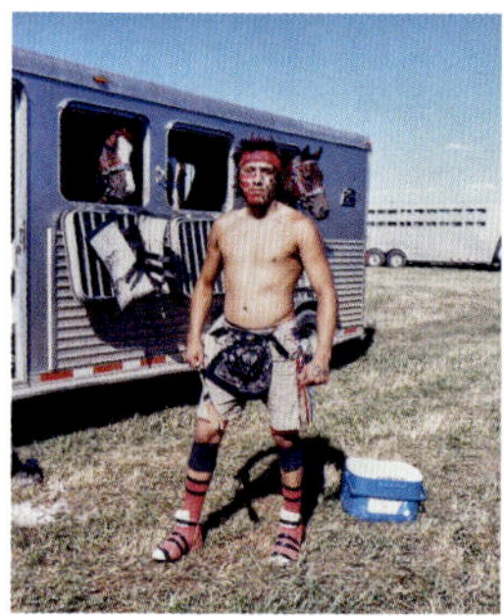

Fort Hall Indian Reservation,
Idaho,
2019

75

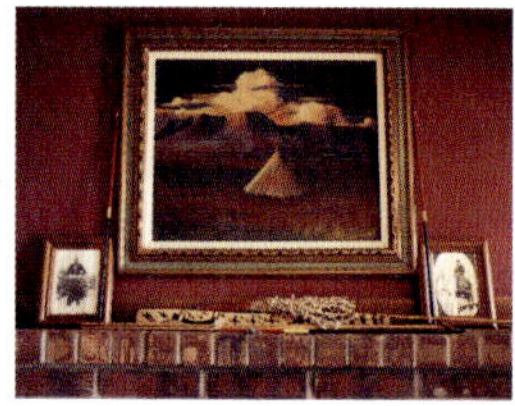

Navajo Nation,
Arizona,
2019

77

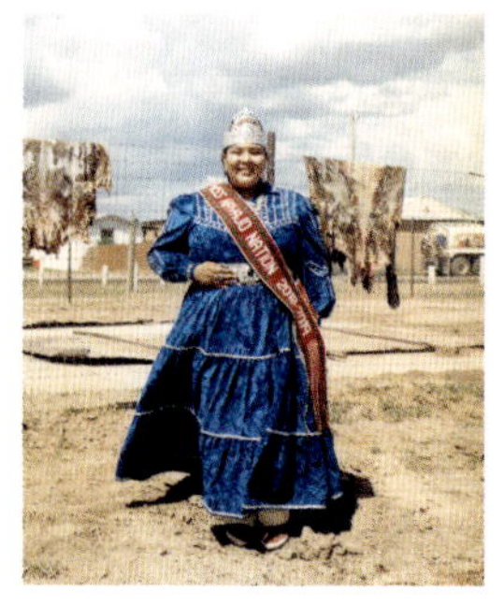

Navajo Nation,
Arizona,
2019

79

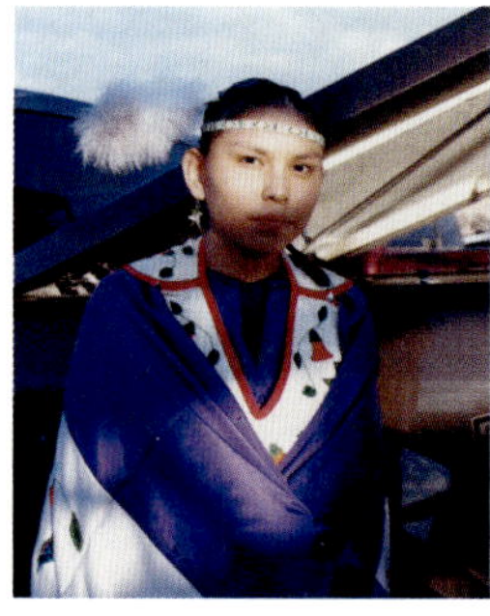

Fort Hall Indian Reservation,
Idaho,
 2019

80

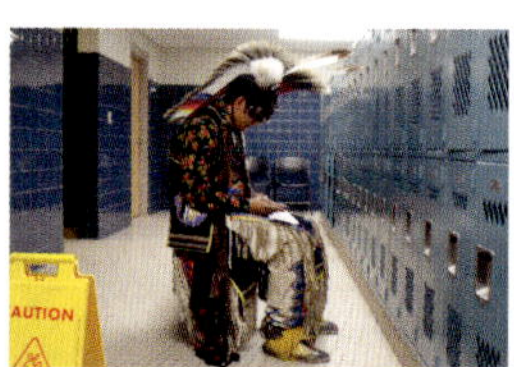

Navajo Nation,
Arizona,
2017

83

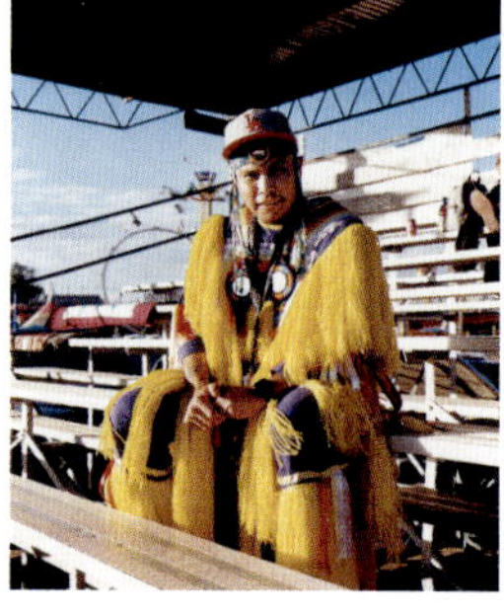

Navajo Nation,
Arizona,
2019

84

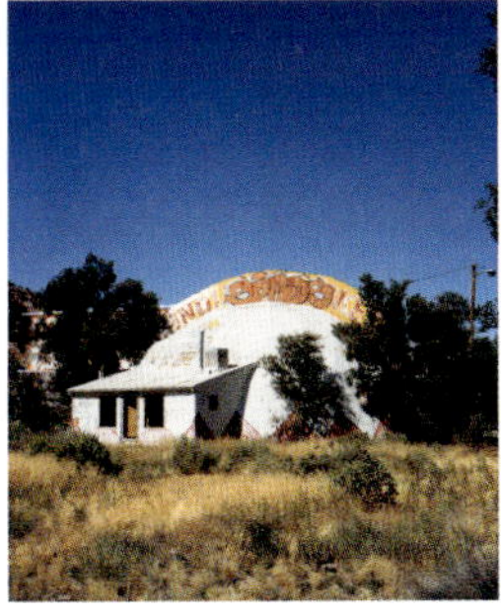

U.S. Route 66,
New Mexico,
2019

85

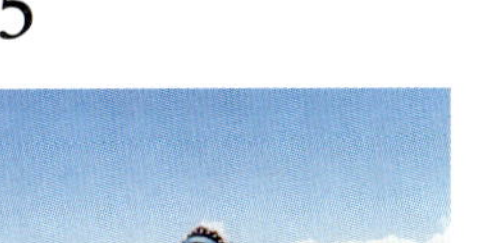

Fort Hall Indian Reservation,
Idaho,
2019

86

Fort Hall Indian Reservation,
Idaho,
2019

87

Navajo Nation,
Arizona,
2019

89

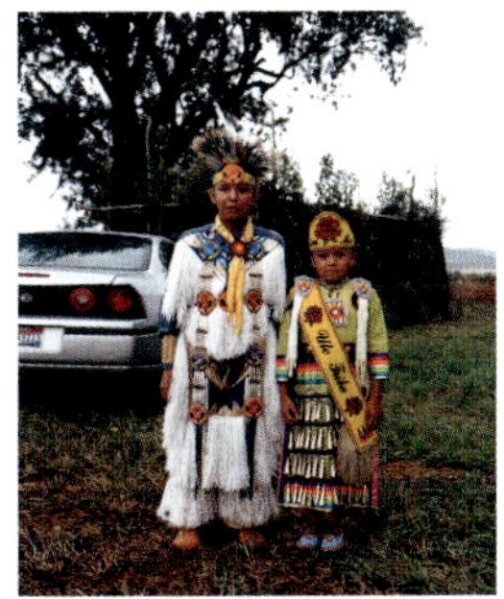

Fort Hall Indian Reservation,
Idaho,
2019

91

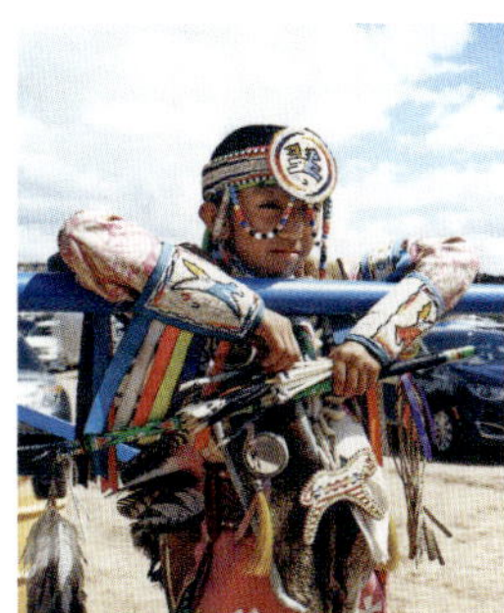

Navajo Nation,
Arizona,
2019

BLACK
SNAKE

96

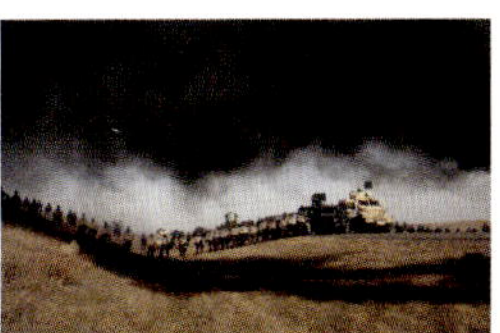

Standing Rock Indian Reservation,
North Dakota,
2016

98

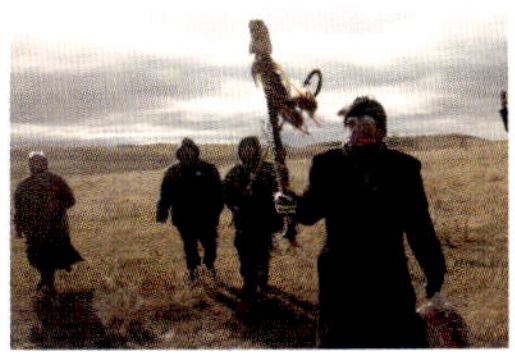

Standing Rock Indian Reservation,
North Dakota,
2016

100

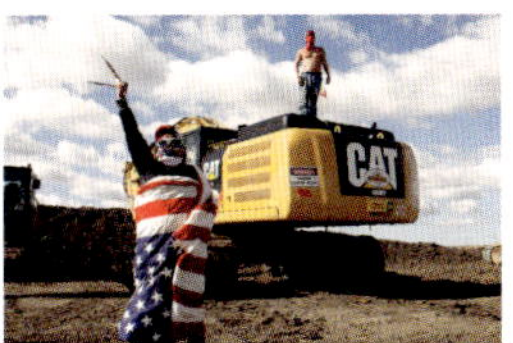

Standing Rock Indian Reservation,
North Dakota,
2016

103

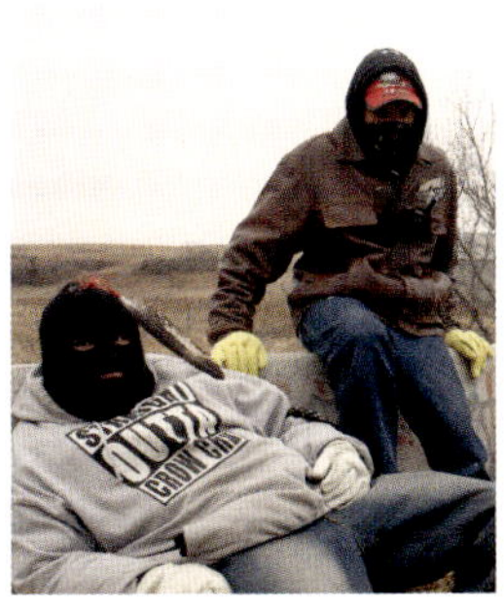

Standing Rock Indian Reservation,
North Dakota,
2016

104

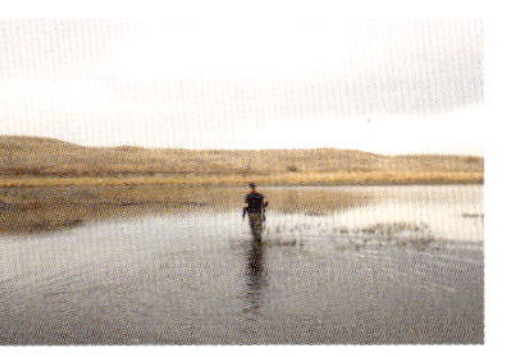

Standing Rock Indian Reservation,
North Dakota,
2016

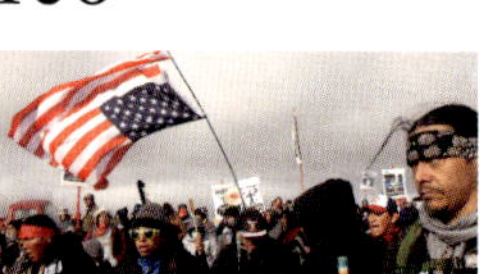

106

Standing Rock Indian Reservation,
North Dakota,
2016

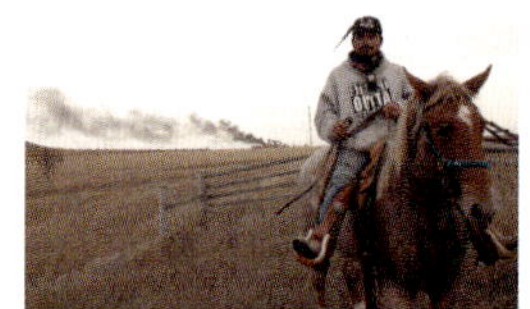

108

Standing Rock Indian Reservation,
North Dakota,
2016

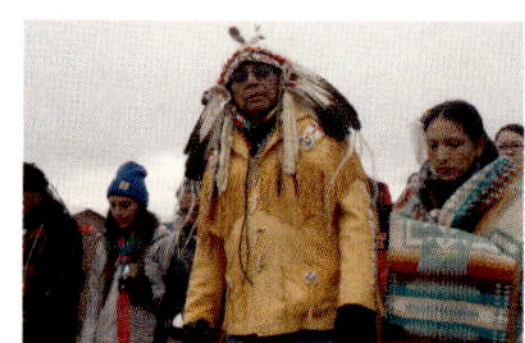

110

Standing Rock Indian Reservation,
North Dakota,
2016

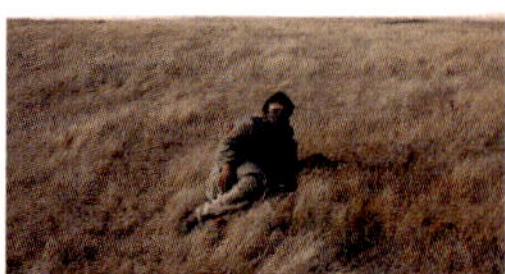

112

Standing Rock Indian Reservation,
North Dakota,
2016

A
BEAUTIFUL
DREAM

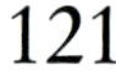

121

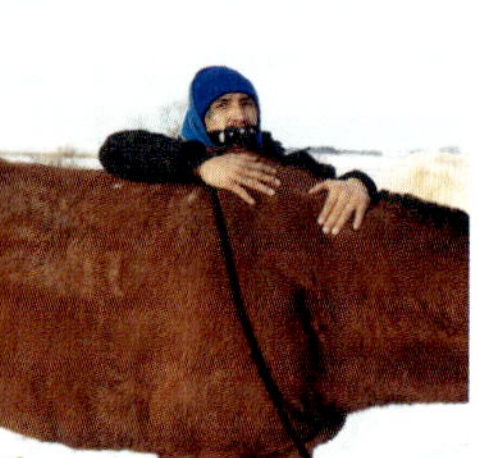

Cheyenne River Indian Reservation,
South Dakota,
2019

122

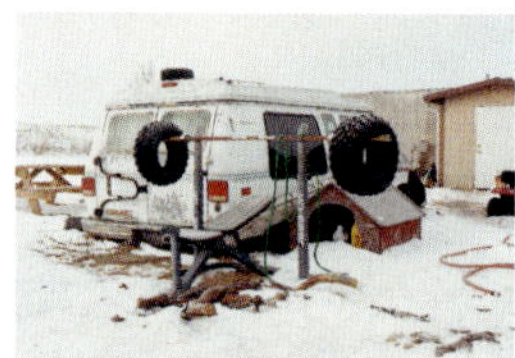

Cheyenne River Indian Reservation,
South Dakota,
2019

123

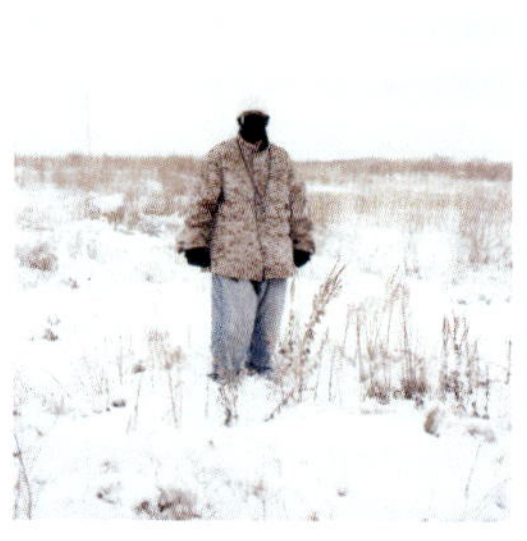

Wounded Knee,
South Dakota,
2019

124

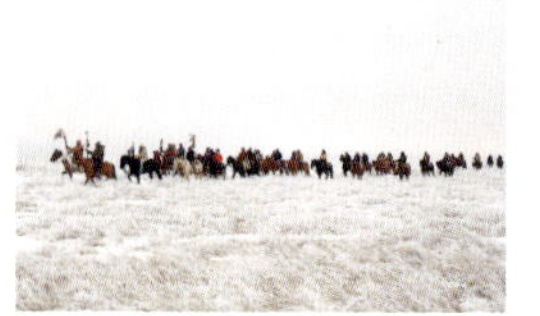

Badlands,
South Dakota,
2019

126

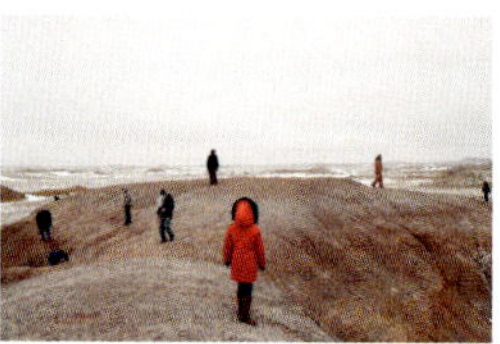

Interior,
South Dakota,
2019

129

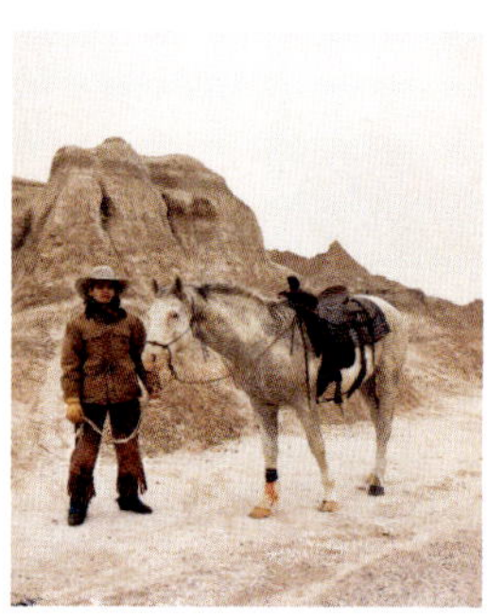

Badlands,
South Dakota,
2019

130

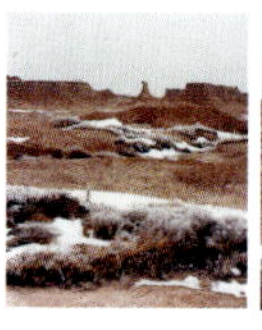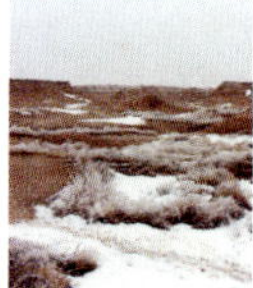

Badlands,
South Dakota,
2019

133

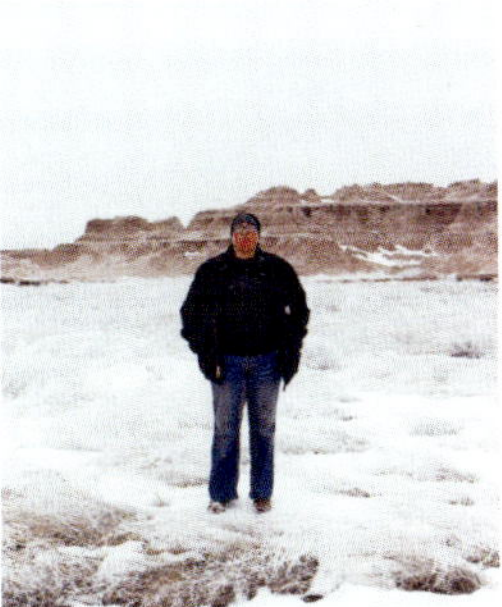

Badlands,
South Dakota,
2019

134

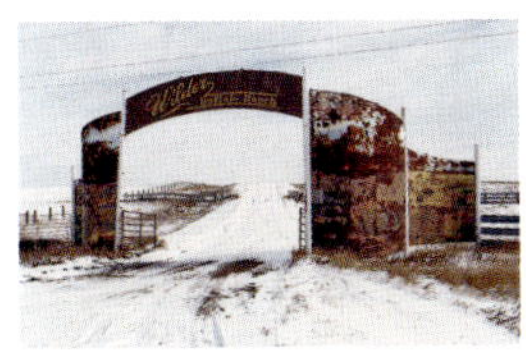

Standing Rock Indian Reservation,
South Dakota,
 2020

135

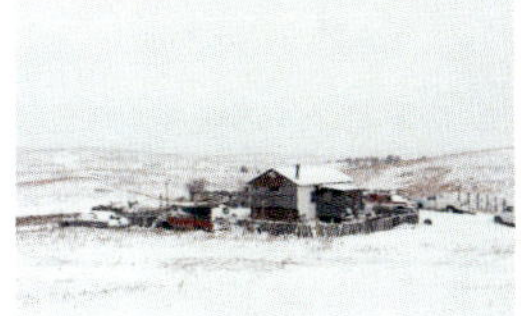

Pine Ridge Indian Reservation,
South Dakota,
2019

136

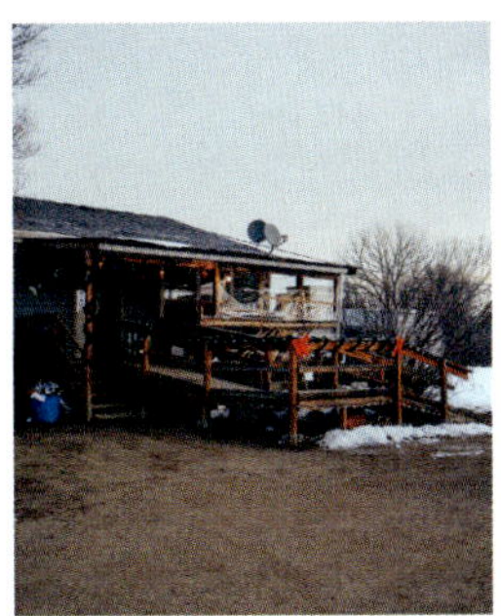

Cheyenne River Indian Reservation,
South Dakota,
2019

137

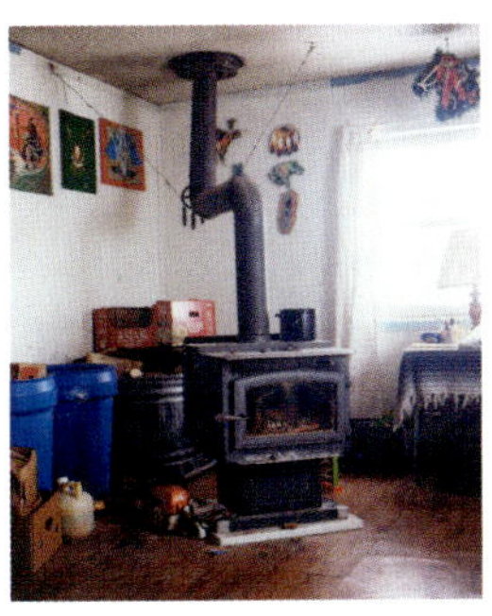

Pine Ridge Indian Reservation,
South Dakota,
2019

138

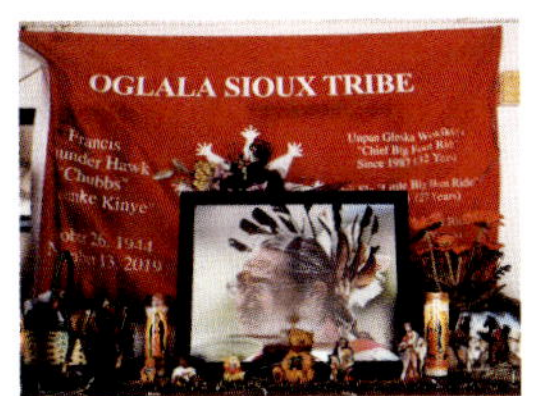

Pine Ridge Indian Reservation,
South Dakota,
2019

139

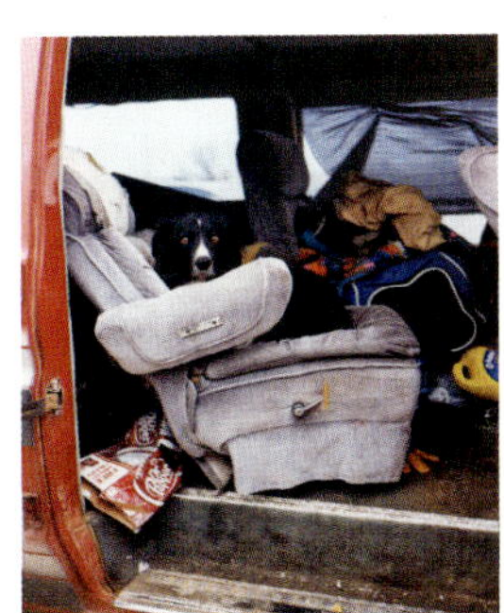

Pine Ridge Indian Reservation,
South Dakota,
2019

140

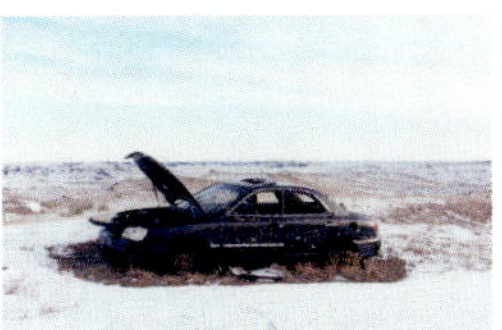

Cheyenne River Indian Reservation,
South Dakota,
2019

142

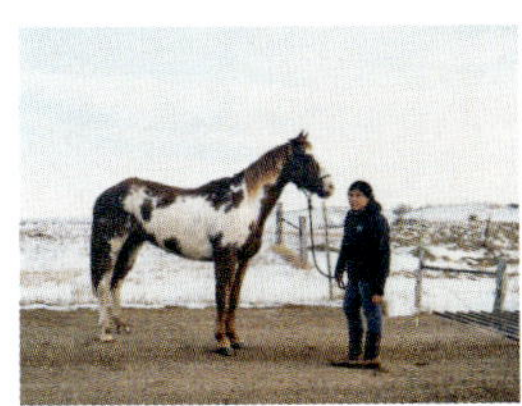

Cheyenne River Indian Reservation,
South Dakota,
2019

143

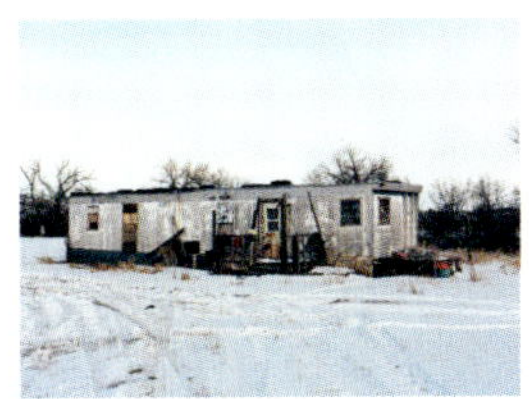

Cheyenne River Indian Reservation,
South Dakota,
2019

144

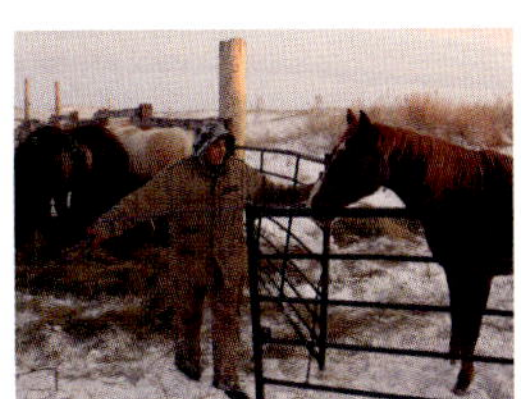

Cheyenne River Indian Reservation,
South Dakota,
2019

146

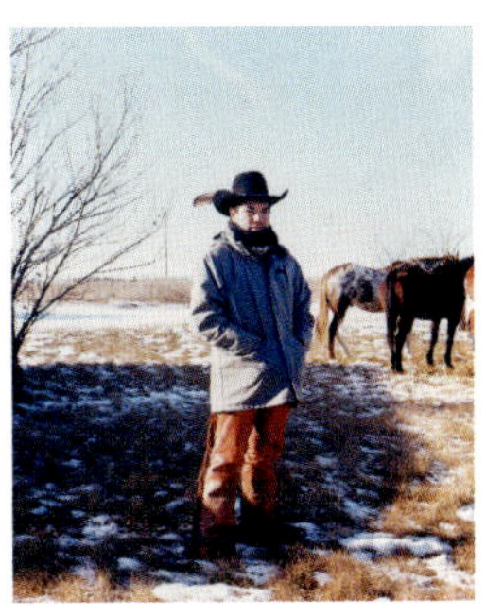

Cheyenne River Indian Reservation,
South Dakota,
2019

147

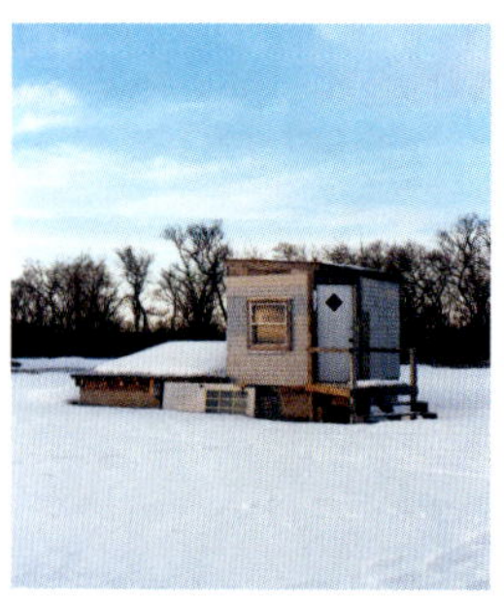

Cheyenne River Indian Reservation,
South Dakota,
2019

148

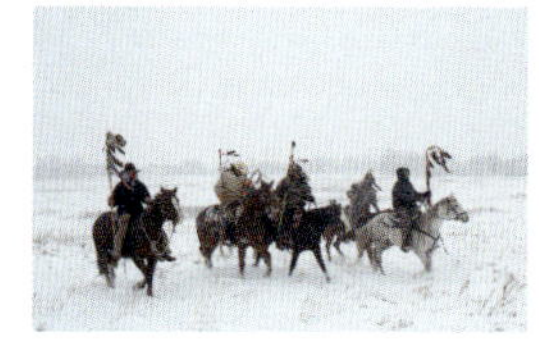

Pine Ridge Indian Reservation,
South Dakota,
2019

150

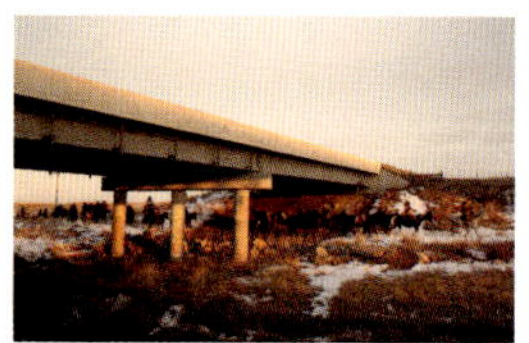

Badlands,
South Dakota,
2019

152

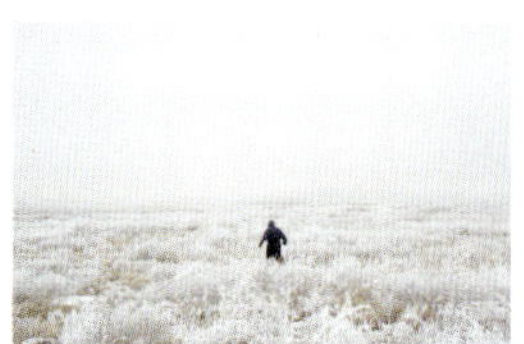

Badlands,
South Dakota,
2019

Photographs: Zen Lefort
Coordination: Lambert Stroh
Graphic design: Studio Mitsu

With the participation of:
Revue Hobbies
Glory Lab
Myop
S.C.A.N. Services
Studio Zéro

Many thanks to:
Akiro
Gregoire Belhoste
Alexandre Bouvron
The Sheap Camp
Jérôme Couderc
Manu Devier
Les Himalayennes Fags
La famille Foster
Pablo Freda
Brandon Iron Hawk
River Iron
Valentin Loubat
La famille Mas
La famille Norcross
Mon père
Alexis Pinguet
Aldo Rossi
La famille Sauret
Paul Schoendoerffer
Anthony Seklaoui
Le château des Tourelles
Heater Water
The Great American West
Alex Withplume
Chanse Zavalla

EDITOR
Nadine Barth

PROJECT MANAGEMENT
Sonja Altmeppen

COPYEDITING
Dawn Michelle d'Atri

GRAPHIC DESIGN
Studio Mitsu

TYPEFACE
Stempel Garamond LT
Balboa

PRODUCTION
Alise Ausmane, Hatje Cantz

PRINTING AND BINDING
Livonia Print, Riga

PAPER
Magno Volume, 150 g/m²

PUBLISHED BY
Hatje Cantz Verlag GmbH
Mommsenstraße 27
10629 Berlin
www.hatjecantz.de
A Ganske Publishing Group Company

ISBN 978-3-7757-5326-5
Printed in Europe